Without a Paddle

WARREN RICHEY

Without a Paddle

Racing Twelve Hundred Miles
Around Florida by Sea Kayak

ST. MARTIN'S PRESS 🞘 NEW YORK

www.stmartins.com

Library of Congress Cataloging-in-Publication Data

ISBN 978-0-312-63076-8

First Edition: June 2010

10 9 8 7 6 5 4 3 2 1

To J.R. and L.F.

The basest of all things is to be afraid.

—William Faulkner

ALABAMA

GEORGIA

ATLANTIC OCEAN

St. Marys River

THE PORTAGE

Fargo

Tallahassee ★

Suwannee River

Big Shoals

Amelia Island: *checkpoint 3*

St. George
Jacksonville

• Branford

St. Augustine

Fanning Springs

Palm Coast

Daytona Beach

Cedar Key: *checkpoint 4*

Kennedy Space Center

The Route

Twelve Hundred Miles

in Thirty Days

...or Less

Anclote Key

Tampa

Sebastian Inlet: *checkpoint 2*

St. Petersburg

Tampa Bay

FLORIDA

START AND FINISH
Fort De Soto Park,
Mullet Key

Stuart

Jupiter
Palm Beach

Placida

Charlotte Bay

GULF OF MEXICO

Sanibel Island

N

W   E

S

Naples

Fort Lauderdale

Marco Island
Chokoloskee

Miami

Biscayne Bay

Everglades National Park

Flamingo

Florida Bay

0 Miles   100

Key Largo: *checkpoint 1*

0 Kilometers   100   200

Key West

© 2010 Jeffrey L. Ward

Without a Paddle

PART I

Consider Yourself Warned:
Paddle or Die

On the Water

At night, alone in the boat, everything feels dangerous. No margin for error. Clouds blot out the stars. No moon. The water, the horizon, the air itself is black and empty. Dry land is a notion somewhere to my left. Navigation is by feel and sound, accepting whatever is offered within the sweep and swell of the sea. The sluggish gurgle at the bow tells me to pick up the pace.

I have been traveling like this longer than I can remember, stopping on white beaches to catch a few hours of sleep in a jungle hammock, but always breaking camp too soon to achieve any genuine rest.

Just keep moving forward.

Sixteen hours. Eighteen hours. Twenty hours alone in the boat.

Did you feel that?

Don't start.

I move my feet to stretch my legs inside the kayak. A butcher's knife is jammed between my shoulder blades. Again.

You must sleep. Sleeeeeeep.

My eyes close, briefly. The paddle strikes something solid in the water.

Did you feel that? You know you felt it.

I pull hard and begin to count strokes. "One . . . two . . . three . . ."

I hear the reassuring sound of water moving at the bow.

"Twenty-six . . . twenty-seven . . . twenty-eight . . ."

Something big. Something hungry.

"Forty-two . . . forty-three . . . forty-four . . ."

I twist around, but I see nothing.

Where am I?

Exhaustion and confusion are with me now almost all the time. They are faithful companions on a journey like this, and a really bad influence. At this point if I capsize, the water grants an opportunity for brief struggle, but no escape. I know this. I know it with every impulse I possess for survival. The problem is I can't stop paddling. I am dead tired, but I can't stop.

Happy Birthday

Some time ago, having arrived at the middle years of my life with little to show for it but a thriving bald spot and a flatulent seventeen-year-old Toyota, I decided to do something completely nuts. I entered a race. It was a fiftieth-birthday present to myself, one of those well-intentioned but somewhat desperate attempts to stir things up a bit, to get the blood flowing again.

This was no ordinary race. It was a contest for small boats circumnavigating the entire state of Florida. I never actually got out a map and measured it, but the event organizer made a big deal out of the fact that it would be twelve hundred miles of round-the-clock racing.

I know, I know. These things rarely end well. I could already hear the *thwack-thwack-thwack* of the Coast Guard helicopter. The newscast would include something like: "Details are sketchy. The man apparently had a huge bald spot and owned a 1989 Toyota with an inoperative muffler."

I didn't care. What did I have to lose?

I've been a newspaper reporter for twenty-eight years, so I have intimate knowledge of failure, doom, and destruction. I've covered suicides, fatal house fires, and bloody car wrecks. And I've learned a few things. Call it reporter's wisdom. For example, always wear your seat belt, keep fresh batteries in your smoke detector, and if you really, really want to kill yourself by drowning in the river but would like to spare your family the grief of having to identify the stinking, bloated corpse, don't wear underwear with an identifying laundry label. Trust me on this.

That's just the easy stuff. The hardest part about being in journalism is working with "newsroom managers" willing to throw reporters under a train, if necessary, to manage their own relentless march toward that corner office. I've worked for a few. Through much of it, I had the last laugh. Every night I went home from work to a beautiful woman and a smart, talented son in a four-bedroom piece of heaven with a swimming pool in the backyard. It is no exaggeration when I tell you I was the luckiest man alive.

Then, one day, it disappeared. Just vanished. When the judge stamped the divorce final, I felt as if I was free-falling into a giant vat of Kool-Aid.

I didn't know what to do or whom to trust. Of course, I wasn't the only one. If you can believe what you read in the papers, one of every two American marriages ends in divorce. They even have a proper name for my condition. Apparently it is called a midlife crisis. Some men buy a Corvette, grow a mustache, and start dating bosomy twenty-somethings. Not me.

I entered a race.

Twelve hundred miles around Florida, and you are thinking, but Florida is a peninsula. How can you circumnavigate a peninsula? Strange. I wondered the exact same thing. Turns out the race rules require that I carry a wheeled cart in my boat. When I run out of water I have to load the boat onto the cart and pull it behind me over land until I reach water again. Among nautical types this maneuver is called a portage, but it sounded like torture to me. The portage in question takes place in north Florida between the St. Marys River and the Suwannee River. The two rivers are separated by forty miles.

But I'm getting ahead of myself. Let me start at the beginning.

The Beginning

It was love at first sight.

There I stood in the center of a palm-shaded kayak shop in the Florida Keys, surrounded by all manner of boating gear. Kayaks to the left, canoes to the right, paddles, life jackets, paddling gloves, spray skirts, and a slew of those pirate-themed T-shirts arrayed around me. "ARRRRR! Where Be the Treasure?" and "ARRRRR! I'm with Stupid."

I had arrived at the shop under false pretenses. This particular kayak shop allowed customers to take sea kayaks into nearby Blackwater Sound for a test paddle. With alimony and child support payments draining my bank account each month, I wasn't exactly rolling around in cash. I figured this would be an inexpensive way to enjoy a few hours of kayaking without having to fork out $50 or more to actually rent a kayak. That was my plan at least. There I stood in the middle of the shop trying to act like a customer, when something caught my eye.

I'm not sure what forced me to look. Maybe it was the glistening radiance. Perhaps it was the flawless smooth skin with curves in all the right places. What I remember most of that first magical encounter was a yearning, a quivering anticipation that welled up from some secret place deep inside. She was as close to perfection as I could imagine.

Impossible, my practical side thundered in protest. It can't happen that fast.

Oh, but the places we could go. The things we could see. The adventures we'd share.

You are not here for that. Cheap fun, remember? Cost-free paddling. Hello?

There would be sunsets. Think of the sunsets. Even better, think of the sunrises.

Look away! Avert your eyes.

I wanted to reach out. I wanted to run the tips of my fingers over those curves, but I worried about leaving unsightly smudges.

You wonder, of course, what it would be like to be inside, whether it would be a good fit. Not too tight, not too loose. You savor the prospect of someday basking in her radiance.

The salesman whispered in my ear like a pimp in a dark alley. "Would you like to try her out?"

It was a short walk to the water. Twenty paddle strokes off the beach, I knew she was the one. I paid by credit card. The salesman helped tie her to the roof of the Toyota. For three weeks, the gleaming seventeen-foot yellow and white sea kayak occupied the better portion of my living room, propped up like a goddess on fluffy pillows. I just sat there on the couch, admiring it.

Some people say I'm crazy. I don't care. I think you can tell a lot about a man by how he treats his boat.

The Dare

At some point it is necessary to stop admiring the boat and start paddling. Thus, I decided to travel around a bit and see the watery parts of Florida.

I'm not talking about a pleasure cruise on one of those all-u-can-eat buffet "fun" ships. Floating crap factories is what the commercial fishermen call them. Or a three-hour tour with a man in a captain's hat and Hawaiian shirt holding a microphone. Blah, blah, blah. "Look, there's a dolphin." Blah, blah, blah. And I'm especially not talking about that "Jaws" ride at Universal Studios in Orlando. That's me sitting in a fake lifeboat attached to a conveyor belt, wedged between seasick Baby Bertha from Ohio and Anthony, the blimp guy from Jersey, who is bellowing "Yo Vinny," as a thirty-foot plastic great white shark squirts a laser beam of water into my left eyeball. No sir. Count me out of tourist excursions, cruise ship extravaganzas, and vomit-soaked amusement park rides. Truth is, my preferred mode of travel is a bit more rustic.

I always liked the idea of backpacking. It's the notion of taking nothing but those few possessions you can't live without, cramming them into a pack, and heading off into the woods just to see what's going to happen. I guess if you put a gun to my head and demanded to know my philosophy of life, I'd tell you less is more. Get rid of all the extra stuff, lighten the load, and be free. That's the way to go. But Florida is not the greatest place for backpacking. You can't walk very far in the Sunshine State without confronting a body of water, and in most places the water is teeming with stuff that bites.

Instead of a backpack what you need is a sea kayak. The idea is to take nothing but those few possessions I can't live without, cram them into the kayak hatches, and paddle toward the horizon—just to see what's going to happen. It's my way of raising a middle finger at the advancing years. Whenever I find myself gritting my teeth instead of smiling; whenever the boss's voice drowns out the inner song; whenever I begin to weigh my lot against those unfortunate specimens of the human condition featured on *The Jerry Springer Show,* then I know it is high time to get into a sea kayak as soon as I can.

It isn't so much about being in the boat as being on the water. There is something about moving across the surface of the sea that sharpens the senses and lifts the spirit. The mind concentrates on the immediate. Part of it is instinct—that unused portion of the brain, residue of our wretched past as prey. You never know what lurks below.

There's more. When you paddle a kayak you move at the rhythm of the earth itself. You leave the man-made world of machines, technology, civilization, and you enter a different realm. You are no longer traveling through the landscape—you become part of the landscape. There is a pull, a connection that binds you to something mysterious, something fundamental.

My story might well have ended right there with me paddling off
into the sunset were it not for a fellow named Steve Isaac. Mr. Isaac
spent his formative years in Vietnam. The experience left an impression as indelible as a Marine Corps tattoo.

Years later, working as a computer consultant in Clearwater,
Florida, Isaac missed the action and excitement of Vietnam. Not the
war. He could live without that. What he missed was the challenge,
the thrill, of being self-reliant in difficult situations. He thought others
might be missing it too, so he conceived and organized a series of adventure races involving small boats. The biggest of them is the Ultimate
Florida Challenge—an event proclaimed "the toughest expedition-style
small boat race in the world." Think of it as a subtropical version of
the Alaska Iditarod, except instead of dog sleds the competition is
among canoes, sailboats, and sea kayaks.

The Florida Challenge is meant to be so tough you can't even call
it a race. It is more a dare. Or a threat. The challenge is to cover
twelve hundred miles in thirty days or less. To travel that distance in
a month means paddling around the clock with little chance to stop
for a good night's sleep or to wait out bad weather. You just have to
keep on truckin' no matter what.

Potential challengers are warned that along the way they may
encounter headwinds, riptides, alligators, sharks, even Burmese pythons. They'll confront clouds of ravenous mosquitoes at night, scorch-
ing sun during the day, and the dismal prospect of facing all of it
alone in a boat about the size of a coffin. It's enough to make you paddle even harder, if you haven't already passed out from sleep deprivation or been knocked unconscious by a leaping mullet.

It isn't just a journey or a competition. In its essence the Florida
Challenge is a full-bore, head-on collision with one's self. I knew there
would be no way to hide or to fake my way through. Whatever weak-

ness existed would be rooted out and then twisted, over and over, to heighten the effect. No one survives unchanged.

It is hard to understand why anyone would agree to endure the kind of physical and mental punishment necessary to compete in such an endeavor. The fact is I was both intrigued and repelled. The idea of it. The in-your-face audacity of it. I wanted to know what it would be like out there. I wanted to know just how brutal the race would be. I wanted to know if I had the mettle to make it all the way around.

There's a word for this kind of thing. Some people were too polite to use it at first, but pretty much everybody I talked to eventually got around to deploying a particular adjective.

"You are going to do what?"

That's the reaction when I raised the subject with members of my family. At that moment a steaming turkey sat at the center of my sister's dining room table. The room went silent. Open mouths, but no sound. Forkfuls of food suspended in midair.

"You are going to do *what*?"

"It's a race around Florida," I explained as my sister urged everyone to eat, eat! "A race for small boats all the way around."

They look at my arms and shoulders to gauge whether I'd be strong enough to do it. They aren't impressed by what they see. I can tell. They aren't saying it, but I'm hearing it nonetheless. Finally, my brother-in-law says it out loud. "Waddaya crazy?"

It's a fair question.

Throughout the ages mankind has taken to the sea—to explore the earth, to hunt whales, to wage war. I could claim no great or noble purpose competing in the Florida Challenge other than to be on the water and content. In that there is glory enough, I told myself. But, truthfully, that is only part of the attraction, and not even the most important part. For to journey alone across deep and wide water under human power, and to do it both day and night in fair weather and foul, is to place a wager against one's own life. Some folks ride motorcycles at high speed down narrow mountain roads. Others jump off perfectly sound bridges with giant rubber bands lashed to their ankles. Still others hunt with Dick Cheney. Me, I entered a race around Florida in a sea kayak.

Some Rules

The beauty of the Florida Challenge is the simplicity of its rules. First one back to Tampa wins. Any size boat may enter provided its captain can drag it unaided off the launch beach into the Gulf of Mexico. Human and wind-powered vessels only. No motors. No tows. No rides.

It is up to each challenger to decide how far and how fast to go, but to beat the thirty-day deadline means covering forty or more miles a day, every day. In addition, once every twenty-four hours the challengers must report their current longitude and latitude position via a handheld GPS unit. There are two reasons for this rule: first, to verify each challenger's current location; and, second, to verify which challengers are still alive.

The primary goal during the challenge is to try to keep the boat moving forward. Sleep is optional, but at some point necessary. Same with food. The best strategy is a version of the parable of the tortoise and the hare. Think turtle. That's because in a monthlong twelve-hundred-mile race, smart but slow almost always beats fast but dumb.

Mine is one of ten boats entered in the event. Six of the boats are kayaks or expedition canoes with a paddle providing the primary propulsion system. All have the capability of rigging a downwind sail to take advantage of certain wind conditions, but they are not sailboats. In comparison, three other expedition canoes are fitted with a mast, full sails, a leeboard, and inflatable outriggers that allow them to tack and sail upwind. The remaining entry is a twelve-foot shallow-draft sailboat.

The race begins at Fort De Soto Park on Mullet Key near the entrance to Tampa Bay. It heads south, down Florida's southwest coast, to Key Largo. Next it turns north, past Miami, Palm Beach, and the Kennedy Space Center. It continues up Florida's Atlantic coast past Daytona Beach, St. Augustine, and Jacksonville. The northernmost checkpoint is at Fort Clinch on Amelia Island. Then the route turns west, up the St. Marys River, across the forty-mile portage on foot towing the boat on a cart over a country highway through the Oke-fenokee Swamp to the Suwannee River. The challengers head down the Suwannee to the Gulf of Mexico. The last stage of the race runs south from Cedar Key back to Tampa.

The concept belongs to Steve Isaac. He wanted to create opportunities for intense, expedition-like experiences for ordinary folks who couldn't break away from work, family, or other pressing responsibilities like cutting the grass for the three to six months it would take to cross the polar ice cap or circle Borneo. He formed a group called the WaterTribe, proclaimed himself "Chief," and started organizing a series of weeklong adventure races for small boats.

Chief's first WaterTribe event was the three hundred-mile Everglades Challenge held in 2001. The race traveled down Florida's southwest coast from Tampa to Key Largo. It has since become an annual event drawing an eclectic assortment of more than forty kayaks, canoes, and sailboats each year. Later in 2001, Chief staged the Oke-fenokee Challenge—a race across the state from the Atlantic coast north of Jacksonville to Cedar Key in the Gulf of Mexico. That was the race that introduced the forty-mile portage between the St. Marys River and the Suwannee River.

It was only a matter of time before Chief started thinking about linking the races up into a single mega race. Thus was born the Ulti-mate Florida Challenge.

It sounds so organized, so rational. Just get in the boat and keep paddling and paddling and paddling until you end up back where you started. That's the idea. Just keep making a left all the way around Florida. You can't miss. All you have to do is get back to Tampa. That's all. I mean, really, how hard could it be?

Death

I wish I could say my decision to enter the race was made without the slightest hesitation. I wish I could say I never felt a molecule of doubt. I wish I could say I was actually looking forward to the event. That would not be entirely accurate. Just between you and me, I dreaded the idea of paddling all the way around Florida.

First, a sea kayak is a cramped, uncomfortable place to live for a month. You don't believe me? Try this little experiment. Go into your bathroom, load your bathtub up with all the stuff you think you might need for a month of camping under the stars, and then crawl inside. Carefully position the gear so that it cuts off pretty much all blood flow to your legs and feet. Now, every two or three hours, turn on the shower to properly replicate an authentic level of rash-inducing wetness, and then sit there amid your perpetually moist and increasingly malodorous gear for the next month.

Here's my point: You'd have to be an idiot to actually look forward to this.

And that's just issue number one: comfort.

Now consider issue number two: death.

I am ashamed to admit it but I gave issue number two a great deal of thought. I imagined every possible fatal opportunity. Call it Murphy's law anticipated, or Darwin's law about to be enforced. For some reason one vision kept returning to me—that I'd end up as a steaming pile of goo emerging from the smelly end of some large toothy creature.

Chief didn't help matters. He seemed to take great delight in the array of nasties that might befall his exalted challengers. There is method to his fearmongering though. He wants to warn potential challengers. He also minimizes any legal liability to himself. He's smart enough to know that pretty much anyone who enters such a race could easily end up strapped to a hospital bed with a perpetual trickle of drool flowing onto a pillow.

"Warning! Warning! Warning! This is a dangerous event," Chief announces on the WaterTribe website. "Do not enter this event unless you are an expert in the small boat of your choice." Then he adds this helpful reminder: "Even if you are a well-prepared expert, you may die."

There it is. The challenge has been laid down. The stakes are established. It's kind of like a bumper sticker that is popular with some sea kayakers: PADDLE OR DIE. Deep down it actually feels more like PADDLE *AND* DIE.

Consider the possibilities:

TEN FATAL THINGS TO LOOK FORWARD TO
DURING THE FLORIDA CHALLENGE
1. Swept out to sea and never heard from again
2. Struck by bolt of lightning
3. Attacked by shark that bites through the entire kayak to enjoy tasty human filling
4. Mistaken for a manatee and run over by sportfishing boat
5. Crushed lifeless by oversexed Burmese python
6. Fall asleep while paddling, capsize, and drown
7. Eaten by alligator
8. Eaten by six or seven alligators
9. While paddling past Miami, shot by stray small-arms fire from minor traffic accident
10. Bad piece of beef jerky

Okay, maybe making lists wasn't the smartest strategy. What I needed was reliable information about each of the most likely threats, information that would help put the risks into proper perspective. So I went to the local library and the Internet. I even found myself watching *Animal Planet*. Big mistake.

What I discovered is that Florida is hands down the most dangerous place on earth. People arrive for vacation and think it is just one giant extension of Disney World, all cement and plastic, sanitized and safe.

Don't be deceived. The Sunshine State is a ruthless, bloodthirsty place. Several years ago there were a series of shark attacks all within a few months. It was just like *Jaws* all over again, except this time it wasn't just a movie. These were real sharks biting real people. Bull sharks were causing most of the trouble. They have this nasty habit of swimming into shallow water and biting anything that looks edible. To a bull shark a human foot apparently looks like a ham sandwich. A human hand—ham sandwich. Human arm—again, ham sandwich. You get the idea.

Bull sharks are big, about as big as, well, a bull. I'm assuming that's why they call them bull sharks. It's not like they have horns or anything. Just the fin and the teeth, standard shark equipment. Female bull sharks can grow to eleven feet long and weigh five hundred pounds. They are curious, intensely territorial, and frequently in a bad mood. Scientists say bull sharks possess extraordinarily high levels of testosterone, which would explain the bushy eyebrows and bell-shaped sideburns.

Another characteristic that makes bull sharks particularly dangerous is their frequent presence in shallow water. They can even tolerate fresh water and are known to swim far up river in search of a meal. Bull sharks have been seen eighteen hundred miles up the Mississippi along the river's shores in Illinois. They've been spotted in Lake Michigan near Chicago. They reportedly travel more than two thousand miles up the Amazon. Shark experts say the bull is probably the most dangerous shark in the world. They say its aggressive presence in shallow, coastal regions makes it a more serious threat to humans than either the great white shark or the tiger shark.

All of this information gave me plenty of food for thought. I tried to imagine what I must look like to a shark ten feet below as I paddle my kayak across the water's surface. Would I resemble a menu item in a restaurant for sharks? That's basically what the ocean is—a seafood place open twenty-four hours. Pretty much everything swimming in or near the sea is a menu item, including me.

The fiberglass hull of my kayak is about one-fiftieth of an inch thick and it wouldn't take much effort to crunch through that shell. I suppose I could carry a harpoon or a shotgun, but I'd still be at a tremendous disadvantage. It is a proven fact that sharks are among the world's most efficient killing machines, right up there with the American tobacco industry.

Being in a boat might improve my survival chances. Or so I thought. Experts keep records on this stuff. Forty-five times sharks apparently confused a small boat with some form of nourishment. It's documented. The International Shark Attack File maintains a list of attacks dating back to the 1800s.

Canoes, rowboats, surf skis, skiffs, catamarans, and, yes, even kayaks have suffered at the business end of sharks. In January 2006, one poor fellow off Maui became the personal plaything of a twelve-foot shark that bumped and pushed his kayak around in open water for fifteen minutes. The guy eventually made it back to shore unharmed, but I suspect he had to rinse out his bathing suit.

In 1995, a fisherman in Fiji didn't fare as well. He was asleep in his boat when a particularly resourceful shark jumped out of the sea and into the vessel. A fatal encounter—for both of them.

Also in 1995, a woman was attacked while kayaking off La Jolla Shores near San Diego. She survived. A doctor reportedly removed a triangular tooth fragment from her face. This is not reassuring. I don't know much, but I know this much: I don't want to be bitten in the face by a shark. Not the face.

In 2000, a local man was fishing for tarpon near Boca Grande Pass, Florida, when a hammerhead shark bit the propeller of his motorboat. This tells me something important. In Florida the sharks can sometimes get so hungry they'll try to eat brass. Bad news for me. Compared to a brass propeller, my fiberglass kayak is the shark equivalent of a Hostess Twinkie.

Sharks aren't the only dangerous wildlife in Florida. More than a million alligators prowl the Sunshine State. Locals will warn you that any body of water larger than a puddle is probably concealing at least one gator.

The tricky thing about alligators is that those you encounter in the most remote corners of the Everglades are by far the safest. That's because they haven't lost their fear of humans. In contrast, the most dangerous alligators are those that live in close proximity to man and have become accustomed to occasionally having one for lunch.

Most people don't know it, but the southern tip of Florida is also home to a flourishing population of American crocodiles. Unlike their highly aggressive relatives in Australia and Africa, these crocs are similar to wild alligators: they would rather run from humans than eat them. That doesn't mean you don't have to be careful.

The crocs' range has traditionally been limited to the southern tip of Florida. The best protected population exists in a network of cooling canals near the Turkey Point nuclear power plant, southeast of Homestead.

Young male crocodiles are believed to be moving out of that area and testing the bounds of their range northward. Crocs have been spotted as far north as Lake Worth near Palm Beach. I'm not talking about a purse, belt, or pair of shoes on Worth Avenue.

In early 2006, three crocodiles took up residence in a lake near a retirement community in Dania Beach, near Fort Lauderdale. The seniors liked watching the crocs sun themselves and prowl the nearby tidal pond. Eventually, someone called the police, as if wild crocodiles were somehow fugitives from New Jersey. The crocs were moved to a park near the Intracoastal Waterway. Homeless folks used to sleep in that same park down by the water. Funny thing, now there don't seem to be as many homeless people down there. Just shoes.

Bliss

I didn't always view myself as a potential meal for finned predators.

In the 1990s, I was living the embodiment of suburban bliss, a married dad who loved spending weekends with his son surrounded by toys on the playroom floor. We'd build cities and major transportation networks with wooden train tracks and blocks. When the city was complete, it was only a matter of time before the earthquake. I provided the sound effects, my son, Jason, made the buildings and bridges fall. The thing about disasters on the playroom floor is that you have to get your face right down next to the carpet to see it at proper scale, to see it the way the frightened passengers on the train would see it. We'd both be down there, our cheeks pressed against the carpet, watching the unfolding disaster.

There were giant sand castles at the beach, Saturday nights at the Chinese buffet, soccer games, birthday parties, violin concerts, school plays, camping trips, outstanding report cards. Jason loved those *Herbie* movies about the talking Volkswagen. Every VW Beetle we saw on the street was a Herbie. He watched a videotape of *Home Alone* so many times he could recite even the most obscure lines five seconds before the actors. "Keep the change, you filthy animal."

One weekend, I ran into a fellow reporter from the newspaper at a spaghetti fundraiser in a local church. He commented later that I had a nice-looking family. He didn't stop there. He went on to mention that my wife was a "babe."

"Babe?" I asked.

He just said, "Man."

I should have seen it coming. I should have known from my experience as a reporter that not every story ends happily ever after. Sometimes people change, sometimes relationships between adults wither and die. It is never first-degree murder. It isn't like someone just pulls out a gun and shoots. The death of a marriage is caused most frequently by subtle forces that lull a couple into complacency. It sets the stage for all that follows. Neglect doesn't carry the sting of cold-blooded murder, but in the end the marriage is just as dead.

There is temptation to apportion blame, to describe in living color the full flagrant violence done to what once was a strong bond between two intelligent, caring human beings. But the fact is, every divorce is exactly the same. It is just the names on the paperwork that change.

Both sides are aggrieved. One party may be more guilty than the other, but the other is always an accomplice. No one is completely innocent. Both sides seek out reassurance by telling a selective version of how things got off track. The reality is that both sides bear responsibility for failing to provide whatever was lacking for the other. Honesty. Companionship. Fidelity. Love. Pick your poison. The start of it is impossible to pinpoint. A relationship that was a glass half full, suddenly becomes half empty. It is a tipping point, a slight shift on a fulcrum. In a marriage facing even the usual challenges, that slight shift in perspective can be the beginning of the end.

Precious things are sometimes fragile, like the flickering life of an infant struggling to breathe in a hospital incubator. That doesn't make it any less precious.

———

Eventually, I moved into an apartment three blocks from my old house. The most prominent feature was a filing cabinet full of divorce papers. There would be no custody fight over Jason, no brutal point-by-point examination of who did what to whom. Under the American legal system the dad never wins. Never.

The only real control I could exert over the situation would be to focus my actions on minimizing the disruption to my son's life. It wasn't the strongest negotiating position. It wasn't a negotiating position at all. Just the right thing to do.

As for me, pretty much all that I once had was gone. It left me dazed and frightened. I had no idea what I would do next. Well, that's not entirely true. I knew I'd have to keep working hard to pay both alimony and child support. I also knew I needed to continue to be a father to Jason. But I had no idea how to rebuild my life.

I resolved to start over. I resolved to strip away all the crap and try to find something permanent, something real about myself. So much of life is just going through the motions, just showing up. You go to school, you get a job, you get married, you have children, you get old, and then you start wearing your pants up around your armpits. There's got to be something more. I wanted to find it. I wanted to experience life, real life, to live deliberately without reservation.

Suddenly, I had a plan. The first thing I had to do was overcome my fear of failure and replace it with the courage to fail. No one ever won anything without facing the possibility of losing. No one ever won big without risking a big loss. It was a kind of pep talk in my soul. It almost worked.

Then I got a good look at that poor schlump in the mirror. A really good look. Reality came crashing down around me. Who am I kidding? What am I going to do?

Water

Before it was over—amid the shouting and the lawyers—I took a day trip to Chokoloskee. It is an island on Florida's southwest coast at the edge of Everglades National Park. There are sun-bleached trailers and rusted pickup trucks between a few modern waterfront homes. It is a funky place populated by fishermen, old dope smugglers, and mosquitoes. Chokoloskee is where the tangled wilds of the Everglades embrace the Gulf of Mexico like interlocking fingers from two different hands, one water, one land. From the first time I visited years earlier, I felt drawn to the mysterious tannin-stained water. There was something unsettling about the dark currents, something menacing.

I paddled an aluminum canoe west from Chokoloskee, through narrow tidal channels that flow between ten thousand uninhabited mangrove islands. I placed my wallet in a ziplock plastic bag and tucked it in with the fishing tackle on the floor of the boat near the life jacket.

This is where I'd come with Jason. He loved paddling to the sandy shoals that accumulate along the fast-flowing channels. He'd used his hands to dig canals through the sand and build castles festooned with shells and twigs. I'd stand nearby casting a green-backed MirrOlure while keeping an eye out for alligators, snakes, and sharks.

This time I came alone. I did not stop on the shoals. I let the boat drift in the falling tide. I slid the paddle down on the floor of the canoe and began to wonder how much weight it would take. I remembered that man back in New Jersey who jumped off the Sea Bright Bridge into the freezing Shrewsbury River and forgot the laundry tag on his boxers. His wife had no comment for us vultures in the press during those few days he failed to come home, before police found the body. She must have known. She must have known that first night when he missed dinner.

In the sixth grade, a girl's father died in their garage. We didn't talk about it. The teacher told us not to. Somehow we heard all the essentials. He'd attached the vacuum cleaner hose to the tailpipe and hung the other end inside the back window of the car. He sat there all night with the engine running. Back then he was just somebody's father. Now I understood it in a different way. I was his age now. I wasn't that kid in the sixth grade anymore. I was old enough, I'd lived enough, to know why a man might do something like that.

I carried a five-pound anchor in the canoe. If I hooked a fish I'd flip the anchor over the side to keep the boat from being dragged into the mangroves, or over the shallow oyster bars, or out to the open Gulf.

Five pounds.

Not enough. Even if it was, the tricky part would be finding a place deep enough. I'd need at least ten feet. Or eight. It wouldn't work to flip the anchor over the side and plunge into the wrong spot. It wouldn't do at all to slide out of the boat and go down with eyes closed and lips pursed tight, only to thrash around a bit before standing up and finding myself in waist-deep water. That's the problem with Chokoloskee and the Ten Thousand Islands: there's shallow water everywhere but the water is so dark you can't tell.

I thought about it. I knew it wouldn't be difficult to cover up. The sharks would do most of the cleanup. Days later, when the Coast Guard found the empty canoe, they'd notice the fishing gear and the life jacket. They'd find my wallet and make an assumption. Boating accident. This is what they'd tell the papers: "If only he'd been wearing his life jacket."

I let the boat drift and examined my five-pound anchor. I could probably swim the three miles all the way back to Chokoloskee with that anchor. That was little comfort. As the current pulled me toward the open gulf, I pushed aside every good thought until there seemed to be nothing good left. I talked myself into believing that every gift, every decent thing in the world had been stolen or destroyed.

It wasn't supposed to be this way. All those things we were going to do. All the places we'd see. The future. Our future.

Large wet dots appeared below me on the floor of the aluminum canoe. I sat down on the wet floor of the boat with my back propped against the seat and cried. The ugly sound of it carried across the water. I sobbed as the canoe drifted in the tide all the way through Chokoloskee Pass and out into the open Gulf of Mexico. It was okay. No one could see me. No one could hear me.

There are deep places out there, and at least I'd be alone. At least no one would see the splash or notice that last line of bubbles as the turbulence on the dark water smoothed out, calm and peaceful like the night sky at the end of a perfect day.

A Date

I had options. More important, I had responsibilities. Jason needed a father. That alone was enough, way more than enough.

And I wasn't finished. Not yet.

I could find someone new. That would be a start. There might be someone out there. I mean, I only needed one person.

I considered enrolling in some kind of continuing-education course. I thought about joining a club. I even thought about signing up for one of those computer dating services. "Newly divorced dad seeks woman with a pulse."

Then I had second thoughts. Perhaps I was being too picky.

I never did place an ad. Never joined a club or took a course. What I did was go to work. That's where I met someone who soon became my best friend.

I had known Linda for many years because we worked in the same office. We were friendly but not friends. I don't even know how it happened. She showed up at a dinner party with her two young children but not her husband. I remember it well because she wore these ridiculous stretch pants that I'm sure must have been very comfortable but looked terrible. Next thing I knew, she was sitting across the dinner table from me, talking about politics and world affairs, and she was interesting and smart.

I asked someone about her husband and discovered she was recently divorced. She just hadn't told many people about it. I knew exactly what that was about. I couldn't bring myself to mention my own divorce.

I don't know why, but at some point I got this idea that maybe, perhaps, just possibly, I should ask her out on a date. A date. I'd been married for fourteen years. I couldn't imagine it. I would rather perform brain surgery on myself with a rusty nail. I had liked being married and having a family and living a relatively quiet life. The idea of going back out into the "relationship market" left me queasy.

I went to a bookstore to build my confidence through research. I bought a book called *The Rules*. I read it and discovered a ton of stuff about women. Scary stuff. I practically ran back to the bookstore and bought *The Rules II*. Of course these are books written for women—ruthless strategies to help snag a man. What I needed was a ruthless strategy to help someone snag me. *The Rules* provided counterintelligence. If I knew how the other side thinks maybe I'd have a better chance of at least surviving. I mean, I was still in pretty bad shape emotionally. I figured, what do I have to lose? I decided to casually phone Linda and ask her out on a date. I sat down and wrote out a nice, relaxed, spontaneous fifteen-page script to read over the telephone.

After two hours of nervous contemplation, I picked up the phone and actually dialed her number.

"Is Linda there. Oh, hi, Linda."

I could barely hear her voice over the annoying pounding in my chest.

I identified myself, offering my first name. When she repeated it as a question, I hastened to add, "You know, from work?"

At that point my side of the conversation went like this: "Yeah. Yeah. Yeah. No. No problem. Great. Great. Great. Okay then. Goodbye."

Not exactly what I'd hoped for. I didn't even have a chance to get into the script. Sweat poured from my armpits. My face looked like I'd just emerged from the shower. She said she was in the middle of something and she'd call me back in a while. The good news is that she didn't hang up immediately. She seemed to recognize my name. She didn't hang up. Did I mention that she didn't hang up on me?

I sat at my desk with the telephone perfectly positioned between both of my clenched fists. I sat watching the phone, waiting for it to ring.

Waiting . . .

Waiting . . .

Waiting . . .

When it rang, the whiplash nearly threw my back out.

"How about dinner? How about a movie? How about dinner and a movie?" The words spewed out.

I'm not sure what was said. I'm not sure whether I even got the question out. There it was. She sort of said yes. Or did she? Was that really her calling? Did she identify herself? Maybe it was a saleslady from the telephone company. Did I just ask the telephone lady out on a date? Did I just sign up for 355 years of high-speed Internet?

Anyway, that's how it started—with a phone call, copious quantities of underarm wetness, and a question. We soon became best friends. When I told her I was thinking about entering the Florida Challenge, she did not express alarm or fear. Her eyes did not suggest doubt or bewilderment. She did not use that word "crazy." Instead she looked at me—right into my eyes—and asked a single question.

"Will you regret not doing it?"

"Only for the rest of my life," I said.

"Then do it," she said.

That's when I started putting together my support team for the race around Florida.

Linda would be my shore contact. Once a day I'd call her by cell phone and report my longitude and latitude position from my GPS unit. We'd be able to talk a little, but not too long because I'd have to preserve my cell phone battery so it would last several days. In addition to sending in my position report, Linda would conduct a short interview and then post a brief narrative updating my progress (or lack thereof) on a race website.

In addition to Linda, I recruited my parents—Marge and Roy—to meet me at two of the five checkpoints. I put a plastic tub full of spare batteries, extra dehydrated meals, and other supplies in their van. I presented them with specific shopping lists. Their job would be to obtain fresh bagels, fresh vegetables, bananas, and orange juice and meet me at the designated checkpoints.

That was the plan, at least, but who knew if I'd ever get far enough around Florida to warrant an actual rendezvous.

Cape May

The Florida Challenge isn't the first time I'd tried something loony.

When I was in the seventh grade and barely an actual teenager I set out on a journey of discovery. I strapped a sleeping bag and a rolled-up sheet of clear plastic onto the back of my ten-speed bicycle, borrowed one of my dad's maps of New Jersey, and headed south from Red Bank down Ocean Avenue and Route 9 into the great unknown.

My destination was Cape May, 110 miles south. I lived off the land like a true wilderness pioneer, surviving on frosted blueberry Pop-Tarts and cans of Mountain Dew purchased at 7-Elevens along the way.

After four days of hard peddling, I arrived at the southernmost point on the Jersey shore. I parked my bike and scrambled up onto a jetty of large black rocks. I hopped from rock to rock past surf fishermen and sunbathers until I was perched at the edge of a jagged overlook at the intersection of Delaware Bay and the Atlantic Ocean.

It was dead calm that morning. The sun had singed the back of my neck and my throat was dry. Somehow I managed to summon the saliva necessary to launch a fairly respectable missile of spit. It followed a high arc skyward above the rocks and fell into what became an expanding circle in the smooth green sea. I watched it float for a few minutes. Then I hopped back over the rocks, past the surf fishermen and sunbathers, to my bike. I turned the ten-speed around and started peddling home.

All told, I might have spent maybe ten minutes in Cape May. Twelve tops. But it shaped my life. Not the being in Cape May part. It was getting there that was important. Mapping the route and seeing it through, enduring whatever had to be endured. It was the delicious idea of a journey well conceived and faithfully accomplished.

That and a couple Pop-Tarts were more than enough to sustain me all the way home.

Jell-O

How do you get ready for a month of the most intense, grueling experience you might ever endure? That's what I wanted to know. To me it seemed like trying to imagine being run over by a freight train. Will I be knocked out by the force of the initial impact, or perhaps instantly decapitated by the wheels? Or will I lie calm and flat and safe on the ties between the raised rails as the train roars over me?

The fact is, it is impossible to prepare to be hit by a freight train, but that's how surreal the whole idea of the Florida Challenge was to me. I could visualize being in my kayak and paddling, but when I tried to comprehend the totality of paddling around the entire state of Florida, my mind went blank. It was like trying to imagine my own death.

It's not as if I had a lot of time to get ready. I didn't actually mail in my $1,500 entrance fee until mid-January—a month and a half before the start. I wasn't in terrible physical shape, but on close examination I was more Jell-O than steel.

I immediately set myself on a strict regimen of push-ups and crunches. And what would a training program be without rigorous roadwork? I covered about two to three wheezing miles a day. At first I alternated between walking and limping. Eventually I had to get serious. I started jogging.

Of course, I also needed to do some paddling. Covering long distances in a kayak is a relatively efficient way to prepare to cover long distances in a kayak. I'm not sure if that is actually true, but it feels true. It's what I did. I loaded up my boat and paddled hard for four, six, eight hours. There are benefits to this. One is that you toughen your hands to the constant pressure of the paddle, building a durable base of calluses to prevent blisters from forming during the race.

I tried to replicate as much as possible conditions I expected to encounter during the race. I kept moving without taking rest stops. I ate on the run, sometimes using one hand to stuff a bagel in my mouth while using the other hand to keep the paddle moving in the water. I tried to get comfortable with the feel of the loaded boat. I began to test myself, paddling hard against an incoming tide or a twenty-mile-an-hour headwind. After much hard work and dedicated thought, I came to the realization that I would never be in good enough shape to make it even halfway around.

Then something happened that made me wish I'd never signed up for the race.

It happened on Super Bowl Sunday—one month before the start of the Florida Challenge. I was on a long training paddle heading south on Lake Worth Creek near Juno Beach maintaining about a five-mile-an-hour pace on the west side of the channel. A sportfishing boat came out of a side canal. He saw me coming. Since I was headed south on the edge of the channel, I assumed he would yield and let me continue my pace.

He didn't. I was forced to jam my paddle into the water to avoid running right in front of his bow. I felt something give in my left shoulder. It didn't seem like a big deal at the time. I kept paddling, catching and passing the jerk in the sportfishing boat. Later that night I knew something was wrong.

With four weeks to the race I figured I had time to recover, but I'd have to cut down on my in-boat training. Better to start the race in one piece than tear up my shoulder trying to get into top condition for a race I might not be able to finish. I continued to jog and perform other general exercises, but I had to lay off my arms. No hard paddling. No push-ups.

I practiced the portage. Twice I packed the boat with bottles of water to simulate a full load, put the kayak on my portage cart, and towed it ten miles on a bike path in a park near my house. Folks driving past thought it was a hoot and started pointing toward the lake, as if I was so mentally feeble I'd lost the ability to recognize an actual body of water—across the street.

Dogs went nuts. Every single dog started barking. Some barked so hard the force of the effort made them turn around backward in circles. They must have thought I was some kind of mutated man-bug with a seventeen-foot yellow and white hemorrhoidal growth extending out of my butt. Arf. Grrrrrrr. Arf. Arf.

I suppose if I were a dog I'd be barking too.

The last month before the race should have been spent in merciless training. I should have been forging my body into a well-honed machine, but I couldn't push hard without aggravating my injured shoulder. It kept me off the water at exactly the time I most needed to be on the water to strengthen my shoulders and back. Instead, on the eve of what should have been the adventure of a lifetime, my mind swirled with fear, doubt, and dread—a condition far more painful than any torn muscles in my left shoulder.

PART II

Sharkchow:
Tampa Bay to Key Largo,
300 Miles

The Challenge

Every sailor, every paddler, who has made an extended journey across water in a small boat, knows a fundamental truth about the sea. It is a living thing with unpredictable moods and deep-flowing emotions. There is no comfort in the fact that these dangers are influenced by phases of the moon. That just makes it even more frightening.

No man is safe. No boat offers complete protection. At the surface, I am captive to every whim and fancy of the wind. Below the surface, I am already dead.

That's part of what makes the attraction so intoxicating. I want the water flat and calm for the entire journey. I hope for it. But I know there will be storms.

I know this also. There are two journeys, and only one of them is in a boat. There is no way to prepare for the other. Not really. There are no checkpoints. No places to rest. No place to hide. No way to escape. On that journey there is peril beyond any imagining because that part of it I must navigate alone, without a chart, without a boat, without even a paddle.

Go

You don't start a race around Florida in a sea kayak thinking about traveling all twelve hundred miles at once. In fact, my goal for the start of the race was much shorter. "First 300 yards off the beach will say a lot," I wrote in my journal in the motel room at 4:30 A.M., two and a half hours before the Florida Challenge was set to begin.

In the days before the race all my doubts multiplied into a kind of crescendo of panic. *What have I done? What have I gotten myself into?* I even rehearsed the words I would say to Chief while dropping out: "I just don't think I can do it."

But sitting in my motel room a few miles from the starting line, the butterflies in my stomach were settling down and there wasn't much that would keep me out of the boat. As long as my arm remained attached to the rest of my body, I was going.

"Worried left shoulder," I wrote in the journal.

I boiled water to make instant oatmeal, slurped down two cups of mandarin orange slices, and drank a small bottle of Ensure, a nutrition supplement made for senior citizens. Ensure is a kind of nectar of the gods for some long-distance sea kayakers, like spinach for Popeye. Every time I crack open a new bottle I hear that familiar Popeye spinach song and visualize anchors appearing in Popeye's ballooning forearms.

"Pace will be critical," I wrote. "Not too fast. Not too fast. NOT TOO FAST."

I showered and started dressing. I forced myself to eat and drink as much as I could hold. It will be a long day. What am I talking about, it will be a loooooooong month.

The race begins at 7:00 A.M., shortly after dawn. That means most prerace preparations must be completed in darkness, usually with the help of a headlamp or flashlight. The dark beach is a beehive of activity; sailboats with rigging in various stages of assembly, frustrated kayakers glaring at gear arrayed beside the boat refusing to fit into cramped hatches, food lists, gear lists, and a fast-approaching moment when preparation yields to a single shouted word: "Go."

There is no uniformity in the effort, just flat-out chaos. The less-prepared challengers find themselves suddenly discovering missing or broken equipment. Duct tape is in high demand.

Many of the challengers loaded their boats the afternoon and evening before and left them on the launch beach above the high-water line. I, too, left my kayak high on the beach the day before, but I prefer to pack the boat immediately prior to the start. That way I know when I push off from the beach I have all the equipment I need and won't waste any time worrying that perhaps a thief or curious raccoon absconded with some key piece of gear during the night.

In packing my boat I position my kitchen supplies and food in the forward hatch. Each meal is separated into its own plastic bag, sort of my version of the military's MREs—meals ready to eat. I also keep a half gallon of water in the front hatch to balance the weight with the heavier cargo in the back hatch.

The rear hatch is where I put most of my water supply, all of my camping gear, and my disassembled portage cart.

In the cockpit, I keep all the necessary emergency equipment within easy reach, either behind my seat, beside my seat, or in a football-sized cargo bag Velcroed to the underside of the front deck, just above my knees. I prefer to keep the deck of the boat as clear as possible. I secure a safety knife under a bungee cord and tie a small waterproof watch to a different bungee cord just in front of the cockpit. I also tie a piece of parachute cord to the bungee and attach the other end to the center shaft of my double-bladed paddle as a paddle leash. A pair of paddle gloves are tucked under the bungee on the deck.

Two critical pieces of gear are a cushion for the seat and a two-foot section of foam backpacker's mattress that I position on the cockpit floor as a pillow for my heels. This may sound luxurious, but it is in no way extravagant. After a few hundred miles the slightest discomfort can be magnified into extraordinary pain.

Packing the boat is a helpful distraction. It postpones the full realization of what is about to happen. It takes some of the edge off the looming disaster. I admit it. The slight breeze off the Gulf of Mexico should have filled my nose and lungs with the heady scent of midlife adventure. I should have been brave, a shining specimen of stoic nautical courage. Instead, the best I could muster was a sort of male-pattern bravery.

You could have overslept—it's the perfect excuse.

An announcement moves across the beach like a breaking wave: "Ten minutes."

I cradle my left arm to try to prevent the inevitable jolt of pain in my shoulder.

What is that slogan in the Nike commercial?

Just go home.

No. That's not it.

The sea awaits below an orange sky. I study the horizon and try to imagine being way out there. Alone. It makes me dizzy.

Save yourself before it is too late.

A fast jog to the men's room, and back. My muscles are warm. Still, my left arm hangs useless at my side. When no one is looking I test it and grimace.

There are brief thoughts of Linda, and a request: "Help me."

Yeah, right, like Linda is going to suddenly emerge from the sea and make everything perfect.

Enough.

I know it is crazy. I know this is the most insane thing I have done in my fifty years, but there's something swirling around me, through me, something big and powerful, drawing me toward the sea. It's as if I've fallen out of an airplane, except this pull isn't gravity. I want to believe life is not an accident. I want to believe I have a purpose, that I'm not just some idiot playing out his existence in a pointless farce.

With all the boats lined up and Chief about to signal the start of the challenge, I tell myself to forget everything—the shoulder, the distance, the danger. Just blast off the beach and fly.

Easy fella. One step at a time.

I had a plan. The first test would be whether I could accelerate and maintain a steady pace at the start of the race. Then I'd see how fast I could cross the wide entrance to Tampa Bay and the shipping channel. Next, I'd try to arrive at the Sarasota Bridge by noon, and then Venice Inlet by 3:00 P.M. Each stage would be a test beginning with the very first paddle strokes off the launch beach.

It was a good plan, a solid conservative strategy. Until the race started.

Three hundred yards off the beach all I remember is being transfixed by the crashing white waves at the bow of a freighter barreling into Tampa Bay. From the seat of a kayak everything on the water looks bigger. But the truth is, this freighter was about the size of Cleveland. I could either stop and wait for the ship to pass or cut in front. I remembered that sportfishing boat and tightened my grip on the paddle.

Oh no you don't.

Go.

What are you doing? Stop.

Go.

Stop. STOP.

Go. Go. GO.

It can take several miles for a freighter to stop, which meant that if my shoulder gave out, or worse, if the boat flipped, there would be little chance for me to escape being run over and ground into bite-sized pieces of fish food. I'd probably drown while scraping and rolling along the underside of the steel hull. On the off chance that I survived that ordeal, there wouldn't be much left after emerging from the backside of the ship's propellers. It would all happen within sight of the launch beach—not even a mile into the journey.

I dug into the water with the kind of frenzy usually exhibited by avalanche rescue teams. The boat lunged forward with each stroke. Spray flew off my paddle blades high into the air as they wheeled around and dug back into the chop.

Shish-shish-shish.

My paddle blades ripped into the water.

Shish-shish-shish.

I turned to see the ship's bow—at dead center. The squawk of the seagulls disappeared into the all-enveloping din of crashing surf where the freighter's bow plowed the green channel into white foam. It drowned out everything as if I was racing a waterfall, except this waterfall was attached to a fast-approaching mountain of steel.

Bits of my boat were about to be scattered throughout the bay, all my carefully packed meals, all that turkey tetrazzini, the warm sleeping bag, my jungle hammock, the GPS with fresh batteries, my emergency signaling beacon. Swamped. Crushed. Shredded. A slick of blood and a trail of blueberry bagels bobbing in the water.

No. Not this day.

I don't know how close I came to getting myself run over. Fifty yards perhaps. Maybe thirty. It wasn't close enough to smell the steel. I only turned once to see the freighter's bow dead-on. Then I put my head down and paddled hard, as hard as I could, and did not turn again to see the ship until it was a couple of miles behind me and approaching the Sunshine Skyway Bridge.

Imagine what that freighter captain in the wheelhouse must have been thinking. If he'd seen the start of the race off the beach to his north he might have concluded he was under attack by some Lilliputian navy, with sailboats, canoes, and kayaks all sprinting with grim determination toward him to pummel him with . . . what? Gatorade and PowerBars, I suppose.

Sarasota Bay

Not too fast. Not too fast. Watch that boat. Turn into the wake. It's gonna break. It's gonna break. Turn. Turn!

Why is the boat so heavy? Why am I going so slow? Come on, paddle. Paddle.

These damn sunglasses are fogging up. I need windshield wipers.

Why am I going so slow? Why is this boat so heavy?

Ugh, my foot. I gotta move my foot. No feeling.

Use your legs. Push. Push. Push.

This is too fast. I can't keep going at this pace. Should I drink now, or wait? I have to pee. When should I stop?

Come on. Come on. Don't start with me. The arm is okay. Who is that? Is he going to pass me? Go.

Is that ski boat coming this way? He is not *going to come over here. You are* not *going to come over here. No.*

I think I gotta pee. Maybe I should eat something. No, really, I gotta pee.

Oh

I remember the first time, the very first moment, I saw her. I was working as the Middle East editor on the foreign desk at a newspaper in Boston. This was 1982. Israel had just invaded Lebanon. Middle of the morning. She walks through the center of the newsroom, blond hair, white shirt, dark tan. She radiated intelligence and confidence. There was nothing cocky or conceited or contrived about her. She did not have to try to be pretty or beautiful or real or smart. She just was.

"Who is that?" I asked.

"She works in features."

"Oh."

I watched her walk across the room—all the way across.

Her hair was cut short but stylish, like Dorothy Hamill, the figure skater. It was a look. She was petite, but not delicate. She carried herself with the grace and strength of a gymnast. Not just any gymnast either, she was the high school balance-beam champion of Wisconsin. She graduated second in her class in college. She lived on fashionable Charles Street near Boston's Beacon Hill. She had a pet cat, black and white, named Lizzy.

It took a little more than two years before I asked her out on a date.

She smiled at the invitation, then closed her eyes slowly in that way that made my stomach fall away every time. "I'm seeing someone."

What?

She shook her head.

I looked across the newsroom—all the way to the windows—hoping for a cruise missile to crash through the glass and explode. Just my luck. Peace. I turned back toward her.

"Oh." On the way back to my desk I walked under about ten other desks without once having to bend over. I think I might have used a pencil to pole-vault a computer power cable. Somehow I got back into my chair.

Way out of my league. What was I thinking?

A few months later, she left the newspaper to accept a job at an interior design firm. While clearing out her desk, she stopped at my desk to say good-bye. I offered to help carry the boxes back to her apartment. We talked late into the night. Within a year, we were married.

Kayaking 101

For those who have never paddled or even seen a sea kayak, a few words of explanation might be useful.

A sea kayak is basically a torpedo-shaped shell with a hole in the middle. The paddler sits in the hole with his or her feet and legs inside the torpedo.

The boat is propelled forward with a double-bladed paddle.

Kayaks ride fairly low in the water, with only a few inches between the surface of the sea and the top of the cockpit. This can be a problem when paddling through waves and chop. The spray and waves can splash up and into the cockpit, leaving the paddler soaked—a prospect that somewhat diminishes the utility of being in a boat. Most kayaks require a piece of rubberized cloth or neoprene that fits around the outer edges of the cockpit and snug to the chest or midsection of the paddler—like a skirt. In fact, it is called a spray skirt and is designed to prevent spray and waves from entering the boat.

Kayaks come in all shapes and sizes. White-water kayaks, the kind that are used to run rapids in fast-flowing rivers, are short and can turn on a dime. Sea kayaks are designed long and skinny. A longer, narrower boat requires less effort to paddle and cruises in a straight line. The drawback is that long, narrow boats require constant vigilance to avoid capsizing. Forward movement increases the stability of the boat—an important point to remember.

The End

Every essential thing I know about fear I saw on the playground watching Jason as a toddler. When he tripped and fell, as toddlers often do, he was too young to know if he had hurt himself. He would not cry immediately. Instead, he'd seek out a familiar face. If he saw fear on that face, he'd cry. If he saw extreme fear, he'd wail.

This is one of the things I loved about his mother. When he fell, she would smile and make a game of it. "Whoops," she'd say, her voice rising into a laugh. For a moment he'd be confused. Then, sure enough, he'd laugh too.

For many years she did the same for me. I loved it, and I loved her more than she will ever know.

But apparently fourteen years is a long time to be married. My lawyer told me I was lucky. If we had remained married one more year, I might be facing lifetime alimony payments. For this I paid him $250 an hour.

She'd stayed home with Jason since his birth. "They'll argue she has no skills, no seniority in the workplace," my lawyer explained.

"She graduated second in her class at college," I countered. "She's way smarter than me."

It had taken years to understand precisely how vacuous my marriage had become. Like an oblivious lobster headed toward a pot, I misinterpreted the hints all around me. Melting butter is an important clue for a lobster, but what should I have been looking for?

One summer evening, a guy in his twenties tagged me on the right eye with a roundhouse sucker punch. He'd thrown a beer bottle in front of my car in the same street where neighborhood kids rode their bikes. This could not stand. I followed him to a liquor store and confronted him. He wasn't alone. There was a woman in the car with a child. A baby. I turned to get a better look at the baby.

Bam!

I staggered backward but stayed on my feet, surprised that I could take a hard, unseen punch like that. I was pretty sure he'd broken my nose. I tasted blood. Instead of returning the favor, I retreated into the liquor store and asked the clerk to call the police. The guy drove away. No problem. I'd already written down his license number.

My wife refused to allow me to press charges. "What if he comes to the house," she said. "What will we do then?" I could hear the fear in her voice. I could see the fear in her eyes. That's all I saw there.

The police officer couldn't believe it. "You have a witness. The clerk saw everything. It is a solid case."

"No, it's okay," I said.

But it wasn't okay. It was the first time I'd looked into her eyes for support and found nothing there. I told myself things would improve—she just needed some time. She'll come around. She'll come back.

Mine was the only real paycheck. Jason was in elementary school, and she was a part-time teacher's assistant. But the fact is, I didn't exist. My sole function was to deposit my paycheck in the joint checking account. For that I got a meal at night.

It is possible for a man to live like that for years, maybe even decades. It takes a toll. It wore me down, it changed me. There is frustration. There is anger. Month after month, year after year, the pressure kept building. I became a different person. Frustrated. Mad. Mean. A few years later, if that guy took a swing at me, I knew exactly what I'd do. I would fight back and keep fighting hard until he was bleeding and unconscious on the pavement. That's not the worst of it. With his blood on my fists I wasn't sure I'd be able to stop. By then I'd become the human equivalent of a loaded gun. I'd graduated from mad and mean to full-on dangerous.

That's when I lifted the canoe onto the roof my car and drove to Chokoloskee, alone.

Crazy Loves Company

I wasn't the only one loopy enough to enter the Florida Challenge. Nine other paddlers and sailors signed up to share the joy. Each brought different expectations to the event. Some came for adventure. Some for competition. Others for the strong bond and camaraderie among WaterTribe members. Ultimately, we all just stumbled into the water not knowing what to expect.

Everyone in the Florida Challenge is required to select a race name. Some names carry deep and significant meaning, while others are merely ironic or just plain silly. Here's the race roster with each challenger's selected race name:

• Sandy Bottom, aka Dawn Stewart, a biostatistician from Chapel Hill, North Carolina, paddling a Kruger Dream Catcher expedition canoe with a one-meter downwind sail. She is the mother of two children, a seventeen-year-old daughter who is a high school senior and a twenty-year-old son attending college at North Carolina State. Her ever-supportive shore-based husband, Paul, goes by the moniker "Dances with Sandy Bottom."

"When Chief announced the race I didn't even think twice. I said I have to do that," she says. "My husband just kind of rolled his eyes." What about her kids? "They think I'm crazy."

• ThereAndBackAgain, aka Dexter Colvin, an avid paddler from Naples, Florida, who lost both his legs above the knee in a highway construction accident twenty-two years ago. He is paddling a Kruger Sea Wind expedition canoe with a one-meter downwind sail.

He switched from his usual sea kayak to the expedition canoe to take advantage of the extra cargo space in the Kruger to carry his wheelchair. It is a piece of equipment he'll need to tow his boat on a cart behind him across the forty-mile portage in north Florida.

"Most people when they see my situation they say, 'He can't go with me, he is going to drag us down,'" he says. But they soon learn the obvious: you don't need legs to paddle a boat.

• Pelican, aka Nick Hall, of Tampa, Florida, a former college professor, medical researcher, and current director of the Wellness Center at Saddlebrook Resort near Tampa. His is the most tricked-out boat in the challenge. The basic boat is a Kruger Sea Wind expedition canoe, but it is outfitted with a mast and full sail, inflatable outriggers and a daggerboard. He has also installed a foot-pedal drive propulsion system designed by Hobie. The pedals push a pair of fins that extend like sea turtle flippers under the boat.

Pelican sees his participation in the race as a way to gather raw material for his work as a motivational speaker and writer. He uses his experiences in WaterTribe adventure races to inspire executives and others to find creative solutions to their work- and health-related problems. For Pelican, the Florida Challenge is the ultimate experiment, with himself as the subject.

• Manitou Cruiser, aka Mark Przedwojewski, of Irons, Michigan, the builder of the Kruger canoes used by six of the challengers. The boats were designed by legendary paddler Verlen Kruger, who covered one hundred thousand miles by paddle during a lifetime of exploration. His boats are hand-built by Mark at a workshop in Michigan.

Manitou Cruiser is competing in one of his own boats, a Sea Wind expedition canoe with outriggers and a full sail. He is also a strong paddler who has participated in every WaterTribe event ever held. He sees the challenges as effective advertising for his boats, which are built and designed for this type of expedition-style paddling adventure. He also views the events as a great excuse to close down his shop and hit the water.

He's familiar with that word "crazy" as well. "Most of my close friends and family they pretty much don't ask me anymore about why I'm doing it," he says.

• Doooobrd, aka Donald Polakovics, a navy engineer from California, Maryland. He is paddling a Feathercraft K-1 kayak constructed of a waterproof fabric pulled tight over an internal aluminum frame. The fabric is a high-tech replacement for the sealskins Inuit hunters stretched over the frames of their traditional kayaks. Doooobrd's boat is also fitted with a one-meter downwind sail.

As an engineer, Doooobrd views the race as a test of logistics and planning. You can bet he's done his homework, checked, and rechecked all the calculations. His one great fear is ripping the fabric hull of his boat on the razor-sharp edges of an oyster bar or a pointy log.

• Dr. Kayak, aka Leon Mathis, a nurse with a home health-care company in Clearwater, Florida. He is competing in a Kruger Sea Wind expedition canoe with outriggers, a daggerboard, and a full sail.

Dr. Kayak is a kayak instructor. He is an expert in a kayak, but traded his beloved kayak for a Kruger canoe to gain the extra cargo space. This is because Dr. Kayak never saw a piece of equipment he didn't want to take along on a trip. "My theory is if I am going to pack everything plus the kitchen sink, I'm going to go with a Kruger," he says. "I've never tried to go light. I just always say I may need this or that, so I've always gone heavy."

• Wizard, aka Matthew Layden, a yacht designer from Jensen Beach, Florida, sailing a shallow-draft sailboat he designed and built from plywood in his backyard.

The boat, *Enigma,* is 12 feet long and 3.3 feet wide. It weighs 180 pounds empty. The boat is designed to carry 200 pounds of ballast that enables the craft to right itself if capsized. Instead of a centerboard or keel, *Enigma* has two wings, or ridges, protruding diagonally underwater from both sides of the hull. They act as a double keel and allow the boat to tack upwind whether the craft is listing to port or starboard. Because there is no center keel, *Enigma* can perform this maneuver in surprisingly shallow water.

Wizard says he designed the boat as a kind of jack-of-all-trades sailboat that could be easily transported on top of a car to a beach launching. He wanted a boat seaworthy enough for ocean island hopping and coastal cruising, yet small and maneuverable enough to navigate rivers and swamps.

He named the boat *Enigma* because those who encounter it on the water aren't quite sure whether it's a sailing vessel or a discarded major kitchen appliance. Wizard knows his stuff. Compared to a canoe or kayak, the cabin in *Enigma* resembles a luxury suite at the Waldorf. With high rails, a well-organized storage system, plenty of open floor space, and protective canvas, *Enigma* offers a dry and steady ride with a cruising speed under sail of about four to five miles an hour. If the wind dies, Wizard can keep the boat moving two miles an hour or faster by sculling.

• Alaskan Seahorse, aka Gregg Berman, an EMS worker and kayak instructor from Half Moon Bay, California, competing in a Current Designs Stratus sea kayak with a one-meter downwind sail.

Alaskan Seahorse is one of the most technically proficient paddlers in the group. He can execute difficult braces, sharp turns, and figure eights with the precision of a figure skater. He uses his kayak to surf giant waves in California that would swamp most of us mere mortal kayakers.

• Wayfarer, aka Marek Uliasz, a university researcher from Poland living in Fort Collins, Colorado, paddling a Kruger Sea Wind expedition canoe with a one-meter downwind sail.

Wayfarer is a talented photographer and veteran of several Water-Tribe events. He trained to complete the forty-mile portage by using Rollerblades to push his boat down the highway at speeds of up to eight miles an hour

• Sharkchow, aka Warren Richey, a newspaper reporter from Plantation, Florida, paddling a seventeen-foot Current Designs Solstice sea kayak with a one-meter downwind sail.

I chose the race name Sharkchow as a reminder to stay in the boat, a kind of clear-eyed recognition of my less than exalted status in the oceanic food chain. That, and it had a more poetic ring than Sharkturd.

I had bought the kayak as a reward for surviving my divorce. It was a declaration of independence, a celebration of moving on. At first I used it to fish and camp in Everglades National Park. I soon discovered I also enjoyed the challenge of traveling long distances in the boat.

On a lark, three years earlier, I entered a three-day hundred-mile race from Key Largo to Key West. The race was called the Rum Runner Challenge. As a staged race, the competition involved paddling about thirty-three miles a day. At the end of each day, the racers were free to rest and eat until the race resumed the next morning. We only got about halfway down the Keys before the organizers called the whole thing off. A storm arrived. The National Weather Service issued tornado warnings as high winds whipped up serious waves and chop.

It wasn't a complete bust. Over dinner on Key West's Duval Street, some of the Rum Runner veterans mentioned another long-distance race called the Everglades Challenge. A few months later, I was paddling the three hundred miles from Tampa to Key Largo. Rather than a staged race like the Rum Runner, the Everglades Challenge is a flat-out push for the finish line. That doesn't mean it is a nonstop sprint. You have to pace yourself. The race format places a premium on efficiency. It isn't just how fast you can move your boat across the water during an eight-hour race. It is also how fast you can find a place to camp, set up camp, eat, sleep, break camp, and get back on the water. It involves seamanship, strength, and endurance, but it also involves planning, logistics, and strategy.

The Everglades Challenge became an annual event for me. I entered it three years in a row. By the time Chief announced the inaugural running of the Florida Challenge, I knew how to get from Tampa to Key Largo, and I knew I could cover that distance in about four days. However, there is a big difference between racing three hundred miles and racing twelve hundred.

When you race three hundred miles your effort takes place over a portion of a single week. You know you will reach the finish by a particular day. Twelve hundred miles multiplies all the unknowns: the weather, the tides, the wind, boat traffic, places to camp. The longer you are on the water, the more likely you will encounter some really horrible situation. Longer miles add something else—physical deterioration. How much of a toll would the first three hundred miles take on a paddler's body and mind? What price would the second three hundred exact? By the time I'd covered a thousand miles would I have anything left to make it home?

Each year after competing in the Everglades Challenge it would take me three or four days to recover. There were a few days of aches and pains in every part of my body, particularly in my shoulders and back. Equally important, it would take one or two nights of sound sleep to clear my mind of the lingering fog of sleep deprivation and the inevitable hallucinations.

After paddling three hundred miles it is not uncommon for kayakers to lose all feeling in their toes. Some even lose feeling in their butts. What would happen after six hundred miles, or a thousand miles? Would the nerve damage travel up from the toes to the foot and then to the ankle and knee? Might the damage be permanent? Who knew? Not me.

Plenty of kayakers have traveled farther—across continents and oceans—and through more treacherous seas. What makes the Florida Challenge unique is the deadline and the constant need to keep going. There are many wonderful books recounting awe-inspiring kayak journeys through interesting and challenging regions, but I could find nothing about completing such long-distance explorations under the crush of a deadline and the kind of round-the-clock paddling required in the Florida Challenge.

It is understandable why there might not be such a book. Racing changes the journey; it alters the experience dramatically. The single-minded pursuit of speed and distance reduces the possibility for exploration and discovery. The goal is ever present with each tick of the clock. The Florida Challenge isn't just a kayak trip around the state; it is hand-to-hand combat with time itself.

Centuries earlier, European explorers plied these same waters in search of fabled treasures—and perhaps the greatest treasure of all, the secret of eternal life. Indian legend talked of a fountain hidden deep in the jungles of Florida that could return a man to his youth. Many have searched for it. In my own way, this month on the water competing in the Florida Challenge represents a similar quest. Will it be possible to push this fifty-year-old body past the limits of time to experience something of those healing waters? More likely my great contribution will be as a piece of dead meat. There's a name for it, not exactly a precise scientific term, but a name nonetheless. Sharkchow.

One ... Two ... Three

At some point paddling down the southwest coast I realized I had a stowaway. She just showed up in the boat.

Go away.

My paddle slashes into the water and I'm already pulling hard and counting strokes.

Go away!

There are benefits if I surrender. Anger can speed a paddler across the water. With a bad arm, I need help. Stir up the memories, churn them, slurp down a fresh brew of adrenaline and dread, then ride the unstoppable burst down the coast. Sometimes I didn't even try to fight back. I embraced it. Sometimes it just felt so damned good.

I have about a hundred versions of the same speech in my head, all rehearsed and ready to go. You might think this would be unnecessary and redundant once the divorce was final.

Nope.

Marriage Is Great

Why would anyone want to get married, anyway. They are all the same. When the honeymoon's over and life settles into the usual mind-numbing routine, that's when you begin to feel like you've made a mistake. Like maybe you came home from the ceremony with the wrong one. Like maybe she was just on her best behavior all that time you were dating. Once you are there and it's official, that's when they know they've got you. Then they can do anything they want because they know the legal system is designed to protect mothers. Get that ring, then get the kid, and they are riding the gravy train.

Divorce lawyers and divorce judges all just play into this game. It has become an industry. Everyone gets richer except the man. They have even incorporated this into the ceremony itself. It's the part where the happy couple repeats "for richer or for poorer." They should change the vows in the interest of full disclosure. The bride should say "for richer." The groom should say "for poorer." Because that's the way it will end up.

Sure, it's probably pretty great at the beginning, maybe for three hours. But you can set your clock, you can mark your calendar, because at some point she will walk into the room and you will see nothing in her eyes. At that point, there's nothing you can do, and that's when you realize that what you really wanted to do is sign up as a deckhand on a slow freighter to the Far East. Or walk the Appalachian Trail from start to finish, all 2,176 miles of it. Or just lie in a hammock somewhere in the shade with a line in the water.

I'm just saying . . .

Southbound

The coast south of Tampa Bay—Longboat Key, Sarasota, and Venice—is an area where the waterfront is jammed with high-rise condos and expensive homes. There are marinas and piers, a few parks, and lots and lots of boats. The heavy boat traffic presents the first major threat. In some places the wakes are huge and the boats don't slow down. Some well-intentioned boaters will race up toward a kayak and then throttle back hard. What they don't realize is that stopping in that way actually throws an even larger wake. Many boats traveling at high speed create no wake at all, and those boats I hope continue to zip past without stopping. Huge motor yachts, on the other hand, can displace massive amounts of water and create waves large enough to flip a kayak.

Then there is the jerk factor.

Any idiot with a large enough checkbook can buy, launch, and drive a motorboat. This is a fundamental law of the sea. There doesn't seem to be any requirement that people at the wheel of such boats follow Coast Guard safety regulations, like yielding the right of way to smaller boats under sail or human power. Instead, a significant number of motor boaters in the section of Florida's Gulf Coast from Tampa Bay to Fort Myers consistently adhere to rules of their own. These are the worst boat drivers in all of Florida. The worst.

Be forewarned. Anyone in a kayak is to be used as an object of amusement, first by turning the boat directly toward the kayak and then at the last moment swerving, to kick up a hilarious rooster tail of water and a corresponding wave flung in the general direction of the kayak. From the wheel of a motor boat this is rip-snorting good fun. From the seat of a kayak, there is nothing particularly amusing about watching the underside of a motorboat approach at high speed while connected to two propellers spinning like twin buzz saws.

It is times like this that sea kayakers dream of carrying one slightly heavy piece of equipment—a deck-mounted missile. One quick flick of the trigger and *pow!* a neat round hole appears in the approaching hull. Then, *kaboom!*

I know this sounds harsh, but it would only happen a few times before word got out. After that life would be good for paddlers. Kayaks could travel right up the middle of the channel as cabin cruisers, ski boats, sportfishing boats, and cigarette boats scattered and stranded themselves on nearby shoals and reefs rather than face missile mayhem. Hey, I can dream, can't I?

The reality is that kayakers are entirely third-class citizens in the boating world. We don't even rank second-class citizenship. I'm not talking about sailboats. In general sailors have a better understanding and reverence for the so-called rules of the road. Maybe it's because they know what it is like to be under sail and vulnerable in a narrow channel or near a bridge with a heavy tidal pull and have a motor yacht driven by some oblivious idiot enter the scene and un-knowingly place the sailboat in jeopardy of wreck and ruin.

It is possible in a small boat like a kayak to avoid the channels and areas where motor and other boats travel, but I'm interested in moving across the water as efficiently as possible. That means trying to stay in water about six to ten feet deep. This is part of the physics of paddling. The displacement of the kayak exerts downward pres-sure through the water. When that pressure interacts with the seafloor it creates a drag on the boat. The kayak becomes noticeably harder to paddle. To avoid this, experienced paddlers try to stay away from the shallows.

There are other issues. If there is a current running in my direction, that's where I'll be too, enjoying the ride. If the current is against me, I'll be at the edge of the channel, using eddies to try to reduce the full force of the oncoming tide.

The point of all this is that by necessity I am frequently in close proximity to motorboat traffic. It is all part of the challenge.

———

There are plenty of sights to see along the route south to Key Largo. The gleaming white high-rise bridge at Sarasota is always a welcome landmark. It means an end to the long, boring paddle down the center of Sarasota Bay. It marks the entrance to a narrow section of the Intracoastal Waterway where there is more to see.

I cruise past waterfront homes and condo swimming pools. There are fishermen, family picnics, and people sitting in aluminum lawn chairs watching the boats cruise past. Mega yachts, sportfishing boats, ski boats, sailboats, and here comes a yellow and white sea kayak. Some of these waterside gawkers may feel sorry for me in my long, skinny, motorless boat. They would be wrong to do so. Many people misunderstand the attraction of sea kayaking. They see it as work. It isn't. It requires effort, but at its core kayaking is an attitude, an ethic. It is a state of mind.

A mile paddled through fresh sea air and across clear, smooth water is far better than twenty miles in a pounding blur enveloped in the stench of oil and gasoline. Gliding silently past mangrove islands and oyster bars teeming with fish is infinitely better than zooming through stretches of water from which all sea life has been driven by the mighty spinning weapon at the stern of the boat. When my kayak crosses a shallow grass bed, I leave no scar on the environment, just a brief wake on the water and some carbon dioxide from my lungs.

It is in these quiet moments that the most interesting discoveries come. The clear eye of a green sea turtle blinking back at me from five feet away a mile offshore. Twenty roseate spoonbills shuffling through the shallows, their coral pink plumage offering a second sunrise in the Everglades. The ten-foot bull shark that followed, single file, a few feet behind my boat for half a mile near Rabbit Key Pass. These things don't happen at twenty-five or thirty miles an hour. To see this, you need a kayak.

Marriage, What Is It Good For?

You trick yourself into believing something is real and it turns out it is all an illusion. In *The Rules,* the big secret is that women must learn how to play hard to get to trick a man into believing they are unattainable. As soon as the man thinks he can't get her, she shows him a little bit of leg or something and then strings him along some more. It's all about man as hunter and woman as prey. It's all about the woman being so much smarter than the man. Allowing herself to be caught in a certain way and making sure her hair is just right. The currency is sexual tension.

What a degrading bunch of horse crap. Somebody should conduct a study to discover how many marriages resulting from intentional deception are still going strong. If they are, it's not because of *The Rules*.

Some people believe men and women can't live together. Sure they need each other at certain times, but men and women want something fundamentally different. Perhaps the women and children should live together in community houses with day care right there on the first floor. The men could live in the woods and sleep in hammocks or tents. Every couple of days or so the men would show up to see the kids and go out on a date with the mom. Dinner and a movie, so to speak. Later the men would go back out into the woods and fart.

What kind of society would that be?

To some men the secret of a long and happy marriage is separate vacations and $500 hookers. Couples stay together for the kids, and end up strangers in their own lives. I'm not interested in that kind of marriage. I want to be friends with a woman. Best friends. I want to be able to look into her eyes and conduct a serious conversation, and then in the next moment be completely lost in those eyes. I want to be so much in love that I'd immediately trade everything to make her happy, to protect her.

Nobody believes that crap anymore. No one. I'm a dinosaur. It's all about appearances, posturing. It's all about setting yourself up financially for old age. That's right, marriage is a kind of pension plan. Not even that. It's just a crappy 401(k). That's all it is.

Stuff

Compared to a backpack, a kayak is downright luxurious in terms of carrying capacity for gear. As a long-time backpacker I know a basic rule of hiking is the lighter the load the more enjoyable the trip. I adopted the same philosophy for the Florida Challenge. I tried to think like a backpacker—to keep all my equipment as small and light as possible.

It isn't knowing what to take. Anyone can draw up the perfect equipment list—one that would anticipate any situation. To do that I'd have to make the trip in a cargo ship. I didn't have that luxury and I didn't want to haul an ounce more than necessary to complete the challenge. For me, the most important aspect of selecting equipment was knowing what I could safely leave at home.

Instead of a five-pound backpacking tent, I decided to use a three-pound jungle hammock with built-in mosquito netting and a covering rain fly. Instead of an eight-pound emergency tarp, I selected a lightweight version that topped the scales at about a pound. The tarp would double as an extra rain shelter in severe weather and as a kind of waterproof blanket if I had to sleep on a beach with no trees to support a hammock.

I'd take a spoon and a knife. No need to carry a fork. My backpacker noodle and rice meals were prepared inside their own packaging, so I needed no dishes, only a single titanium pot to boil the two cups of water necessary to rehydrate and cook the meals. Every other item of food in my boat could be eaten by hand.

Instead of a cup, I would drink through a tube in a CamelBak hydration system or directly from plastic bottles of water.

For cold nights in my hammock I carried a pair of SmartWool

socks, which I would also wear combined with a pair of silk sock liners inside my running shoes while walking the forty-mile portage.

My Gore-Tex paddle jacket would double as a rain jacket and triple as an emergency layer to be worn in my sleeping bag if the temperature plunged to subfreezing during cold fronts in north Florida.

I also carried three bandanas, each a different color. The red and blue were both large and could be used as a towel, a bandage, or even a head covering. Sometimes I used one to protect my thighs from the sun while paddling on calm water with the spray skirt pulled back. The white bandana stayed handy in the cockpit to wipe the salt spray from my sunglasses. To keep it dry I'd tie it around my neck, which would also save my neck from overexposure to the sun.

When empty and resealed, my plastic gallon jugs of water would become extra floatation compartments in my rear hatch.

Of course most of the stuff I carried had only one real use and so I brought it along because I knew it would be essential. My primary paddle, for example, was constructed of lightweight carbon fiber, which is important when you are planning to paddle up to twenty hours a day. Carbon fiber paddles are also expensive (about $360), so my backup paddle, made of fiberglass, weighed a little more but was cheaper.

I brought three hats: one made of straw with a broad brim for paddling under a blazing sun, a baseball-style cap for night paddling, and a fleece ski cap for staying warm while sleeping on cold nights or to warm up in a hypothermia survival situation.

Some pieces of equipment are more important than others. A good sponge is essential. Comfortable paddling gloves are vital. My night-paddling system included the potential of using four different lights, but only one would be lit all the time. It was positioned on the back deck. I kept a headlamp on my forehead, but would only turn it on when another boat came too close or when I had to consult a chart. A very bright, thumb-sized diving flashlight hung on a cord around my neck. I kept my brightest flashlight—again, designed for diving and thus waterproof—under a bungee cord within easy reach on my front deck. I also decided to wear a reflective jogging vest to boost my visibility on the water.

I never added up the weight, but my rough estimate is that the boat, fully loaded, weighed 110 to 120 pounds. I tried and tried to get the weight down even lower, but at some point function trumps weight.

Linda

A new relationship is like an entire week of Saturdays. Everything is fun and the possibilities are endless. That's how it was with Linda. Just going to the store became an adventure. I even went shoe shopping with her.

Then, out of nowhere, a Monday rolls around.

We've only had one fight—I'm not even sure what caused it. She just started crying. We were driving up Sixteenth Street in Washington toward her house after work. Next thing I know she's crying and I'm feeling like I'm somehow responsible. We sat in her kitchen without talking. I walked home. We didn't talk for two days. She never explained it. I don't remember if I apologized. I don't think I did because who knows what caused it. It wouldn't have been much of an apology.

"Gee, I'm really sorry for whatever it is that I did."

I know, I know. I should have talked to her, but it ticked me off and scared the crap out of me all at the same time. She'd never done that before. After a few hours of walking in the city, I felt terrible.

This is the thing. Since we became friends I have never felt alone—even when I was in Florida and she was in Washington, or when I was off on reporting assignments in the Middle East. In Baghdad, after the U.S. invasion of Iraq in 2003, I was embedded with the army. I'd climb the stairs to the roof of the cigarette factory headquarters to make a call on the satellite telephone. Sometimes snipers with night-vision goggles were posted up there watching for truck bombs. I went to the other side of the roof so they couldn't hear me. I kept my head down. Anyone in the city with an AK could squeeze off a few rounds. Occasionally a bullet or two would tear through the sky overhead. They were usually too far away to pose any real threat, but I kept my head down anyway.

We couldn't talk long, satellite calls are expensive. All I needed was to hear the excitement in her voice when she knew it was me on the phone and I'd feel loved. All I wanted was for her to hear the excitement in my voice when I heard her on the phone and to feel loved. We don't say a lot of mushy things to each other on the phone.

"You be careful," she'd say. I could hear in her voice that she meant it.

I had a Kevlar combat helmet and a flak jacket that supposedly could stop an AK-47 round. But thirty seconds on the phone with Linda gave me all the protection I needed.

It is hard to describe Linda. To me she is a feeling, the feeling of being safe and at home, even when I'm neither. She is a journalist and a news reporter, a divorced single mother with two children. She is the quintessential helicopter mom who would drop everything at midmorning on a busy day at work to deliver a forgotten lunch or press the back of her cool hand to a small forehead. She organized major school fundraisers and baked enough birthday cupcakes to choke an elephant. Teachers know her by her first name. So do principals. It's not just public service. She intentionally infiltrated the DC public school system to help get her kids into the best schools with the best classes and the best teachers. Like I said, helicopter mom.

Linda is smart and beautiful. Strong. Interesting. No frilly dresses. In some ways she is more like a guy than a girl. She roots for the Red Sox and actually knows the game. She loves politics. She has a wild side, but hides it. Not fussy. Down to earth. Funny. Taxi driver to her kids. Best friend, lover, everything, to me.

We never spoke about that fight, about why she burst into tears driving home. We should have sat down and talked it out. I know that. Instead, after two days of miserable silence, we just pretended it never happened. I'm not certain what it was about, but I can guess. Linda wanted to know whether she'd ever be more than just my girlfriend. She was wondering if someday I'd get tired of her and leave to try to find a different, younger version. I'm pretty sure that's what brought the tears and the silence.

I just wish I'd talked to her about it.

Placida

The first checkpoint in the Florida Challenge is near Boca Grande at a place called Placida, about sixty-seven miles south of the starting beach. The rules require that racers present themselves with their boat at designated checkpoints to sign the race logbook and use a time stamp to record their time of arrival.

The Placida checkpoint is located up a tidal creek on the east side of Gasparilla Sound. By placing the checkpoint several miles inland from the Gulf of Mexico, Chief forces his competitors to navigate through or around a variety of potential hazards. There are sandbars swirling with tricky currents and crashing surf, long stretches of extraordinarily skinny water, a draw bridge, and other hazardous structures.

The channel leading to the checkpoint is narrow and flows under a twelve-foot concrete-and-steel bridge and then around the remains of an older wooden bridge. Sailboats in the race must take down the mast, lash it to the deck, and then paddle, scull, or row the quarter mile up the creek to the checkpoint. This is another of the "filters" built into the race to keep the field competitive and prevent those with large, fast sailboats from dominating the competition. For me in my kayak, my only concern in the creek is to avoid scraping the kayak's smooth white hull on submerged, oyster-encrusted pilings near the wooden bridge. At night there is no way to detect them just below the surface. As I pass the bridge on my left I just have to hope for the best, hold my breath, and glide through.

The checkpoint is located at a canoe and kayak rental business in Placida. It sits on the west bank of the creek under several massive oak trees. It features a boat ramp covered with AstroTurf, a real luxury compared to the hull-scraping concrete on most Florida boat ramps.

It felt good to arrive at Placida. A small crowd cheered and applauded as I paddled up to the ramp. I signed the logbook and time-stamped my entry. Then I pulled my boat farther up the ramp and headed off to take a freshwater shower. This is a luxury that would only be available at the checkpoints and I intended to make the most of it. After the shower, I cooked a full dehydrated noodle dinner and tried to get some sleep.

I covered the sixty-seven miles to the Placida checkpoint in a little over thirteen hours that first day. I arrived first among the ten Florida Challengers. I wasn't alone for long. An hour after I arrived, Wizard appeared in his sailboat *Enigma*. He came ashore and we chatted for about twenty minutes before he got back in his boat and headed off into the darkness. Although there was no commentary or recognition of it, I had just been passed in the race and now occupied second place.

Doooobrd arrived at Placida in third place. He paddled his sea kayak into the checkpoint just before midnight. Manitou Cruiser arrived a half hour later. Pelican landed at about 1:30 A.M. The rest of the Florida Challenge roster wouldn't sign in at Placida until after dawn.

I decided to get a few hours of sleep in a bunkhouse at the checkpoint. When I awoke I could barely lift my left arm. The arm felt fine just lying there, but when I tried to lift it, pain jolted through as if I'd inserted a wet finger into an electrical socket. I couldn't imagine spending the entire day—or twenty-nine more days—enduring that kind of pain. Again, I considered dropping out of the race.

What would I tell Chief? I couldn't think of an acceptable excuse. "It hurts," just sounded so pathetic. Worse, I knew that if I dropped out now I'd hate myself probably for the rest of my life. There had to be a way to get this done—to keep going, to keep fighting.

Sunday, Day Two

It is odd the things that get you through the tough parts of a journey. Sometimes a comment by a stranger is helpful. Sometimes it is an idea that arrives from who knows where. Sometimes it's a major motion picture. That's what happened to me at Placida.

When I launched into the darkness at 5:00 A.M., I thought about a scene from the classic film *Lawrence of Arabia*.

Young T. E. Lawrence lights the cigarette of a fellow military officer and then makes a show of letting the flame from the match burn down to his thumb and forefinger before snuffing it out. His colleague is impressed and tries it himself, burning his fingers. "It damn well hurts," the colleague says. "Well, what's the trick then?"

Lawrence responds: "The trick . . . is not minding that it hurts."

It isn't that T. E. Lawrence was some kind of masochist. (Although some historians actually believe that was the case.) The point is that there are some things that are more important than pain. Actually, pretty much everything is more important than pain.

Fear has something to do with it. Fear is what gives pain its power. I had to recognize the real enemy and overcome it. I told myself nothing bad is going to happen. I repeated it. Then I repeated it again. *Nothing bad is going to happen.*

That's what got me onto the water and warmed up enough to cross the often treacherous Boca Grande Pass in the predawn darkness of that second day. The wind blew steady, maybe fifteen out of the east-southeast. It meant I had to pay close attention to avoid being swamped by the occasional breaking wave. Now and then a wave would crest and crash over the boat, but as long as I kept moving I remained stable and the wash just ran off the deck.

This was Boca Grande Pass—a place infamous for strong tides and treacherous currents. The mile-wide cut ranges from thirty to seventy feet deep and is scoured four times a day by a tidal rush that can whip up formidable waves and chop in even a slight wind shift. Boca Grande is also well known as one of the best places in the world to catch monster tarpon. I'm talking about two hundred-pound silver kings. The mother of all sport fish. Fishermen aren't the only ones drawn to the pass by giant tarpon. Sharks are also known to show up for a meal. More sharks than you could shake a paddle at. Hungry sharks. Monster sharks. I couldn't see them, but I could feel them. Right there, moving under the boat, circling around me, and sometimes even flying out of the dark water and then knifing back into the sea without leaving so much as a ripple. Giant sharks capable of snapping off an arm and then disappearing into the black void. It happened all around me in the darkness, I was sure of it.

A splash.

What was that? Over there.

I couldn't see anything. Too dark. But I could hear them, feel them. Big as eighteen-wheelers.

I had a strong incentive to be careful, to keep the upside of my boat facing the stars. *Just keep going. Just keep moving forward.*

The sky lightened as I reached the south side of the pass. This was Sunday morning—less than twenty-four hours into the race. I didn't look back. Once across the pass my thoughts turned to another potential disaster. What if the wind builds and the weather turns really bad? Do I have enough drinking water? The prospect of being short of water kept nagging at me. It wouldn't be a problem if the wind set down. If that happened I knew I could get to the next checkpoint at Chokoloskee Island by Monday afternoon. But who knew what weather I might face between here and there. When you spend a lot of time alone in a small boat it is important to figure out how much respect to grant those little voices in your head. Chances are you will be hearing them often.

Think

As in any activity involving extreme levels of endurance, I expected there would be a mental side to the Florida Challenge. Just as I had no idea whether my body could sustain a month of physical punishment, I also had no idea how my mind would hold up under the strain.

Psychological studies have shown that solitary sailors frequently encounter a mental condition similar to the effects of being isolated in a solitary-confinement prison cell. They see things. They hear voices. The mind begins to play tricks.

Man is a social animal and a lack of human interaction is a form of sensory deprivation that can be disorienting and even mentally destabilizing. If prolonged and combined with little sleep, it can lead to hallucinations and delusions, according to mental health experts.

Nothing strange there. That just sounds to me like a typical night of nonstop racing in the Everglades Challenge. What I really wanted to know is what might happen during the longer race around Florida.

The leadership of the former Soviet Union used isolation in a prison cell as a psychological technique to break suspected political dissidents. The U.S. government used the same tactic in its war on terror after the 9/11 attacks. Suspected terrorists were kept in isolation cells to soften them up for interrogations. Some tried to commit suicide. A few succeeded.

The precise procedure for this isolation technique is outlined in cold war–era top secret Defense Department documents on Soviet interrogation methods. The KGB refined it to an art form. Agents would arrange an arrest, then confine the detainee in an empty, windowless room. Four walls, a bed, and a lightbulb.

The confused target is at first indignant. "Why have you arrested me? I have done nothing wrong."

The investigator asks no questions. He says only: "You know your crimes."

The statement is designed to set a mental trap. The interrogator seeks to turn the subject's mind against itself. The Soviets rarely used physical force. They didn't need it. Anticipation of terrible things that might happen during the interrogation was worse than any beating. The Soviets knew this. They knew the detainee would rack his or her brain, first to discover the source of the infraction and then to try to formulate a plausible explanation.

In this way, the Soviet interrogator was not prompting a specific inquiry. There were no questions to ask. The subject would be driven to the edge of insanity and then invited to make a full confession. With experience, Soviet jailers learned that the average man could be broken in four to six weeks. In that time a detainee could be reduced to a whimpering, suicidal idiot sitting in his own waste, eager to confess to anything that might ease the massive pressure crushing his mind.

Four to six weeks. Now there's an extra bit of incentive to beat the Florida Challenge's thirty-day deadline. Finish the race and retain the ability to think rational thoughts.

Traveling alone in a small boat for a month is not a form of torture, I kept telling myself. But I wondered whether it might become torture—or worse—if I wasn't careful.

Cabbage Key

I stopped at the Cabbage Key Inn, a famously remote waterside restaurant on a small mangrove island near Cayo Costa State Park. It is only accessible by water. The Cabbage Key Inn includes a few rooms, cottages, and a marina. The island was purchased in the 1930s by the family of mystery writer Mary Roberts Rinehart, whose work inspired the phrase, "The butler did it."

In 1938, her son built a Florida old-style house with a tin roof and a wide porch on a grassy palm-shaded hill. The hill is actually a shell mound, a remnant of the ancient Calusa Indians. This spot had been sacred to the Calusa. Later it would be revered for entirely different reasons—proximity to good fishing, excellent food in the restaurant, and a well-stocked bar.

Ernest Hemingway fished and drank here. Perhaps he even drank like a fish here. Katherine Hepburn visited. So did John F. Kennedy and his brother, Bobby. Julia Roberts. Walter Cronkite. And me.

The bar and back dining room are wallpapered with dollar bills signed with names and hometowns. It is a tradition that began in a simpler time when a fisherman flush with cash tacked a dollar to the bar wall to insure that he'd have beer money upon his next visit. By some estimates there are now seventy thousand dollar bills taped to the walls and ceiling.

The restaurant is the real draw. This is supposedly the waterside lunch spot that inspired Jimmy Buffett to write the song "Cheeseburger in Paradise." Who knows if it is true. I do know from experience that the food at the Cabbage Key Inn is delicious, but I wasn't about to waste time eating when I should be in my boat and moving south fast.

I paddled into the marina and pulled the kayak up on a small sand beach in front of the inn. It was still early and I found no one at the marina. I jogged up to the inn and asked if I could fill up my gallon bottle with water. A waitress obliged after warning that all she could offer was groundwater from the Cabbage Key well. Having once stayed two nights at the inn, I knew what that meant. The water is perfectly healthy, but the taste is hard to describe. It is a swizzle of discarded redfish innards flavored with decomposing Brillo pads, a smidgen of rotten egg, and fortified with condensation from the underside of a turtle's tail. It's an acquired taste—like kerosene. "No problem," I told her, and gave her a $5 tip. The waitress didn't ask for money. The fact is, $5 was a bargain just to get those voices in my head to shut up.

After stowing the extra water (eight additional pounds), I started across Pine Island Sound. It is a shallow bay several miles wide between a line of barrier islands to the west and Pine Island to the east. A dredged channel runs down the middle. The fastest way across is to follow the edge of the channel and that means spending most of the day a few miles from the nearest dry land.

I pressed on through the day, maintaining a steady pace but trying not to push too hard. Although my shoulder hurt, I still had enough power to keep the boat moving at a good pace.

"I can do this," I told myself.

When I reached the southern tip of Sanibel Island, I pulled my kayak up on a beach to eat lunch and called in my position report to Linda. I'd been anticipating these few moments all day.

"How are you?" she asked. It was always a significant boost just to hear her voice. I closed my eyes to try to see her.

"I'm doing alright," I said. "Not great, but alright."

I didn't say anything about my arm. I didn't want her to worry.

We talked for about a minute or so. "I miss you," I told her. It was too fast. I wanted to talk to her much longer. To really talk. I wanted to tell her all the things I'd been thinking on the water. Things about her and us. I was afraid I wouldn't be able to remember them or say it all in the right way.

"I miss you too," she said.

No. Don't hang up.

But it was already over and I felt a terrible emptiness, like I'd missed my chance.

I love you.

Alone and empty. I had to get off that beach, fast. I couldn't stand being there alone.

What Is Important

Before the race I took special care to cut my cargo weight. I didn't want to carry one ounce more than necessary. What I hadn't counted on were all the extra passengers. I thought I'd be alone. My ex-wife proved me wrong. So did Linda. The great thing about Linda, though, is that every time *she* arrived, the boat felt substantially lighter.

In 2003, I went on assignment as a newspaper reporter in Iraq shortly after the U.S. invasion. I was embedded with the army's Second Armored Cavalry Regiment. One of the last articles I wrote before I returned to the United States involved talking to soldiers about the importance of having someone at home. Many of these soldiers were rugged war vets, scarred and tattooed. Some were fierce and belligerent, clearly disappointed that there hadn't been more combat. They'd trained hard for warfare and were ready to kick Saddam Hussein's ass. However, when I sat quietly with them one-on-one and asked about the importance of having a wife and children, or a girlfriend, waiting for them to return home, it didn't take long before their voices began to crack and their eyes filled with tears.

Soldiers in a dangerous place form a bond. They develop faith in each other. They will fight for each other, and in some cases, they may even die for each other. It is an intensity of devotion that easily outshines many marriages. But warriors also need a reason to come home.

A year after I returned from Iraq, one of the soldiers in the regiment called me with a sad story. It involved a special-operations officer, a major. I remembered him. He was popular, the kind of guy who was fun to work with, the kind of guy who got things done, a fixer who pulled strings behind the scenes and made stuff happen despite army bureaucracy.

I remember him because one day as I walked near the Baghdad cigarette factory where the regiment was camped, he invited me to sit down and join him and a few others relaxing in the shade. He offered me a glass of Pepsi—with ice. This was a time when Baghdad was still trying to recover from the U.S. invasion. There was no electricity, and thus no refrigeration or ice. We were all still eating MREs and digging holes in the dust to crap in. Somehow, somewhere, the major found ice—and shared it. That was my first cold drink in at least three weeks.

He just sat there smiling, enjoying my enjoyment of such a small but significant luxury. He was a good man, and I admired him. I could tell that pretty much everyone admired him. Later he was awarded the Bronze Star and promoted to lieutenant colonel.

However, when he returned home to the United States, something was wrong in his marriage.

Within months of his return, police arrested him twice for driving under the influence and once for domestic assault.

Impossible, I thought, this couldn't be the same man I'd met in Iraq. We were based in Sadr City, a sprawling Shia Muslim slum considered so dangerous that Saddam Hussein's ruthless forces rarely ventured there. Raw sewage ran in the streets, with trash and garbage scattered everywhere. City services were an afterthought in this forgotten corner of Baghdad, until the U.S. Army arrived.

Where many of us saw a slum, the major saw something else. He organized a massive cleanup, hiring a small army of local men and teens. Within two weeks the trash was gone. Soccer fields were built. Schools were refurbished. The sewer pipe was fixed. Work began on the power station. For the first time in their lives, the oppressed Shia of Sadr City were no longer under the thumb of Saddam Hussein. Life began to improve.

The major wasn't the only one who made it happen. This was a big part of the work of the Second Armored Cavalry Regiment in Iraq while I was with them, but the major was in the middle of it. He deserved that Bronze Star.

That's what made it such a shock when I heard the news. Here was a man who was so full of life in Iraq, a man who survived a place filled with death, but when he went home something was wrong. First, he was arrested for drunk driving and domestic assault. Then, early one morning, a neighbor found his body hanging from a bridge near his home.

To Marco

From the southern tip of Sanibel Island to Naples is about twenty-five miles. The most direct route is straight across open water, which means, once again, paddling for five or more hours several miles from shore, but this time in deeper water in the Gulf of Mexico. It is possible—and safer—to turn east and follow the coast. That would add at least an hour to the trip and require navigating through the busy boating traffic near Fort Myers Beach.

I didn't want to waste the time. I went for it. This crossing holds a special level of concern for me because a friend of mine, Marty Sullivan, flipped his kayak while trying to make this same crossing during the 2002 Everglades Challenge. It happened as a cold front swept through the region with high winds from the northwest blowing in thick swells. Marty, whose WaterTribe name is Salty Frog, used the wind and waves to propel his boat forward at eight, nine, ten miles an hour. At some point as he surfed his kayak down the face of a breaking wave, his boat turned sideways and flipped. It happened faster than the time it took to read this sentence. He tried to get back into his boat, but couldn't. Cold and wet, all he could do is cling to the boat. The wind and waves eventually pushed him ashore at a state park, where he bailed out his kayak and fought the cold. He bought a cup of coffee. Then he went to the men's room and crouched under the hand drier. He hunkered down in a growing puddle of water and had to keep reaching up to press the button to maintain the flow of hot air blowing on him. Outside, the temperature plunged. Marty ended up renting a motel room and dropping out of the race.

Although Salty Frog has made the crossing quickly and safely many times since, the episode sticks in my mind as a warning to stay alert. My own crossing was just a long slog across deep and open water. I reached the pier at Naples sometime between 8:00 and 9:00 P.M., being careful to paddle a hundred yards beyond the end of the structure to avoid getting snagged in fishing lines. I paddled into the yellow-white halo around the lit pier and then back into the night with about four more hours to go. By midnight I'd covered more than sixty miles, and set up camp on an island of dredged sand near the entrance to the Marco River.

It's Got Character

The first time I saw Linda's car on the street in Washington, D.C., I began to suspect we might be soul mates.

My flatulent Toyota was a cream puff compared to her dented and dinged-up 1992 Dodge Spirit. It hurt my eyes just glancing at it. Pockmarks and deep slashes everywhere, it appeared the vehicle had survived a tiger attack. At some point she must have parked thirty yards deep on a golf course driving range or in close proximity to a gauntlet of talentless Little League pitchers. Two hubcaps had fled in embarrassment. The body paint was one of the least attractive shades ever developed—Hoary Hue of Crematory Ash. The upholstery in the backseat resembled Jackson Pollack's best work, except this masterpiece was created by Linda's children through hundreds of episodes of spilled oatmeal, fumbled milkshakes, ground-in bacon strips, and the occasional splash and ooze of projectile vomit. Four doors. Manual transmission. And a most pleasant surprise: Linda is, without any doubt, the best parallel parker I have ever seen.

"It's just a car," she said, a bit defensive, as I positioned myself in the passenger seat.

She had not yet seen or heard my flatulent Toyota, and she had no idea what I was thinking.

I love this woman. I do.

A Proposal

When I awoke in the hammock, I could barely lift my arm. Again, I thought of dropping out. It just wasn't much fun. I loved being on the water, but I was paying a high price for the privilege, and the pain was an enormous distraction. All of my thoughts, all of my energies should have been locked like a laser beam on one goal—to just keep that boat moving forward. Instead, I kept wondering when my arm would fall off into the water, and, when it did, whether it would sink or float.

I dealt with it by setting small goals. Get on the water. Get to that bridge. Get to Goodland. Get to Indian Key. Get to the checkpoint at Chokoloskee. Just keep going.

It was a great strategy in part because the farther I went the more incentive I had to keep going. I got on the water. I got to that bridge. I got to Goodland. Then, when I reached the water, the bridge, and Goodland, I told myself, if I made it this far I can make it a little farther.

What I tried to do is to see past the injury, to look right past it. To see it as unimportant.

Sometimes I just have to trust that I am going to make it even when the immediate evidence strongly suggests otherwise. Folks might say racing around Florida with an injured shoulder is stupid and reckless. They might say I was tempting fate. But that's not it at all. There is a big difference between tempting and trusting. To tempt is to give power to something dangerous, something destructive, something terrible. To trust is to place faith in something better, something stronger, something more powerful. To tempt fate is to try to sneak through a door. To trust is to expect the door to be open and to remain open long enough. To me, this is the key. When you trust in this way, that's when things start to happen. Amazing things.

Alone in my kayak in the Florida Challenge I had a lot of time to think. Instead of dwelling on my shoulder I spent much of that morning thinking of Linda, and as I rounded the tip of Indian Key and headed toward Sandfly Pass, I sensed for the first time that I might be able to make it. I started to believe that maybe I could do this.

That's when I made a deal with myself, a pledge. I resolved that if I made it back to Tampa and found Linda standing on the beach when I arrived, I'd immediately drop to one knee and ask her to marry me.

I had plenty of reasons already to get to Tampa, but this was by far the best I could imagine. It boosted the stakes, and gave me something wonderful to anticipate that would be much more significant than finishing the Florida Challenge. It was, of course, a fantasy. But I didn't see it that way. It's what I felt in my heart. For me it was effective motivation. It associated the finish line in Tampa with the greatest prize ever.

I should mention that I never suggested to Linda that she come to Florida for the race, or to Tampa for the finish. It would be logistically difficult. Linda lives in Washington with her two children. She had important obligations and responsibilities to fulfill in that city while I paddled around Florida. Her role as my shore contact did not involve her having to actually come to Florida. I telephoned in my position reports long distance to Washington and she relayed them back to race officials in Florida.

But the more important point is, she didn't need to be physically present in Florida. She was already with me in the most important way. But I confess, I loved the idea of it, that I might finish the race and win her hand.

Everglades

When you pass Marco Island, it means the end of high-rise condos, seaside mansions, and fancy hotels. In fact, it means the end of most signs of civilization. This is the beginning of the Everglades. Here Florida looks much as it did when Spanish explorer Ponce de León sailed up the coast in 1513.

The landscape is a trap. Mangrove islands are separated by tidal channels and serpentine creeks forming a system of inscrutable mazes. Water surges through the wilderness four times a day, ebbing and flooding over the mangrove roots and providing shelter for small fish and crabs during high tides. Low tide is a dinner invitation for wading birds of all shapes and sizes. They are beautiful from a distance, but don't be deceived by their exquisite and elegant plumes. Up close it is a scene of unimaginable carnage. The herons, with their digni-fied blue-gray feathers, stand statuelike at water's edge, an ambush in the making. Ibises jab their curved orange beaks into the muck in search of crabs, fish, insects, and worms. Roseate spoonbills offer a splash of exotic color amid the unfolding slaughter. They sweep their spatula-shaped beaks from side to side through the mud.

Elsewhere in the channels, the swimming birds—cormorants and anhingas—float low in the water, searching below the surface for prey to chase. They can stay under water for nearly a minute and dive as deep as sixty feet. Their feathers are not as water-repellant as other birds'. This gives them better speed and maneuverability in the underwater hunt, but it also poses a risk. When they are wet, they have difficulty flying. The best they can do is skim along the surface flapping furiously for a hundred yards or so. They are easily recogniz-able on branches and logs holding their wings out to dry in the sun after a swim and a meal.

Historically, Florida panthers prowled not only the central Ever-glades, the river of grass made famous by Marjory Stoneman Doug-las, but also coastal areas, including the Ten Thousand Islands. The big cats can swim. They are also extraordinarily shy. In all my years in backcountry Florida I've never seen one in the wild. Just tracks.

One of the most troublesome animals in the Everglades is the raccoon. Unwary campers have lost much of their food to these night-time bandits. A few years ago, two deputy sheriffs from Tallahassee camped in the national park on Pavilion Key—an island known for its particularly aggressive population of raccoons. To protect their food they decided to keep it in the tent with them. The first night, one of the deputies awoke nose-to-nose with a raccoon. The wily thief snatched a complete loaf of bread and disappeared out a hole he had chewed in the side of the tent.

Although I knew of the threats posed by raccoons, I wasn't particularly worried about them during the Florida Challenge. Five months prior to the race, Hurricane Wilma, a Category 3 storm, made landfall on the gulf coast of Everglades National Park. Most of the raccoons on the outer islands never had a chance. What is remarkable is that any survived. Forecasters predicted a tidal surge of up to seventeen feet. The tallest trees on Pavilion Key max out at twenty-five feet. Those treetops would have been exposed to steady 125-mile-an-hour winds with driving rain and wind-whipped spray. Hanging on would be like clinging to the top of a flagpole while being blasted by a hundred fire hoses. Somehow, the strongest raccoons survived. It must have been the loaf of Wonder Bread those deputy sheriffs lost. "Builds strong bodies twelve ways," according to the old advertisements.

Python Pete

Raccoons are annoying and they can carry rabies. But there just aren't that many reports out there of killer raccoons. I took precautions against the inconvenience of having hordes of hungry and curious raccoons around, but I never felt personally endangered.

Pythons are a different story. A full-grown adult python can kill a man with brutal efficiency. Good thing pythons aren't native to Florida. I'd have to go all the way to the Amazon, or Africa, or Burma to be in python territory.

Or I could just go down the street anywhere in the United States to the nearest pet supermarket. A Burmese python doesn't cost much at all—less than $50. The little guys are so cute at eighteen inches when they hatch. Two years later they are six feet long and fully capable of dispatching not only every pet in the neighborhood but every child under five. Suddenly when the poodle goes missing, it's time to get rid of the snake. By then the reptile is a member of the family, and the snake's "parents" do what any parent would do when a troublesome kid becomes too much of a burden: they release him into the real world to become someone else's problem. In this case the real world for snakes is Everglades National Park.

Since Florida is about half a world away from Burma there are no predators even remotely capable of eating a giant snake, at least not since *T. rex* roamed the earth. The pythons are pretty much getting bigger and bigger.

Here's where we're headed. A few years ago someone posted a photograph on the Internet showing a thirteen-foot python that had apparently burst open after swallowing a six-foot gator—whole. The photo was taken by a park naturalist and is a prime topic of conversation among nervous backcountry campers in certain parts of the Everglades. I mean, let's face it, if a snake is big enough to swallow an adult gator, it is more than big enough to make short work of a juicy camper.

Just to paint a full picture, I usually sleep in a jungle hammock while camping in the Everglades. So if a python should slither into my campsite it would encounter what would appear to be a large bag of hot meat conveniently suspended between two trees—a sort of piñata for pythons. So much for enjoying a deep and satisfying snooze in the Everglades.

My plan was to sleep well armed with a filet knife in one hand. I figured a Burmese python is a constrictor, so if I could reach a sharp knife I could always cut my way out if necessary. A fine plan, I thought. Then one day while using my TV remote to watch three television programs and a basketball game at the same time, I happened upon *Animal Planet*. It featured a report about a zookeeper attacked by a Burmese python. The snake didn't just slowly wrap around the zookeeper and start putting on the big squeeze. No, it unleashed a lightning-quick strike, clamping down with its teeth on the zookeeper and then quickly wrapping its foot-thick body around dinner. The so-called snake expert was about to be demoted by natural selection.

This can't be, I thought, momentarily releasing my white-knuckled grip on the TV remote control. It was the most horrible thing. Pythons prefer to go for the head. They have a triple row of razor-sharp teeth curved inward. Their jaws can open 180 degrees and once they close, they aren't opening up until that snake decides to burp or yawn. At the last minute a fellow zookeeper with a big knife came to the rescue of his colleague. Others haven't been so fortunate. A pet python killed a fifteen-year-old Colorado boy in 1992. A nineteen-year-old New York City snake owner was done in by his pet in 1996. And a forty-three-year-old Colorado man was squeezed to death in 2002.

Pythons can grow to twenty-five feet and weigh more than three hundred pounds. Scientists say they are seeing all different age groups in the Everglades, with the largest captured so far measuring sixteen feet. The giant snakes are already battling alligators for top carnivore status in the Everglades. It is only a matter of time before things get totally out of control.

The National Park Service says folks don't have much to worry about with pythons. But I bet they haven't seen that program on *Animal Planet*. What I do know is that they are pulling out all stops to bring the giant snakes under control. They brought in a beagle.

That's right, one beagle. Python Pete is his name. He is led around the backcountry by a leash, sniffing for snakes. I'm kinda worried about the little fella. To the ever-expanding population of giant snakes in the Everglades, Python Pete is little more than a wiener on a toothpick. Arf.

Most recently, scientists at Everglades National Park have gone high-tech. When they catch a big snake they implant a tracking device. Then during the spring mating season they follow the slithery Romeos to other snakes. But something tells me it's not going to work. I mean, the snakes are *having sex*. It won't be long before all of south Florida will be like that Samuel L. Jackson movie *Snakes on a Plane*. I guess you could look on the bright side: it might slow down the onslaught of snowbirds moving to Florida. Or at least thin out the population a bit.

Chokoloskee

I arrived at the checkpoint at Chokoloskee Island in mid-afternoon, about four or five hours behind my intended schedule. Unlike the checkpoint at Placida, there is no convenient bunkhouse. The checkpoint is at a beach near a small marina, gas station, and convenience store. The purpose of the checkpoint is to sign and time-stamp the logbook. It is a chance to refill water bottles. In addition, I wanted to use the last real toilet I'd encounter, probably until Key Largo.

Although there is great temptation to relax and socialize with race officials, my plan was to get through the checkpoint as quickly as possible and use the remaining daylight to cross the distance to my next campsite. The quick pace in and out of Chokoloskee was aimed at avoiding something else. Nearby Chokoloskee Pass is where I spent that grim morning drifting in my canoe.

There are three other passes through this part of the Ten Thousand Islands. I know them all. Indian Key Pass, Sandfly Pass, and Rabbit Key Pass. I used Sandfly Pass on my approach to the checkpoint and I took Rabbit Key Pass back out to the Gulf of Mexico. They were more efficient, more direct than using Chokoloskee Pass. I've made scores of trips through the area, but I haven't been through Chokoloskee Pass since that morning. Not once. At some point I know I'll go back to try to erase the memory. But I wasn't ready. Not yet.

Before reaching Chokoloskee, I stopped at the park ranger station at Everglades City and obtained a camping permit for New Turkey Key, about twenty miles away. The place I really wanted to stay was the campsite at Graveyard Creek, about forty miles away. But getting there can be tricky, even with two good shoulders.

The weather report settled the issue. It called for winds from the north building overnight to twenty. This section of the gulf included long stretches of shallow water. Sustained twenty-mile-an-hour wind would whip the gulf into a frenzied, dangerous place with chop and breaking waves. While I could probably safely paddle through it in the daylight, I didn't want to test my skills in complete darkness. I decided to stop at New Turkey. I'd sleep and then leave as soon as the wind fell or the sun came up, whichever happened first.

There was just one problem—I ran out of daylight before I reached New Turkey. I've camped on the island many times, both alone and with others. I've arrived at all times of day and night. That evening a thick fog descended and there was a complete lack of moon or starlight. I could not find New Turkey Key. I paddled south to where it should have been and found only a curtain of black wrapped in a pea soup fog. I paddled north and knew soon enough I was lost. As forecast, the wind began to blow. I felt the sea starting to churn. Finally, I pulled into the lee of an island to examine my chart. Reassured. I headed south again.

The weather report was accurate. Soon after I pulled my boat ashore at New Turkey Key the wind began to build. It grew from a rustling in the trees to a steady roar. I'd made the right decision to stop. I lay in my hammock, listening to the tarp flapping furiously overhead. I was happy to be on dry land and not out on the open water. But dry land has its perils too.

Pythons are good swimmers. I wish I didn't know that. With that little bit of knowledge, I began to consider the possibilities.

Since the hurricane had significantly reduced the raccoon population along the coast, perhaps there wasn't enough prey to sustain a python. Pythons don't require three square meals a day. All a python needs is one 170-pound kayaker every three weeks or so. That would be more than enough to satisfy a twenty-foot snake on New Turkey Key. The idea of a hungry, twenty-foot snake lurking in the bushes gave special meaning to the name of the island. I guess the new turkey would be me.

This is not a smart thing to be turning over in one's mind while trying to enjoy a night of deep and peaceful sleep. On a windy night, leaves and twigs move around in the brush. It is a natural occurrence. It is also a problem. How am I going to hear that python slithering toward a nylon bag of hot, fresh meat suspended between two trees? Imagine this problem from the perspective of the hot, fresh meat. It is vital to be able to differentiate between routine wind noises and the telltale sound of a snake on the prowl.

The more I listened, the more I could hear him out there, just waiting for me to doze off. The evidence was unmistakable. Twigs moved. Leaves crinkled. There was only one rational explanation—a twenty-foot Burmese python. Maybe bigger. And lightning fast. Three rows of needle-sharp teeth. Not just one row, or two. Three rows!

Did you hear that?

I aimed my flashlight into the bushes. I saw nothing.

What did I expect? They are smart, cunning. They don't show themselves until the last moment. Then it is too late.

What was that? Just over there.

Twenty feet long, or longer. A snake as big as an eighteen-wheeler. Bigger.

What was that? That's not just wind.

Around 5:00 A.M., I decided it was time to go. I packed the boat, forced down a couple of bagels, and pushed off.

Not a minute too soon.

Tuesday, Day Four

By the time I left New Turkey Key my shoulder was no longer an issue. I'm not sure if that was because I'd already maxed out on the amount of pain a single shoulder could produce or sleep deprivation and the chorus of other emerging aches and pains were simply drowning out the complaining shoulder. I'd like to believe that my thoughts of Linda played a role and my strategy was paying off. The important thing is I had enough strength in the arm to keep the boat moving at a good pace and my shoulder seemed to be getting stronger each day.

This was huge. I'd been chewing on the idea of having to endure intense pain for a month, all the way around Florida. Now, it seemed to be better. Much better. I felt as if my kayak were suddenly one hundred pounds lighter. I still had a long way to go. And there were plenty of other issues to worry about. Like navigation.

It is difficult to explain to folks who have not experienced it themselves, but a major obstacle in the Florida Challenge is trying to deal with the cumulating effects of physical exhaustion and sleep deprivation, combined with the gnawing desire to keep going as fast as possible. At some point, something has to give. It is usually the mind that goes first. Confusion reigns supreme.

That morning paddling south from New Turkey I kept thinking maybe I shouldn't have stopped so early the night before. Maybe I should have kept going and pressed on through the night. I was behind my anticipated schedule. The nonsense with the shoulder had slowed me down. I needed a way to make up lost time.

At the same time, I tried to justify the stop at New Turkey. I needed the rest, and, perhaps more important, my shoulder needed a break from the constant pressure of paddling. It was time efficiently spent. True, I kept waking up on python alert, but I did get some sleep in between. I just didn't feel refreshed and mentally sharp. That should have been a warning.

The trick—if you can call it that—to traveling through this section of Everglades National Park is to try to aim just west of the farthest piece of visible land. From the seat of a sea kayak that generally appears as a small dot on the horizon. When I left the cluster of islands near New Turkey, I was already several miles from the Florida mainland. It would be a waste of time to try to hug the coast. Instead, I located the smallest bit of land I could see to the south and aimed for it.

The advantage of this strategy is that the shortest distance between two points is a straight line. The disadvantage is it took me so far offshore there wasn't much to look at. As always, there was plenty to think about.

Due West of Lostmans River

Back then, your kids were in second and fourth grade. Jason was a little older, in fifth. But they were all too young to watch their parents fall apart and divorce.

My first solid memory of Evan is from that hamburger place at the shopping mall. We sat in a booth, me on one side and you and your kids on the other. There was no discussion or seating chart. This was their design. They sat on each side of you, leaning in toward their mother so there was slight contact.

Rebecca was just happy to be out on the town and ordering from a menu like an adult. Evan took the dining experience very seriously. He pursed his lips when asked what he'd like to drink. You could see the wheels turning as he gave the question thoughtful consideration. But that wasn't the most important question of the night.

Rebecca talked about school. Evan talked about the Redskins. I talked about Jason. The food arrived. At some point, I excused myself and went to the men's room. A few minutes after occupying the second stall, I heard the men's room door open and then light footsteps padding across the tile floor. They went up one side, then down the other. An eyeball pressed up close to the crack near the sliding lock on the stall door. Just an eyeball and behind it a small, dark shadow.

"*Yes?*" *I asked.*

"*Are you in there?*" *Evan asked.*

"*I'll be out in a little bit.*"

He waited, washing his hands several times. I could hear the sink going on and off. When I emerged, I stood next to him at the sink. I turned on the hot water and gave the soap dispenser several pumps. Evan just looked at me. I could see him in the mirror looking up at me.

Then he asked: "*Do you like my mom?*"

There is a part of me that just wants to outlaw divorce altogether. Parents need to behave like adults and put the best interests of their children ahead of their own selfish motives. But parents aren't perfect—or anywhere close to brave enough. Once lawyers get involved, that's it. There is no turning back. Reconciliation is impossible. Marriage doesn't mean what it used to mean. It isn't even a contract anymore. Children get caught in the middle of the breakup. They see the two people they love and trust most, trying to destroy each other. For this little wide-eyed boy to feel the weight of that disaster on his own shoulders is almost too much to bear.

"*Do you like my mom?*"

I will remember until the day I die the look on my son's face when I told him that his mother and I were getting a divorce. Just watching his heart break. The tears in the corners of his eyes. A little light there, going out. We were in a park. I know the exact tree, the exact spot where we stood, near an empty park bench. I told him that I was his father and I would always be there for him. I told him I would be moving out of the house but that I'd found an apartment just a few blocks away. He could come see me whenever he wanted. Things wouldn't be much different. But that was a lie and he knew it. I knew it too.

"What about Mom," he asked.

Sons worry about their mothers. For the first ten or so years of a boy's life Mom is the most beautiful, most important person. She is everything. Fathers can be important, but mothers are essential.

It was the hardest thing I have ever done, moving out of the house to live alone. Hard, because I had no idea what I would do, whether I would ever find anyone close to the woman I had married fourteen years earlier. Hard, because I had no idea whether some other man might appear and attempt to raise Jason as his own son. But what made it incredibly difficult was the thought of Jason suffering through this disaster and worrying about his mom.

"Do you like my mom?"

"Yes, I do."

We walked together back to the table, where you and Rebecca waited. We ordered a piece of apple pie à la mode with four forks. Everyone took a few quick bites, trying to finish dessert before the ice cream melted.

Shark Point

There are two points of land that help guide me south. The first is Highland Point, at the northern end of Highland Beach. The second is Shark Point, ten miles farther south. Shark Point is important because it marks the entrance to Ponce de Leon Bay and the back route to the race checkpoint at Flamingo.

Reaching Shark Point would be good news and that morning of the fourth day I certainly needed some good news. I came upon a prominent point in my paddle south and immediately and confidently assumed it was Shark Point. I checked my watch. Wow, I was really flying. At this point I may be able to get to Flamingo in midafternoon, I thought. The good news was a real boost. I stepped up my pace.

As I paddled down the coast, I kept an eye out for the Graveyard Creek campsite. I knew it was just past Shark Point. But after about a half mile, I hadn't seen it. I wondered where it had gone. That's not all. This shoreline didn't look anything like my memory of the northern shoreline at Ponce de Leon Bay, where tall trees came right to the water's edge, their roots providing a tangled barrier—as effective as prison bars—to prevent any attempt to safely land a kayak in rough weather.

It didn't look right. It didn't add up. Had I not spent the past three and a half days trying to move a kayak as fast and far as possible down Florida's west coast, I might have figured it out. But this is what the Florida Challenge does. I am always tired, always a little confused. The question is, what am I going to do about it?

I could have gotten out my GPS. I could have consulted my chart. Instead, I was so confident in my ability to navigate without a chart or other aid, I rationalized the evidence. Hurricane Wilma had changed everything. It had swept the trees away from the water's edge and created a broad beach where none existed before. I made a mental note to always respect the power of a hurricane to change a wild landscape. Graveyard Creek, the waterway for which the campsite was named, didn't exist anymore.

When I reached the far end of the beach, I turned up a waterway that I assumed was the Little Shark River. Again, I did not open my chart. Again, I did not consult my GPS. At this point I could hear the water peeling off my bow. About a mile upriver, nothing looked right. Then it hit me. Wrong turn.

The realization came at once. I knew that I'd made a stupid error.

I turned the boat around and paddled back out to the Gulf of Mexico, where I did what I should have done an hour earlier: I turned on my GPS. It told me I still had more than eight miles to Shark Point. My chart showed that I'd just gone up the Broad River—in exactly the wrong direction.

Now I really was traveling fast. I was so angry at my stupidity that I tore into the water and the boat responded by surging forward with each pull on the paddle. My mind raced. *How much time did I lose? How far out of the way did I go? Can I even make it to Flamingo before dark?*

I saw Shark Point up ahead. That wasn't all. An orange sail appeared about a mile behind my right shoulder. It had to be someone in the race. I entered Ponce de Leon Bay and slowed a bit to allow Manitou Cruiser to sail up beside me. We traveled together for a couple miles, trading stories about our experiences over the past three days. Then at Oyster Bay he continued into Whitewater Bay for the straight-line sail across the open bay to Flamingo. I turned south toward the Joe River, preferring to take a slightly longer route that would be more sheltered from high winds. I didn't want to get caught in the middle of turbulent Whitewater Bay in a gale.

Flamingo was only about fifteen miles away, but I couldn't afford any more wrong turns. My concern wasn't time as much as daylight. I wanted to get through the Flamingo checkpoint and well out into Florida Bay before it got too dark. This was essential because the tide in Florida Bay was low and to successfully cross the bay I would have to find a series of channels, passes, and cuts through miles of shallow mud that could easily swallow a person to midthigh. There was a particularly tricky channel called the Twisty Mile that I wanted to locate before nightfall. My repeated mistakes were squandering what little daylight I had left.

I finally pulled my boat ashore at Flamingo at 5:57 P.M. There is a dam at Flamingo that separates the freshwater backcountry from saltwater Florida Bay. To get my kayak to the Florida Bay side I had to drag the boat over a three hundred-yard portage to the saltwater boat ramp. I used a lightweight pair of plastic wheels. Manitou was still at the ramp preparing to leave. I signed the checkpoint logbook at Flamingo and then prepared my boat for a night trip across Florida Bay.

Mud

Manitou and I agreed to paddle together for the thirty-five miles across the bay to Key Largo. We left at about 6:15 P.M. With a west wind and an incoming tide, we flew across the first section of the bay, navigating several narrow channels before sunset. At 9:30 P.M. we stopped at a place called Dump Key to eat some food. Everything was going well. I told Manitou that I'd just experienced perhaps the worst day of paddling in my life, but that the day would be redeemed with our safe arrival that night in Key Largo.

What I failed to notice as we paddled east from Dump Key was the arrival of a cold front. The wind started to shift from west to north. By 11:00 P.M. we were almost halfway across the bay and approaching the appropriately named Twisty Mile Channel. Ominously, the temperature plunged as the wind picked up.

It can be a long and difficult way across Florida Bay to Key Largo. To the casual observer the route appears to be a straight shot across open water between the few mangrove islands that dot the horizon. But closer examination reveals a bay subdivided into a series of forty shallow basins. These basins can easily trap an unwary boater. Imagine a cluster of giant soup bowls. The water in the center of the bowl is four to six feet deep but each basin is surrounded by wide banks of thick, sticky mud. In some places the mud sits less than six inches below the surface of the water—at high tide. At low tide, milewide mud banks emerge all around. This isn't lackluster mud. Regular mud may swallow an ankle or even a knee. I can slog my way out. Florida Bay mud goes on forever. In some places, according to scientists, the mud is six feet deep. That means if I jumped in with enough force I might sink to midchest or higher.

These conditions didn't happen overnight. The mud in Florida Bay has been accumulating for four thousand years. It is primarily silt and clay and comes in a variety of textures, from soupy, to gelatinous, to sand-and-shell porridge. The bay exists in the trough of ancient limestone that underlies most of Florida. The slow flow of water southward from Lake Okeechobee through the Everglades originally emptied into Florida Bay. It provided the ecosystem with a steady supply of fresh water. But "progress" put an end to that. Beginning in the late 1800s, would-be developers dredged a series of canals through the coral rock to try to drain the Everglades. The effort was successful near Lake Okeechobee, but failed farther south. The land never did drain properly, but the harm was already done. Much of the water that once flowed slowly and uninterrupted to Florida Bay is now diverted via manmade canals to the Atlantic Ocean. Estimates are that during the past hundred years the flow of fresh water from the Everglades to Florida Bay has been cut in half.

Help is on the way. Federal and state officials have undertaken a $2 billion ecological restoration project to restore much of the natural flow of water down through the Everglades and back into Florida

Bay. If successful, it will mark the largest environmental restoration project in the history of mankind. But even under the best projections, the project will do nothing about the mud in the bay.

Every time I paddle in Florida Bay I carry in the back of my mind grim thoughts of a Florida version of quicksand. The worst-case scenario starts by getting stuck in the mud. In trying to get unstuck, I get out of my kayak to push the boat. Somehow I lose my balance, the kayak slips out of my grip, while I sink deeper and deeper into the sticky ooze. Struggling only makes me sink deeper. I watch my kayak drift out of reach and blow away across the shallows. Within minutes I am alone in the mud. That's not the worst of it. The tide is rising. I can't get enough leverage on the bottoms of my feet to free my torso, hips, and legs. I calculate that I have maybe three hours to swim free or face the prospect of drowning in the rising tide.

Maybe I could contort my way out of it. If so, I could swim to a channel marker and wait for a fisherman in a motorboat. If not, the tide might rise to my neck or my mouth. I could still breathe through my nose. No one would hear my cries for help, even if I could make a sound beyond gurgling in the water. By the time they found me, I'd still be stuck in the mud like a human fertilizer spike.

When I look at Florida Bay I see a series of traps and a few doors. The best strategy to get across is to avoid the mud altogether. Pinpoint navigation is essential. Fishermen who crisscross the bay in search of redfish, snook, tarpon, and blacktip sharks have established a series of channels through repeated churning of their propellers while crossing the mud banks. Hit the channel and then aim for the next. That's the way across Florida Bay.

Twisty Mile is right in the middle of it all. There is no easy way to retreat from Twisty Mile. You just have to go for it.

I'd taken this route several times in both daylight and at night without any difficulty finding the channel and staying in it. But now, at 11:00 P.M., with Manitou nearby, I couldn't see any of the markers showing the way through the pass. The wind blowing hard from the north made it difficult to stay in one place while trying to get my bearings.

We both knew the channel was nearby—we just had to find it in the dark. Manitou went north. I went east. In what seemed an instant, the gusty north wind and the falling tide left us on different sides of an emerging bank of mud. The mud seemed to appear instantly from nowhere.

I saw deep water to the east and pushed across by using my hands as paddles stuck deep in the muck. At one point I got out of my boat and held tight to both sides of the cockpit to avoid sinking to my thighs. Don't let go of the boat, I told myself. Don't let go. I managed to push the kayak to the edge of deep water. Then I washed the mud off my legs, got back in the boat, and turned on my GPS. I could see that I had a clear shot over open water to the next channel, about five miles away. But Manitou (Mark) was about seventy yards away on the other side of what now looked like a mound of dry land. "Hey, Mark, come over here. I have deep water," I shouted. "Hey, Mark. Mark!"

He couldn't hear me over the roar of the wind. But from where I sat, poised and ready to continue, it looked like he was stuck in the mud. I knew his boat was much heavier than mine and I assumed he couldn't move it.

What I didn't know is that Manitou wasn't stuck at all. In the time it took me to push over the mud bank, he had found the channel and was ready to continue. I could hear him yelling. But I couldn't hear *what* he was yelling. In fact, I discovered later that he was yelling: "Warren, I'm in the channel. Let's go." I just couldn't hear it over the roar of the wind.

With the wind blasting down from the north, the temperature fell fast and kept falling. Exposed in my kayak, I began to shiver. I knew that I had to do something to preserve my body heat. I wrapped myself in a light plastic poncho. The temperature continued to fall. The shivering did not stop. I was under no illusion about the potential dire consequences. If I couldn't get the shivering under control by stabilizing my core body temperature I could be dead before dawn. Hypothermia is relatively easy to avoid, but once it takes hold it can send the unwary into a fast, deadly spiral.

In February 1995, more than a hundred U.S. Army Rangers were undergoing grueling combat and survival training in the swamp on Florida's panhandle near Eglin Air Force Base. The men had been in the field for four days. The water level in the swamp was unusually high, and the Rangers ended up spending significant amounts of time in fifty-two-degree water. When some of the trainees began to show signs of hypothermia—uncontrollable shivering, blue lips, etc.— the trainers called in a helicopter. Two men were flown to a hospital. By then others started showing symptoms that their body temperatures had fallen too low. Thick fog rolled in, grounding the helicopter. The trainers tried to walk the others to a waiting ambulance, but the men were wet and tired. Seven were taken to the base hospital; three died. The body of a fourth Ranger was discovered the next day out in the swamp.

Ranger training is designed to push elite soldiers to their physical and mental limits. These men are among the toughest in the country, and the training is designed to show them how to become even tougher. In addition to being given limited food, they are expected to function on only a few hours of sleep and to keep going in all kinds of weather conditions. To me, that sounds familiar. It sounds like the Florida Challenge.

I had plenty of options. The first thing I did was try to clear my mind. "Keep your wits about you," I told myself. Immediately I wondered: "Who even uses that word, 'wits,' anymore?"

This is good, this is good. Stay calm. Keep thinking of solutions. If necessary, I could push out into the deep water and paddle to keep warm. I had enough food to fuel the effort. I could even paddle the sixteen miles to Key Largo and back, if necessary, to get help for Mark.

But he wouldn't know that was what I was doing. To him it might look like I was abandoning him. There is an unwritten code among WaterTribe challengers. We will come to the aid of anyone in distress and will not leave them until we are sure they are safe. If that meant spending an uncomfortably cold night sitting up in my boat, then that's what I'd do.

I carefully turned around in the kayak and got my dry camp clothes out of the back hatch. I put on every piece of clothing I had, including a fleece ski cap. In addition, I knew that if the temperature continued to plunge I could get out my sleeping bag, a reflective space blanket, and two waterproof tarps. But I hoped the extra clothing would be enough to stop the shivering.

It was cold, too cold to sleep. But at some point exhaustion takes over.

————

What if we just went down to city hall and got someone to say the words, signed the papers. That would be something.

"To have and to hold, for as long as we both shall live." We could be together. We could get a place, or stay in your place.

I'd have to move to Washington. I can't do that yet. Not with Jason in school.

But it would be great. Just a small ceremony. Just family. Okay, maybe Nadine. The cats, too, as ring bearers. Tie little pillows on their backs like saddles. Don't you think?

Or maybe we just take an afternoon off and go to city hall. Sign the papers. Surprise! Do you want the dress and the cake? If you do, that's fine. I'll do that. It would be great.

That would be something. That would really be something.

———

At dawn, the wind still blew hard, and although I could see Mark I still couldn't hear him. The tide had come up somewhat. I pushed out into deep water, and when Mark saw it he paddled out through the channel. That's when we both learned that we'd spent the night on the mud bank for no reason. He was never stuck and neither was I. Amazed, I asked him, why he didn't just paddle through the channel and on to Key Largo.

"I thought you were stuck in the mud," he said. "I wasn't going to leave you."

We headed toward the rising sun and Key Largo having spent nearly seven hours sitting on that mud bank. Seven hours. Some folks might see it as a colossal waste of time. I saw it as a useful bit of education. I learned something important about Manitou Cruiser. I also learned that even in the worst situation I could always sleep sitting up in my boat and survive until daylight.

That's one way of looking at it, but I still had more than nine hundred miles to go.

Mohammed

We paddled the rest of the way across Florida Bay side by side. We talked during part of it. There were also long periods of quiet. It was only sixteen miles to Key Largo, but at some point twenty-six years fell away.

In the summer of 1980, my friend Mohammed Saleh invited me to travel with him into the Arabian desert. It was more than just sightseeing.

That year I worked as a reporter at an English-language newspaper in Jeddah, Saudi Arabia. I took a week off. We drove east from the city, to the so-called Heathen Highway around Mecca, then south through the Asir Mountains and down into a remote, hot corner of Saudi Arabia near the Yemen border. At a certain point, Mohammed turned his white Peugeot off the paved highway. We raced across a wide plain. Flourlike dust hung in the air behind the car in a roiling mass of suspended powder. He parked the car in a cluster of rocky hills. I tried to brush the dust out of my hair and off my shirt while looking around for Mohammed's relatives. All I saw were rocks and sky, not a hint of living vegetation other than an occasional dust-covered acacia tree.

The route was too rugged for the car. Mohammed opened the trunk and took out a pistol in a black leather shoulder holster. He strapped it across his chest. We gathered the rest of our things and began to walk.

We trekked through the rocky hills. My eyes kept moving between that pistol and the surrounding hilltops. I wondered who or what might be out there that required the presence of a loaded gun. All I could see was rock and sky.

"You are with me now," Mohammed said, talking over his shoulder. "Whatever I need to do to protect you, I will do it, even if I might die." When he said this he turned and looked at me to gauge my reaction.

We had spent hours back in Jeddah talking about Islam and Saudi Arabia and Arabs. We were friends and I understood that this was part of his tradition. "I will do the same," I told him. "I will protect you, too."

He smiled that broad, irrepressible smile that I saw every time we met; the smile, a firm handshake, and a slight bow.

It is tradition; it is the way things have always been in Arabia. One man alone in the desert could easily die. Two men together in the desert had a chance to live.

Life in the United States is different from the Arabian wilderness. It would be absurd to head off for a hike in the American woods and have your friend offer a solemn pledge to fight to the death to protect you. Imagine the hike after that, the side glances, the awkward silence, wondering whether during the next pregnant pause your buddy might pull out a .44 Magnum and demand that other hikers on the trail back off. "We're walking here. We're walking here."

In Arab culture it is essential that everyone know his place in the hierarchy. God, family, tribe, country. With my friend Mohammed I had been elevated into a very important spot. I fully intended, if necessary, to live up to my responsibilities.

In American culture, such devotion is no longer much of a priority. Sometimes it seems the governing principle is every man for himself. I like the Arabian way.

Until I took that trip into the desert I never thought about the possibility of actually fighting to the death to protect someone. I never considered the notion of trading my life to save a life.

Parents of a gravely ill child know this issue from the core of their being. It is the ultimate expression of love. Yet it remains a question largely unexamined by most.

What if I had to make a list of those people I would trade my life to save, who would be on it?

Filling out such a list is significantly harder than assembling the seating chart at a wedding. And much more revealing. Who is worthy of such sacrifice, such devotion? Who is unworthy? What makes the difference? Would you make the sacrifice for your child, but not your spouse? Is anyone on your list?

It is not a question of whether I would try to protect someone in a life-threatening situation. Pretty much everyone would try to do something. The ultimate issue, the hard question, is whether I would make a clean and even trade, my life for someone else's.

This is what I pondered as I walked with Mohammed through those hot, dry hills. I came to the conclusion that it was more than just a hypothetical inquiry, that there was truth in the question and power in the answer. This is what I decided: the value of my life would increase in direct proportion to my selfless devotion to someone else. It's all about who's on the list. And whether I am on their list.

I had talked for hours with Mohammed at an outdoor coffee shop in Jeddah's old market near the Red Sea. We were friends, best friends. But when we went to the desert, we become brothers.

Day Five, Key Largo

The seven hours spent in the mud at Twisty Mile left both Manitou and me tired and dragging throughout the day as we tried to prepare for the second stage of the Florida Challenge: the two hundred-mile run up the east coast to Sebastian Inlet.

We decided to continue traveling together for the trip from Key Largo to Miami and the long crossing of Biscayne Bay. But first there were showers to take, clothes to wash, food to buy and pack, a few meals to eat, and most important, many, many hours of catch-up sleep to enjoy. Our plan was to leave Key Largo by 4:00 A.M. and, hopefully, take advantage of a forecast wind shift from north to southeast.

Wizard had already been cooling his heels at Key Largo for nearly a day by the time Manitou and I arrived. We were both surprised to see him. A couple of hours after greeting us, he set sail for Sebastian Inlet. There wasn't much we could do about it other than wish him well. I figured that was the last I'd see of him.

My prerace prediction was that Wizard would win the Florida Challenge, and nothing I'd seen so far altered that assessment. He was the only WaterTribe member whose race name had been changed by Chief and bestowed like an honorary university degree. Wizard had already become a legend in the group after completing a three hundred-mile race around much of Michigan in a two-man inflatable raft purchased off the shelf at West Marine. He somehow rigged a sail and rudder and navigated through headwinds and storms in Lake Huron and Lake Michigan to a second-place finish in the race. It was a magical performance befitting, well, a wizard.

We all knew Wizard's strategy. His approach to the race was simple and effective. He just kept going. He would set a course five or more miles offshore, raise his sail, and catch short cat naps while underway. It meant that even though his boat might only average two and a half or three miles an hour in light wind, he could cover significant distances while the rest of us searched for a piece of dry land to cook a meal and catch a few hours of sleep.

Wizard's plan was to build up as much of a lead as possible during the open-water portions of the race. He knew he'd be at a disadvantage on the portage and in the north Florida rivers, but he figured if he could amass a big enough cushion it might keep him in the lead long enough to get back to the open water of the Gulf of Mexico and the finish line at Tampa Bay before the rest of us caught up to him.

The most ambitious—and potentially dangerous—part of his plan involved sailing in the Gulf Stream about ten miles offshore in the Atlantic Ocean. He'd get an extra three-mile-an-hour push from the warm water current while heading north from Miami to Sebastian Inlet. It was a gutsy move considering the size of Wizard's boat.

It didn't seem like it at the time, but all three of us getting to Key Largo when we did was fortuitous. It became the first major turning point in the Florida Challenge. Early Thursday morning, as forecast, the wind shifted from north to southeast. Weather reports said the wind would build to twenty miles an hour and that it would blow out of the southeast for several days.

Seven challengers were still on their way to Key Largo. The wind change meant the gusty southeast wind would help push Wizard, Manitou, and me quickly northward. At the same time the relentless blast would hit the seven other challengers smack in the face, slowing their progress to a crawl.

Hit hardest was Marek "Wayfarer" Uliasz of Fort Collins, Colorado. He started the Florida Challenge at a significant disadvantage. In the weeks immediately prior to the race he faced a crush of work overseas. His last-minute return to the United States left him barely enough time to pack his boat and car. He drove from Colorado to Florida and arrived just before the start of the challenge, without any opportunity to catch up on his sleep.

Sleep deprivation is a standard feature of every WaterTribe event. It is to the WaterTribe what Heartbreak Hill is to those who run the Boston Marathon. Wayfarer took sleep deprivation to new levels by arriving at the starting line with a substantial sleep deficit.

When the headwinds arrived, that pretty much sealed his fate. Wayfarer got halfway across Florida Bay and just ran out of gas in the grip of an unforgiving counterforce. His GPS later revealed he endured fifty-four miles of corkscrews, circles, and figure eights churned out during two nights and a day of paddling over the same twenty-five-mile section of windswept water in the central part of Florida Bay.

The wind took a toll on Alaskan Seahorse as well. Both Wayfarer and Alaskan Seahorse dropped out of the Florida Challenge at Key Largo.

Meanwhile, Wizard's plan to sail quickly up the east coast soon encountered trouble. The seas were higher than he anticipated with gusts over twenty. The Coast Guard intercepted him south of Miami on his way out toward the blue water. They didn't know anything about Wizard and his sailing abilities. To them he was just some nut trying to sail a floating refrigerator out into the ocean in very unforgiving conditions. After checking his safety gear they let him continue sailing toward the Gulf Stream, but only on condition that he make frequent radio contact with Coast Guard headquarters.

A few hours later, with the wind still building, that decision was rescinded. The Coast Guard told Wizard to reroute his trip from the Gulf Stream to the Intracoastal Waterway. It cost him valuable time. More important, it kept a door open for those of us behind him.

PART III

Heading North:
Key Largo to Sebastian Inlet,
200 Miles

Day Six

Manitou and I pushed off from Key Largo at 4:45 A.M., just as the first puff of a breeze started to blow from the southeast. By midday we were in the center of Biscayne Bay with a steady wind at our backs and the Miami skyline growing larger and larger on the horizon.

Although the race follows the Florida coast, there are several places that offer the possibility of saving substantial time by cutting across open water. Now we faced the longest crossing yet, about thirty-five miles from the Card Sound Bridge to downtown Miami.

The water in Biscayne Bay was bright turquoise from a distance but crystal clear when looking straight down into it. Visibility appeared to be about twenty feet or more. The wind swirled this way and that when we first entered the bay, so I kept my sail down and just paddled. Manitou reduced the size of his sail somewhat and we both headed toward open water at about the same speed. I, of course, paddled and worked hard to maintain a good pace. I felt obliged to keep up a brisk cadence with my paddle stroke because I felt Manitou might be holding back as a courtesy to me. Every half hour or so I'd look over and he'd be eating a snack or making a cell phone call or yawning and stretching. He wasn't paddling. The wind filled his sail nicely. He moved at about four and a half to five miles an hour. It wasn't killing me to keep up, but I was paddling, sometimes pretty hard. With gusts to twenty, thick swells pulsed across the bay. Small waves broke and washed over the deck several times. If I hadn't been paying attention these conditions could have sent me over in a flash. About midway across the bay, we turned slightly toward the northwest bringing the wind more directly behind us. This slight adjustment gave me a bit more stability and confidence. I put up my downwind sail and continued to paddle. For much of that last run into Miami we were probably moving at about six miles an hour or a little faster.

The approach to Miami is a slow-motion event. When I rounded tiny East Arsenicker Key in the southern part of Biscayne Bay I couldn't even see the Miami skyline. It isn't even a notion. Then, a few miles north, it appears as a tiny dark block on the horizon—like the faintest bar signal indicator on a cell phone. Gradually as I continued to move north, one block became two, then four. Eventually the beginning of a skyline emerged. Nothing prepared me for the dramatic scene of approaching the city up close, as we did in the late-afternoon sunlight. A modern glass and steel metropolis seemed to rise out of the bay and then loom over us like a wave about to break.

We made it. From about a mile out we began taking pictures of each other with the city in the background. Once we got to downtown Miami, Manitou had me take a picture of him in his boat with his arms stretched above his head. He said he'd seen a similar photo of his mentor, Verlen Kruger, stretching his arms after a long paddle into downtown Miami during one of his epic trips. Out of thousands of admiring paddlers, Kruger had selected Manitou to carry on the business of building and selling Kruger expedition canoes. Manitou wanted his own version of the photo. He handed me his camera. I framed the shot and took it.

"Awesome." Manitou kept saying it. "Awesome."

We didn't pause very long to celebrate our arrival. We continued north under a series of draw bridges and stopped briefly on a small spoil island just across the water from the Miami Herald Building. A spoil island is a pile of sand left behind from dredging the channel to create the Intracoastal Waterway. The "spoils" had to go someplace. Sometimes they just dumped it a few hundred yards to the east or west of the new channel through Biscayne Bay. Over time these islands sprouted vegetation and became popular destinations for weekend boaters. I was hoping one would also provide a safe urban camping spot for a few hours.

Ah Yes, Miami

The air in Miami is sultry and electric, and I'm not talking about the frequent lightning storms. This place vibrates—it trembles. What is happening in Miami is extraordinarily important. Miami is the capital of Latin America—and the future of America.

It is anti-Castro exiles shaking their fists in the air, and Guatamalan moms making beds in the Sheraton. It is "businessmen" from Colombia moving money into numbered Brickell Avenue accounts and rickety boats filled to the brim with dreams of any place other than Port-au-Prince. It is Santeria chicken parts left on the courthouse steps to help deadlock the jury and a sun-bronzed American top model Rollerblading through art deco South Beach. It is Al Capone in the 1940s, and Jackie Gleason's "sun and fun capital of the world" in the 1960s. This is where Ed Sullivan came for his second nationwide telecast of the Beatles—live from the Deauville on Miami Beach in February 1964. It is the 1972 undefeated Miami Dolphins. It is two detectives, Sonny Crockett and Rico Tubbs, wearing linen suits with T-shirts chasing bad guys in fast, exotic cars in a music video packaged as a television show called *Miami Vice.*

Famous residents include Latin pop queen Gloria Estefan, tennis star and eye candy Anna Kournikova, Clinton administration attorney general Janet Reno, and football superstar and acquitted murder suspect O. J. Simpson. Deposed Panamanian dictator and convicted drug conspirator Manuel Antonio Noriega has been a longtime resident of the federal lockup.

In 1969, rock and roll poet Jim Morrison came here. In an alcohol- and drug-induced live concert in Coconut Grove he stumbled through his lyrics and at one point opened his trousers to free his spirit—so to speak. The city fathers were not amused. In September 1970, he was convicted of indecent exposure and sentenced to eight months' hard labor. Morrison never served a day in jail. Instead, his lawyers appealed. He went to Paris and died nine months later in a bathtub.

The tragedy is Parisian, but the sin is 100 percent Miami. Miami vice. A version of law and order in a city with an unlimited appetite for corruption.

Miami is temptation and danger. It is steam. Desire. It is a beautiful naked woman pointing a gun at my heart and applying slight pressure to the trigger. But all I can see is the single bead of sweat on her left nipple, waiting to drop.

That's Miami.

Voyage of a Thousand Bridges

A "haulover" is a narrow strip of land used to carry or drag boats from one body of water to another. Along Florida's Atlantic coast there are several historic haulovers. One is Bakers Haulover.

Bakers Haulover was the domain of a man named Baker, who in the early 1800s, kept a team of mules on a sandy sliver of land between the northern end of Biscayne Bay and the Atlantic Ocean. A tow across the sand from bay to ocean could cut a half day or more off a boat's journey to lucrative fishing in the Gulf Stream. A century later, in 1925, engineers dug a channel through the sand. Bakers Haulover suddenly became Bakers Haulover Inlet, which is a contradiction in terms. Still, the name enjoyed the benefit of local recognition. Everyone knew of Bakers Haulover, so now they knew the inlet's location, too.

The engineers also built a bridge with arched columns extending over the cut to connect Miami Beach with the emerging communities of Hollywood and Fort Lauderdale via an oceanfront road that later became known as A1A. In 1926, a massive hurricane hit, destroying both ends of the bridge. Only the central portion remained standing in the midst of the washed-out inlet, like some misplaced Roman aqueduct. Engineers fixed the bridge, reinforced the banks of the inlet, and built a series of moorings and docks just north of the cut. In the 1930s these docks became the backdrop for one of the most famous sportfishing venues. World-record marlin, swordfish, sailfish, tarpon, and dolphin were hauled up and weighed on the famous scales of the Metropolitan Miami Fishing Tournament.

The docks were dark and lifeless at 2:20 A.M. as we paddled past the charter fishing boats. We'd stopped for about five hours on a small spoil island at the north end of Biscayne Bay. Now we were back on the move. We did not debate whether to take Bakers Haulover Inlet to the ocean. Had the wind dropped down to a whisper we might have considered heading up Florida's east coast via the offshore route. Overnight the wind remained steady at twenty miles an hour with higher gusts. The Coast Guard issued a small-craft advisory. We knew the surf would be high and the ocean itself would be difficult or impossible for us to navigate. We also knew we could remain behind the barrier islands and stay sheltered from the strongest winds by following the Intracoastal Waterway. If necessary we could follow the waterway the entire 360 miles to the checkpoint at Fort Clinch near the Georgia border. In fact, that was my plan.

The Intracoastal Waterway is a marvel of engineering and a monument to man's often misguided desire to shape the natural world to his purposes. Any beachgoer who has tried to build a castle in the sand with a protective moat in the face of a rising tide understands this. It is sheer folly to attempt to train sand to stay in one place in the path of rushing water. Predictably, the moat fills in and the castle collapses. The entire Florida coast is like that ill-fated castle and the Intracoastal Waterway is the doomed moat.

What gives the waterway the semblance of permanence is the U.S. Army Corps of Engineers. This is an entire government agency that has managed to make the digging of ditches into a hundred-million-dollar industry.

To really appreciate it, one should view the Intracoastal Waterway from an airplane or a helicopter. Internet satellite images are
cool too. It is a continuous underwater ditch. The dredges cut right
down the center of shallow bays and rivers, depositing the sand and
muck spoils a few hundred yards away creating a line of man-made
islands in the shallow bays.

Of course there are sights to see along the way—Miami, Palm
Beach, the Kennedy Space Center, St. Augustine—but anyone who
has traveled the Intracoastal Waterway in Florida from one end to the
other most remembers the bridges. The trip from Miami to Georgia
involves passing under eighty-two bridges, but it feels more like a voy-
age of a thousand bridges. There is always another bridge up ahead.

The hour-to-hour strategy along the entire east coast can be
summed up in four words. Get to that bridge. That's it. Once I arrive
at a bridge I adopt the same strategy all over again. I squint toward
the horizon and give myself a new assignment. Get to that bridge.
Eighty-two times.

It could be worse. Paddling a kayak I had no trouble gliding under the bridges. It is a different story for sailboats.

Manitou's mast measured just under twelve feet. I know it because
I was with him when he approached the Venetian Causeway, the historic and scenic bridge that leads from Miami to Miami Beach. The
bridge is marked with a twelve-foot clearance. In an abundance of
caution, Manitou radioed the bridge keeper and requested that she
open the drawbridge. She refused. She told him he didn't need the
bridge open.

I paddled ahead and then turned around in the channel to watch
the unfolding drama. It looked close. I actually held my breath as
Manitou paddle-sailed through the center of the bridge. He positioned his boat to follow the highest point of the arched drawbridge.

He had about six inches to spare. One small boat wake and the tip of his mast would scrape the underside of the bridge. A significant wake might have bent or broken his mast.

The original Venetian Causeway was built in 1926. It replaced the 1913 Collins Bridge, said at the time to be the longest wooden bridge in the world. In 1999, the Venetian Causeway underwent a $29 million renovation and, nonetheless, remained one of the lowest bridges along the entire length of Florida's Intracoastal Waterway.

The trend along the Intracoastal Waterway is to replace the smaller drawbridges with sixty-five-foot permanent flyover bridges. Of the eighty-two bridges from Miami to the Georgia border, thirty are now in the sixty-foot range.

The two lowest bridges along the waterway are railroad bridges, with clearances listed at five feet and seven feet. Unlike roadway bridges, railroad bridges are always open until a train approaches. In a way, they don't count as bridges. They are more like temporary obstacles.

The lowest drawbridges are those with a nine-foot clearance. They are located in Boca Raton, Delray Beach, and Titusville. For some of these bridges Manitou took down his mast and paddled under, although he was within his rights to request the bridge to open.

What Dads Are For

It wasn't always the paddling. My body adjusted. My mind tuned out. First, I settle into a rhythm and the next moment I'd be years younger, or years older, or about to relive something that should be dead and gone.

Not all of it was bad. Sitting alone in a boat day after day, mile after mile, forced me to confront myself and examine my life.

I've spent my entire professional existence chasing news stories, some of them tragic beyond words. Just a few weeks after being hired as a rookie reporter at the *Red Bank Register,* I watched a fireman pull a young girl's lifeless body from an icy creek. A few weeks later, a little boy disappeared in the Navesink River. Those stories were hard to write. Years later, when I became a parent, the faces of those dead children started coming back.

When my son, Jason, was about five years old, "Santa Claus" brought him a plastic car big enough to sit inside. It was designed to permit a kid to propel the car forward by moving his or her feet against the ground like Fred Flintstone. Jason spent hours in that car. He'd race through the house at top speed, providing an effective laxative for the cat.

Often he'd drive his car outside on the patio near the pool. The swimming pool provided the centerpiece of the house and was one of the reasons we bought the place. The living room, family room, and master bedroom all looked out through sliding glass doors at the tranquil blue water. Of course, we knew pools and young children can be dangerous. We did two things to reduce the threat. First, we installed a kid fence around the pool, so Jason could play and drive his car near the pool without us worrying about him falling in. Second, Jason learned to swim. From a very early age he was encouraged to feel comfortable in the pool and not be afraid to swim underwater.

One day, in the rush of ordinary events, the pool fence remained open. Jason was on the patio competing in the Daytona 500 in his car. He drove the car into the pool. No one saw it happen. He was on his own.

He did not panic. For him it was just another opportunity to swim underwater. Another adventure. He reached the stairs and ran soaking wet into the house to report the unusual presence of an automobile in the swimming pool.

I wasn't home. Jason told me the entire story when I returned from work. Next, I heard the story from his mother. Then from Jason, again.

"I did it. I did it," he said, the pride swelling in his throat.

"Yes, you did."

He ran back and forth between his mother and me. A celebration.

I tried to avoid the terrible temptation of thinking what might have happened. How it might have ended. I did not want to tarnish the victory. Later, standing at my closet after hanging up my tie, I closed my eyes and exhaled. The air came out of me. Almost all of it. It was as if I'd been holding my breath for years.

The story of the car in the pool is one of my favorite stories about my son. I especially like it because he did it himself. He saved himself.

This is part of what I pondered paddling a kayak around Florida. At some point in his life, Jason may find himself alone and in danger. There is no way to know beforehand the what, the where, the when of it. Someone has to get him ready. Someone has to show him how to work past the fear.

Mothers love and nurture their sons to prepare them for life. Fathers condition and toughen up their sons to protect them from death. Love is the better gig, no doubt about that. But consider what it takes to teach a child how to swim underwater. Swimming is only half of it. The other half is trusting that he will make it safely back to the surface every time.

Imagine the courage it takes to try to raise a son to be fearless.

Imagine the courage. And the love.

The Nation's Waterway

Florida is not unique in boasting an inshore water route. The Intracoastal Waterway extends nearly three thousand miles along the Atlantic coast from Boston to Key West and follows much of the Gulf coast from the Florida panhandle to the Rio Grande. It wasn't all geographical serendipity. In some places canals had to be cut through dry land to tie the waterway together. The finished result makes it possible today to travel by boat from Key West all the way to Point Pleasant, New Jersey, without ever having to enter the Atlantic Ocean.

The waterway represents one of the nation's first major engineering projects. In 1808, treasury secretary Albert Gallatin proposed an interconnected inland waterway spanning the east coast. His vision included four man-made canals. One sliced through the Dismal Swamp linking North Carolina's Albemarle Sound to Chesapeake Bay. Another cut across Maryland and Delaware linking Chesapeake Bay and the Delaware River. A third, bisected New Jersey between the Delaware and Raritan rivers. The forth cut through Cape Cod in Massachusetts to speed the trip to Boston. All but the Delaware-Raritan canal in New Jersey are still in use.

Secretary Gallatin's vision provided a cheap, safe, and reliable form of transportation along the coast. It also came in handy during World War II when German submarines parked off east coast beaches and turned the offshore waters into a shooting gallery. Supplies could be securely shipped from state to state via the relatively secure (and shallow) intracoastal system. Once American cargo ships and tankers left the inlets for the deeper Atlantic, however, they were vulnerable to torpedoes.

While much of the Intracoastal Waterway was in place along the mid-Atlantic seaboard by the early 1800s, the Florida section of the waterway wasn't even contemplated until much later. Florida became a state in 1845, but with sparse population there was little economic incentive to dredge channels and dig canals.

The first organized effort to create what would become the Intracoastal Waterway in Florida began in 1881. This was no public project. A private firm, the Florida Coast Line Canal and Transportation Company, undertook to improve the state's waterways. Of course, the effort would benefit the state, but the primary motives were land and money.

The state legislature granted the company a million acres to lubricate the wheels of progress. Back then it was a million acres of marshes and remote beaches. Today, that million acres includes some of the priciest beach and waterfront real estate in the country.

Work on the Florida East Coast Canal started in 1883. By law, the resulting channel had to be fifty feet wide and five feet deep. The dredging extended through creeks and bays. About fifty miles of the waterway required excavation through dry land. With heavy tides and shifting shoals the waterway required constant maintenance. Geology and geography weren't the only obstacles to the construction of a reliable east coast waterway. The dredging company had to fight off the competitive efforts of former Standard Oil tycoon Henry Flagler, whose vision for the state centered on his Florida East Coast Railway— not some watery ditch capable of carrying mountains of cargo at a fraction of the cost of a freight train.

At the same time the dredges slung slop, Flagler built a railroad system headed roughly in the same direction—south. By 1894, Flagler's railroad ran from St. Augustine to Lake Worth. He knew the rails weren't enough. He needed to give people a reason to ride his trains deep into the Florida wilderness, so he built the Royal Poinciana Hotel on what had been a mosquito-infested mangrove island between Lake Worth and the Atlantic Ocean. The place was called Palm Beach.

The Royal Poinciana was advertised as the largest wooden structure in the world. It required 5 million board feet of lumber and 2,400 gallons of paint. After two expansions, the hotel could accommodate two thousand guests each night. The grounds were a pristine study in tropical opulence. The hotel featured wide porches lined with rocking chairs and shaded walkways to the beach. Flagler took Victorian splendor to a new level.

In 1896, Flagler built a second hotel on the ocean side of the Royal Poinciana grounds. The hotel was initially named the Palm Beach Inn, but that name never stuck. Guests at the Royal Poinciana kept asking to stay in that other building—the one over by the breakers.

In 1904, a room at the Breakers cost $4 a night. With it, a guest was entitled to breakfast, lunch, and dinner.

Flagler's strategy worked. Palm Beach was no longer a quiet haven. It soon became the preferred retreat of those with money and power—a kind of winter version of Newport, Bar Harbor, or Tuxedo Park. The guest lists included Rockefellers, Vanderbilts, and Astors. Many guests liked the view so much they decided to buy property in the neighborhood and build mansions.

Flagler did pretty well himself. Under Florida's land grant system, he received eight thousand acres of undeveloped land for each mile of new railroad track he built. Eventually he amassed 2 million acres.

Under Flagler's plan, the railroad would end at Palm Beach. Communities farther south well understood the importance of reliable transportation. So did land speculators, who tried to anticipate any future path of Flagler's tracks and set themselves up to extort a small fortune.

Julia Tuttle, owner of a 640-acre citrus grove, tried to persuade Flagler to extend his rail line from Lake Worth to Biscayne Bay. At the time, her south Florida settlement was known as Fort Dallas, named for the old Seminole War military encampment on her property.

Flagler wasn't much interested in plunging deeper into Florida's untamed swamps and rejoining the battle against land gougers. Mrs. Tuttle wasn't about to give up. Following the Great Freeze of December 1894 and February 1895, she made it known to Flagler that the icy winds that destroyed most of Florida's citrus crop never blew far enough south to chill the oranges in her grove. Flagler was intrigued.

Work soon began on an extension of his rail line. It reached Fort Dallas in April 1896. Grateful residents wanted to rename their tiny town in his honor. He suggested they use an Indian name instead— Mayaimi, which became Miami.

The railroad was only the beginning. Flagler also dredged a nine-foot-deep shipping channel across the shallow bay to the open ocean. He built roads, created a waterworks and a power plant, and underwrote Miami's first newspaper, the *Metropolis*. Within a year, Flagler's 350-room Royal Palm Hotel opened just north of the Miami River. It boasted two electric elevators.

Flagler wasn't done. With word out that construction would soon begin on a canal through Panama, Flagler decided to extend his Florida East Coast Railway another 138 miles to the south. In 1912, Flagler himself rode the first train into Key West.

As for the Florida East Coast Canal, the dredging project reached Biscayne Bay in 1912—the same year Flagler celebrated in

Key West. There were no grand hotels associated with the canal. America's rich and famous were not flocking to the waterway. But the accomplishment was important. It opened up Florida's east coast for further development. The project had taken twenty-nine years and cost $3.5 million. For the first time it was now possible to follow an inland water route from Miami to the Georgia border.

Congress took over the Florida coastline canal in 1927 and authorized an improved channel seventy-five feet wide and eight feet deep. The dredging was done piecemeal over many years. In 1931, Congress directed that the channel be widened from seventy-five to one hundred feet across. In 1939, lawmakers authorized a twelve-foot depth along the entire length of the waterway. It was an ambitious goal. By 1965, the Intracoastal Waterway was twelve feet deep and one hundred feet wide from Jacksonville to Fort Pierce. That's where the project stalled. The southern section, from Fort Pierce to Miami, remains only ten feet deep to this day.

Up the Intracoastal

We had been following the Intracoastal Waterway since we left the checkpoint at Key Largo almost twenty-four hours earlier. But to my mind, the trip up the Intracoastal really began when we left Biscayne Bay and encountered the long, narrow passage up Florida's heavily populated east coast. There are over a million boats with access to these cramped channels. We arrived on a Friday, anticipating heavy weekend boat traffic. Fortunately for us, at 2:30 A.M., pretty much everyone else was asleep.

Gliding through the towering condos of North Miami in the predawn darkness felt like we were floating down the Grand Canyon on a moonless night and someone had positioned fires at random intervals along the face of the cliffs. At that hour—in the darkness—my eye was attracted to the two or three lighted windows in each building. While most of the condo commandos were sound asleep, every high-rise building included a few night owls. They were surprisingly consistent. Lights burned in every large building. No high-rise was totally dark.

The water was ink black and swirling in places. The barrier island between the waterway and the ocean is only a few hundred yards across, and I could hear the roar of the surf crashing on the beach. The steady wind had whipped the ocean into a combination of rolling breakers and wind-tossed whitecaps. The palms swayed under the pressure, the fronds all pointing north and vibrating. A plastic grocery bag flew down the street and then shot fifty feet up into the dark sky.

I had raised my sail to try to get a little extra push from the wind. At places between the apartment towers, the wind wrapped around the structures and was somehow funneled back toward me in a single, almighty burst. These blasts came from the north—ahead of me—not the south. The first time it happened it just flexed the sail backward briefly. The wind stopped. The sail refilled from behind, and I continued forward. A few minutes later I was hit full force in the face by a massive and prolonged wall of wind. The sail bent sharply backward. It stopped my forward progress and then began to turn the boat. I could feel the boat about to go over. I braced to counteract the force. "No. No. No." Somehow, I managed to stay dry. That close call provided all the warning I needed. I took down the sail.

I knew I could keep the boat moving at a respectable pace with my paddle alone.

Swirling blasts from above weren't the only dangers lurking in the condo canyons. The Intracoastal is narrow here and lined with concrete bulkheads. I'd paddled my kayak along this route once in the middle of a busy boating day. I vowed never to do it again.

In most places in Florida when a large boat cruises past, it generates a wake that radiates outward in a trailing V. The motion creates a swell that rolls through the water and is usually no big deal for paddlers. It lifts the kayak and then the energy is expended in the form of waves breaking on a beach or swells pushing up into a tangle of mangrove roots.

But, in a narrow channel with concrete bulkheads like this section of the Intracoastal Waterway, there is nothing to dissipate the energy of the wake. It rolls up onto the concrete bulkhead and then comes right back out toward the center of the channel. It is not particularly dangerous to face the wake of one or two boats, but multiply it by the scores of boats that zip or chug past on a busy weekend and some sections of the Intracoastal start to resemble the deep-dirt cycle of a Maytag washing machine.

It doesn't have to be dangerous. The confused seas can be fun to paddle—for about twenty minutes. Try doing it at the end of an eighteen-hour day of hard paddling. I do not want to capsize in the Intracoastal Waterway—at least not in southeast Florida. There are strong tides that could pull me into barnacle-encrusted bulkheads and piers. There are scores of intoxicated boat captains behind the wheels of half-ton speeding buzz saws. The raw sewage alone would likely be fatal.

That's what it would have been like to paddle through this section of water during a Saturday afternoon. Instead, at 3:00 A.M. on a

Friday morning we had the water to ourselves and our trip was pretty close to perfect.

Just before dawn, we reached Port Everglades. On weekends it is a bustling cruise ship terminal. Thousands of sunburned passengers disembark, only to be replaced by thousands of pale-skinned newcomers. On weekends there can be as many as seven ships in the port at once. Security is very no-nonsense.

A few months earlier I paddled my kayak up the Intracoastal and into the port. My tiny boat looked like a floating toothpick compared to the giant cruise ships. Within moments I was confronted by a Marine Police officer. He sped up to me with his blue lights flashing and his siren blaring. Then, with me bobbing in my boat, he began an interrogation. He asked me what I thought I was doing. I restrained myself from providing the obvious answer: "Why, officer, I'm paddling a kayak. It is a vessel originally designed by Inuit hunters in the Arctic. It is propelled forward by means of a double-bladed paddle. It is also a form of recreation and an enjoyable way to spend a delightful weekend afternoon."

An astute observer of human behavior, I could tell such a response would not be appreciated. I also resisted the urge to raise my hands above my head in a sign of surrender. I just sat still and looked back at the officer. This was Barney Fife in a boat. Before I could gather my thoughts to render an appropriate response, the officer spoke again. "You need to stay on the east side of the channel. You can't come over to this side of the channel."

I looked around for a sign that might have warned me—or anyone else—of this regulation. There was none. I suppose some high-priced security consultant from Halliburton advised our government that such a sign might tip off a band of al Qaeda kayakers. I am not opposed to security or those who provide it. What bugs me is an attitude by some security officials that anyone who doesn't carry a badge is automatically a terror suspect.

I paddled to the east side of the channel. As I did it I could feel the ever-vigilant police officer's eyes on my boat. I could well imagine he had his hand on his pistol and his finger on the trigger, just in case. Yea, right, like I'm going to suddenly double back and ram my seventeen-foot, fiberglass kayak into some nine hundred thousand-ton cruise ship named *Jackass of the Seas.*

Allahu Akbar, indeed.

As we paddled north, I warned Manitou of the tight security at Port Everglades. "We need to stay on the east side of the channel," I told him, fully anticipating another delightful encounter with America's homeland security blanket. "They take security very seriously here."

We arrived at the port just before dawn. All the cruise ships were still at sea and there didn't appear to be any security. We paddled on the east side of the port just in case the west side had been seeded with submerged mines to thwart kamikaze kayakers. We took special care to paddle like Americans.

Fort Lauderdale

The sun rose as we crossed the inlet and entered Fort Lauderdale. The sight of streaks of yellowish light blazing across the morning sky like a phalanx of Star Wars light sabers reminded me I'd entered hallowed ground. Years ago, this place was world-famous as the location of *Spring Break.* The movie *Where the Boys Are* was filmed here in 1960. Each year around the sacred Christian celebration of the arrival of the Easter Bunny and some other religious event, millions of collegiate scholars descended on the beach for a weeklong celebration of alcoholic beverages and tiny bathing suits. Nothing wrong with tiny bathing suits (on women), but the single-minded pursuit of dead brain cells seemed to trigger an unbelievably high incidence of public urination and involuntary lunch loss. All over town ornamental plants started dying, even the fake plastic orchids.

The city decided enough was enough. An ordinance was passed outlawing the public consumption of beer. It worked. Within about thirty minutes, everyone grabbed their coolers and drove to Daytona Beach. Now you can walk on the sidewalk in Fort Lauderdale without risking a nasty slip-and-fall injury. There is still a lot of public urination, but the offenders are all over eighty and wearing Depends, so you can't really tell it's happening.

Fort Lauderdale was founded back in the 1830s on the banks of the New River. It was wild back then. Anyone will tell you. The city has a long history of marauding Indians, ruthless pirates, and carpet-bagging Yankees—and that's just the baseball teams arriving for spring training.

I had lived and worked in Fort Lauderdale for several years, but I'd never seen the city from the water. Not like this. We paddled past the Bahia Mar Marina, where John D. MacDonald's intrepid sleuth Travis McGee lived at slip F-18 aboard the *The Busted Flush*.

Some of the houses fronting the water are pretty glitzy. A few appear to have been designed to host a three-ring circus, complete with vaulted ceilings to facilitate the high-wire act. Some have guest rooms for the guest rooms. There are swimming pools shaped like lima beans or various letters of the alphabet. One house was surrounded by life-sized statues of teenaged girls who had apparently misplaced their bathing suits. Very classy.

Every house had a boat. Every boat had a name. These weren't just houses and boats; some were bold and brassy declarations of wealth. "Look at me, I've got more than you." The winner of the most appropriately named yacht in Fort Lauderdale goes to a chunky sport-fishing boat named *Poverty Sucks.*

Boating has always been near the center of life in the city. Just about every house—including the smallest bungalow—fronts on a canal and has a place to park a boat in the backyard. There are so many canals in Fort Lauderdale it is actually called the Venice of America.

The Venice of America? They've got to be kidding. It's a nice thought, but about the only thing Fort Lauderdale has in common with Venice is the quality of the water in the canals. Venice is exquisite architecture at Piazza San Marco, centuries of history, and breathless romance in a gondola. Fort Lauderdale is cigarette boats, "high-stakes" Indian bingo, and a quickie in the backseat of a Chevy Cavalier.

The Mall

One day in the mid-1990s, we went to a crowded shopping mall, the three of us. We weren't there to spend money. This was a spontaneous outing, a shared adventure. Jason would run up ahead and then look back to make sure we were coming. We walked side by side about a foot away from each other, but it could have been a thousand miles. She did not speak to me. She did not look at me, she did not look in store windows. It was as if she was there to fulfill some dreaded community service obligation.

Tell me what I did to deserve this? I'd tried to have that discussion before. She shook her head and left the room.

I pondered what I could do to get things back on track. I wondered what I could do to rekindle the flame. *Tenderness. Let her know how you feel. Reach out to her.*

I took her hand in mine. Jason was up ahead, running between shoppers. We walked like that, hand in hand, for about three seconds. She jerked her hand away and scoffed: "What are we, in high school?"

I couldn't speak. I could barely breathe.

In nearly three decades as a newspaper reporter I have seen terrible things. I was at Sabra and Shatila in Beirut after the massacre in 1982. Survivors held my elbow and led me through the narrow streets to show me the places where the dust was still stained black and littered with body parts. One man held up a thick chunk of skin and hair and made a sound like an American Indian in a western. Those responsible for the massacre used knives, machetes, and axes because gunfire would have made too much noise. Some suggested they didn't want to waste bullets. "Tell the world," the survivors said. "Tell what was done here."

Years later I arrived at a Kurdish village in Iraq where Saddam Hussein used poison gas to wipe out the local population. Most victims died in their basements. Dead mothers clutching dead babies. Dead children nearby. Those who ran died in midstride. The Kurds who discovered the massacre kept repeating the same thing: "Tell the world."

In Beirut, as in the Kurdish village, the victims were mostly old men, women, and children. The able-bodied men were off fighting or preparing to fight. These massacres were intended in large part for the able-bodied men. Not to kill them. The purpose was far more insidious. It was to crush them by taking away what they cherished most.

This is one of the lessons I learned as a reporter. When you wade out into that river of human suffering, you must put on a kind of armor to protect yourself against all the horror and brutality you encounter. It is not a journalist's job to grieve or feel the pain too deeply. The assignment—the calling—is to tell the truth.

I've worked as a local reporter at small newspapers, and as a national-affairs writer in Washington, D.C., and I've traveled around the world as a foreign correspondent. Nothing I'd seen as a reporter prepared me for that moment in the suburban shopping mall. It was the realization that as a husband and a father I was completely vulnerable to the horror of losing my own wife and child, not to a massacre in some distant war zone, but to a different kind of atrocity.

Revived

With the wind at our backs pushing us north, we were flying up the east coast. My original plan was to travel from Miami, past Palm Beach, to a small spoil island just north of the Lake Worth Inlet. This would transport me through the cramped waters of Miami, Fort Lauderdale, and Palm Beach County before the busy boating weekend. I felt pretty good about our progress. So did Manitou.

As we entered Lake Worth, Manitou talked to his shore contact on his cell phone and received an important piece of information.

"Wizard's not out in the ocean," he yelled across the water. "He's in the Intracoastal."

"Really? How far ahead?"

"South of Stuart."

"That's close," I said. "Real close."

Manitou wanted to make a run to try to pass him. I wished him luck and told him I would probably follow my original plan to camp near the north end of Lake Worth.

I enjoyed Manitou's company. He travels fast and doesn't complain about anything. Nonetheless, I felt I was slowing him down. When he told me he would press on to try to catch Wizard, I felt relief.

I told him it had been great paddling with him and that maybe I'd see him up ahead—or not. I wished him a fast trip to the finish line in Tampa. He said the same to me, or something like it. He waved. I waved. I kind of expected him to zoom off toward the horizon. I kept up a steady, comfortable pace, paddling and sailing. He had his sail up and paddled. But we just continued to travel side by side. It created one of those extended awkward moments like you've just delivered a heartfelt farewell to your wife or girlfriend or significant other at the airport but then your flight is suddenly delayed for two hours.

Eventually, as we moved into the middle of Lake Worth, the wind picked up and Manitou made the most of his larger sail. He began to pull ahead.

It had been a perfect day. I was ready to stop. I paddle-sailed up the east side of the channel with West Palm Beach on my left and the mansions of Palm Beach rolling past on my right. As I cruised under the Royal Park Bridge I could see the Flagler Memorial Bridge a half mile ahead.

The sun, low in the western sky, threw dramatic light over all of

Palm Beach. Flagler's former mansion, Whitehall, looked like a movie set, surrounded by green grass and lush, tropical landscaping. Even more impressive was the majestic sight of the twin towers of The Breakers, each tower topped with a flag flapping briskly.

I'd been to The Breakers a few times, pulling up to the front entrance in the flatulent Toyota. Guests in the hotel must have assumed an entire biker gang had just arrived. I would just hand the valet my key and walk inside as if I'd just pulled up in a Maserati. Several guests would stare. I didn't care. I like my car.

The Breakers is an architectural gem. Inspired by the Villa Medici in Rome, it includes examples of all the finest touches of Italian Renaissance style. Hopefully, it also includes smoke detectors. The hotel has twice burned down, once in 1903, and then again in 1925. The existing hotel was rebuilt in 1926 and has so far managed to avoid spontaneously combusting.

For a brief moment I was tempted to pull my boat up on The Breakers golf course, stride up to the front desk and inquire about a room for the night. I'd have cut quite an impressive profile in my baggy orange bathing trunks, diving booties, and straw hat. The flies circling my reeking body might also have raised a few eyebrows. It would have been great fun in an anarchistic kind of way, but I had places to go.

As Manitou's sail disappeared on the water up ahead, I pulled my boat ashore at Peanut Island County Park. The park has a beautiful view of the nearby inlet and Palm Beach. For me, the real attraction was the restroom.

Peanut Island is the product of three different dredging projects. The large spoil island is comprised of sand and muck from the Intracoastal Waterway, Lake Worth Inlet, and the Port of Palm Beach. Until 1996, this was home to a working Coast Guard station. The building is still there and now serves as a museum and landmark. Peanut Island is perhaps best known as the location of JFK's presidential nuclear fallout shelter.

Everyone knows about it—now. Back in 1961, a top-secret contingent of navy engineers arrived on the island and proceeded to construct a bomb shelter for John F. Kennedy and his top advisers. President Kennedy spent many weekends at his family's estate on nearby Palm Beach. During the Cuban missile crisis all sense of decorum evaporated. One could no longer be sure that the Soviets would confine hostilities to the workweek. Not only might those godless Communist bastards attack on a quiet Sunday morning, they might also lob a thermonuclear device or two toward our young president.

The bomb shelter isn't much to look at. The Seabees built it below a sandy hill in a forest of tall Australian pines. There is a pipelike shaft leading to a small underground room. The steel door is covered in camouflage paint and flanked by air intake vents. It was built in the backyard of the Coast Guard station to resemble a munitions storage facility. That was the cover story. In the event of an actual emergency—like nuclear Armageddon on a weekend—Peanut Island would have been the nerve center of American efforts to resist, recover, and respond.

My arrival on Peanut Island was related to a different kind of mission—a need to use the "facilities." The island features a really nice restroom, newly built and spotlessly clean. In addition to using the toilet, I decided to rinse out both my paddling shirts, including the shirt I was wearing.

I wasn't about to miss this opportunity to do some laundry. There I stood shirtless in the men's room hoping no one would come in.

It didn't take very long. I rinsed out the shirt and put it back on. I walked into the sunlight, soaking wet and trying to act like any other park visitor.

I'd been paddling since 2:15 A.M.—about fifteen hours—and was ready to stop. But when I put on that wet shirt to help it dry, the coolness was surprisingly refreshing. It was so refreshing, in fact, that twenty minutes later as I approach my anticipated campsite, I decided to keep going. I felt pretty good. I rigged my boat for night paddling and aimed for the entrance to Lake Worth Creek.

Disaster at the Inlet

A few days after I paddled through Fort Lauderdale with Manitou, Pelican arrived at the same place. He was in a big hurry, trying to make up for the twenty-six hours it took him to travel the thirty-five miles across Florida Bay to Key Largo against a relentless headwind. Now, with the wind at his back, he wanted to try to make up some lost time. To do it he decided to take a big risk. He left the shelter of the Intracoastal Waterway to try to sail in the ocean.

"It was exhilarating," he told me later. "I was making darn good time."

The wind had been blowing from the southeast for several days. The ocean was a choppy, foaming mess. He didn't care.

By 11:00 P.M. Pelican was about two miles offshore, surfing between whitecaps, when he heard a banging at his stern. A flashlight inspection revealed that much of his rudder had snapped off. Gone. He had just lost the ability to steer his boat.

Let's review. Pelican is two miles out in the ocean in wind-whipped seas in the middle of the night with no steering. The surf is too rough to attempt a beach landing. What should he do?

He checked his chart and aimed for the Boynton Beach Inlet. His plan was not without peril. The inlet is a boil of swirling currents lined with jagged, unforgiving rocks. Pelican used every bit of his acquired seamanship to guide the rudderless vessel to the center of the inlet. Just as the smooth, sheltered water of the Intracoastal Waterway came into clear view up ahead, he discovered something heartbreaking. The tide was running hard against him. Millions of gallons of water were hell-bent on returning to the ocean—and carrying Pelican along for the ride. He refused to give up without a fight. He gritted his teeth and went to work. There was too much water moving too quickly. Soon his boat was swept backward into the dark, storm-tossed ocean. "It was like a washing machine, the water was so turbulent," he said. On a second attempt he came close to wrecking on the rocks. Instead, he plunged through the surf and managed to land safely on a nearby beach.

The following morning, Pelican installed a spare rudder, but while he was trying to relaunch into the ocean, a spectator grabbed hold of the aluminum brace supporting one of his pontoons. It broke. It cost him. Time was ticking away. The assorted mishaps ate up about twenty-four hours before Pelican was finally able to get off that beach and resume his journey.

Lost in Space, or How Do
I Get to Jupiter?

Sometimes there is nothing more frustrating than a stranger who decides to mind his own business.

Around 9:00 P.M. I was somewhere in Lake Worth Creek approaching Jupiter Inlet. That's about all I knew. I'd paddled all the way from Miami, about six hundred thousand miles away. I still felt pretty good and began to think I might be able to make it all the way to Stuart and a beautiful spoil island campsite I knew near the St. Lucie Inlet. If you'd asked me a day earlier whether it would be possible to paddle from Miami to Stuart in a day, I'd have said you were crazy to suggest such a thing. By 9:00 P.M. I started to believe I might be able to do it.

Then something bad happened. I got lost. I hate to admit it. Messy business, getting lost.

What got me lost was my faulty memory of this section of the route. I'd never actually paddled here before. I'd spent time studying the Intracoastal Waterway on my charts and made a mental note to turn east (toward Jupiter Inlet) when I reached the Loxahatchee River rather than proceeding straight ahead under the bridge and up the Loxahatchee. A detour up the Loxahatchee could cost me valuable time—and maybe more.

There are alligators up there. The water gets dark and the trees get jungle-thick. Spooky stuff. Locals know all the stories. In June 1993, a ten-year-old boy was on a canoe trip down the river with his family. They reached a place where trees had fallen across the water. The boy got out of his canoe to wade around the tree. An alligator got hold of him with jaws that can exert a force of a thousand pounds per square inch. It happened very quickly. His father grabbed hold of the boy's feet and tried to pull him free, while others in the group swatted the eleven-foot, 350-pound gator with canoe paddles.

The gator eventually let go. Family members wrapped a T-shirt around the boy's head to stop the bleeding and then paddled downriver to get help. It was too late. The boy died.

Fatal alligator attacks are rare—about two to three a year. When they happen they have an understandable tendency to attract media attention. They also have a tendency to concentrate the mind of those of us who like to paddle in the most remote corners of Florida. It always makes me wonder what I would do in a situation like that.

But it wasn't the prospect of an unfriendly encounter with gators that had me wary of the Loxahatchee. My biggest enemy was inefficiency. I couldn't afford to take a wrong turn. It would take too much effort and eat up precious time. That's why I spent time prior to the race studying the charts, finding the fastest way to get from here to there. My primary objective at this point was to avoid going under the Loxahatchee Bridge.

It sounds simple enough. Don't go under the bridge. Turn right before the bridge. But after covering sixty to seventy miles on the water, an otherwise simple route can become daunting for the smallest reason. I had developed a flawlessly direct set of instructions to keep from going the wrong way. When you reach the bridge over the Loxahatchee, take a sharp right turn and do not go under the bridge. Do *not* go under the bridge.

When I reached a bridge I followed my simple, fail-safe instructions. I did not go under it. I turned right. But after turning, I found myself following a watery detour that circled around and eventually took me back to the same channel I had just paddled, except now I was about two hundred yards south of where I took the turn before the bridge. At first I thought this was déjà vu. Everything looked familiar. *Unbelievable,* I thought. *I feel like I've been here before—like just a few moments ago. This is not good. This is not good.*

Had I just arisen from a night of sound sleep, I might have quickly discovered my error. But what's the fun in that. A big part of the Florida Challenge is trying to survive stupidity. I had been awake and pushing hard in my kayak for nineteen hours. Between the exhaustion, the darkness, and the swirl of lights from nearby buildings and roads, my IQ was down in the single digits.

I remembered passing a marina, so I backtracked, hoping to find someone who could point me in the right direction. Local knowledge. I just needed a little reassurance. I couldn't possibly be lost, could I?

I paddled into the marina to the first boat on the right, a sailboat with the recognizable flickering light of a television in the cabin. The curtains were drawn.

"Hello. Hello. Is anyone home?"

I repeated it, this time a little louder. "Hello. *Hello.*"

No answer.

Maybe I need to yell a little louder, but not so loud that whoever was on the boat would be afraid to come out to see what I'm yelling about.

"Is anybody home?"

Nothing.

I paddled east down a line of very expensive yachts. None of the other boats showed any signs of life. No lights. No music. No people. No crew.

I paddled to the end of the row of boats hoping for a store or an office—anything to get directions. I sat motionless in my boat, debating what to do. Then I looked up. The marina was apparently attached to a high-rise hotel or apartment building. Thirteen stories above me a man stood on a balcony leaning against the railing. He wasn't just enjoying the night air. He was looking down—at me.

"Excuse me," I said, trying to hack my way through a thick jungle of mindless boobosity. "Excuse me. Which way to Jupiter Inlet?"

The man could see me. Of course he could hear me. His balcony stood high enough in the building that he probably could have looked out and seen the inlet. Did he offer any help? Did he suggest a solution?

"How do I get to the Jupiter Inlet from here?"

Idiot man on the thirteenth floor continued to look directly at me, but that's all. He couldn't even lift his arm and aim a finger in the appropriate direction.

"Jupiter Inlet?" I shout.

Nothing. He walked into the apartment. Once again, I yearned for a missile. I decided to try the sailboat again. I paddled to the edge of the marina, figuring I'm going to have to actually get up on the dock to knock on the cabin door. I can't just stay in my boat and pound on the side of the sailboat. There is just something so undignified about pounding on the side of a sailboat. True, I was desperate, but not *that* desperate.

I discovered a small beach near the end of the pier. I got out of the kayak and was immediately confronted with the prospect of having to climb a fence to reach the sailboat. My mind raced between two closely related issues. How will I get the attention of the people inside the sailboat? What if they have a gun and start shooting?

I crashed through some bushes and reached up toward a railing near the fence. That's when I got an idea. *You should check the map.*

I have maps?

Sleep deprivation strikes again.

I searched the area beside my seat in the kayak where I store my charts for each day. That's where I found the map of Jupiter Inlet. The map revealed that the bridge I encountered was the Indiantown Road Bridge, not the Loxahatchee Bridge. The Indiantown Road Bridge was only the first bridge. I had to go under it to reach the second bridge over the Loxahatchee. That's where I needed to make the right-hand turn to the east.

I shoved off the beach, happy to be back on my way again. As I approached the first bridge I saw a sign: INDIANTOWN ROAD. I knew this was the right way now. In a few minutes I saw the Loxahatchee Bridge and made my turn. The tide ran fast and pulled me quickly toward the ocean inlet at the southern end of Jupiter Island. Now I had to really pay attention. I tried to fire off a few electrical impulses into my brain.

Come on, concentrate. Wake up!

Huh?

What I had to do next was avoid the inlet. This was not a minor issue. The Intracoastal turns north just before the inlet. If I missed this turn I would be swept into the full force of the outflow, straight into standing waves large enough to swallow my kayak. I glanced toward the dark inlet and saw a flash of white water. I heard the waves, the relentless suck of the tide through the narrow cut. Beyond the inlet the dark Atlantic Ocean churned with whitecaps and waves. The outflow would drag me a half mile offshore in a few terrifying moments, if I was lucky. Less lucky would be getting caught in a side current and thrown into the surf zone. I'd end up sprawled in the rocks clutching the few remaining pieces of my shattered kayak.

I stayed on the north side of the channel and made the turn up the Intracoastal. As I did it, I discovered a new problem. I was now paddling against the outflowing tide. The swift current required

genuine effort and concerted thought. I pulled hard with each stroke.
I appreciated not being sucked out into the ocean to my death, but
this involved hard work.

Oh, crap. I hate paddling against the tide.

I suppose you'd rather drown?

You are always so dramatic. I'm not going to die.

Shut up and paddle.

Fighting the tide, I paddled hard under a drawbridge and then
began to contemplate the spectacle that is Jupiter Island.

There are mansions, fancy lawns, and plenty of security. This is
where Greg Norman, Nick Price, and Tiger Woods have homes.
Woods paid $38 million for his place, and he's treating it like a tear-
down. Singer Céline Dion has a house here. The real estate on this
very exclusive barrier island isn't just expensive. It's so expensive that
just asking the price will touch off alarm bells and trigger deploy-
ment of a special realtor swat team. It is trained to maintain Jupiter
Island as an exclusive enclave of the Super Rich. Potential buyers
who are merely rich or even comfortably wealthy can expect to be
shown the door.

Jupiter Island is also famous for its rigorous security force. A few
years earlier I paddled my kayak around the island on a day trip. At
several points, security guards appeared to be watching me as if I was
some kind of waterborne burglar. Security would be even better at
night. At that moment they probably had night-vision goggles trained
on my kayak, and a group of commandos assembled in the bushes. I
knew better than to even think about trying to find a spot to camp
on the east side of the Intracoastal.

I wasn't sure how far I might get that night. I had been hoping to
reach the St. Lucie Inlet, another twenty miles to the north. But all
this paddling against the tide had pushed me to the edge. I couldn't

seem to catch a second wind. I tried a little late-night sightseeing. I passed Greg Norman's house to my right on Jupiter Island, and then I passed what I believed to be Burt Reynolds' place to my left on the mainland side of the Intracostal. After that, my eyes would not stay open. I knew I had to get to shore. But where?

I aimed toward a wooded section of the western shoreline. No houses or lights were visible and it looked to be a perfect place to stop for a few hours.

I made it to within sight of the Route 708 Bridge. Then I found a place in a grove of Australian pine trees to rig my hammock. I pulled the boat up under the hammock, got out my sleeping bag and went to sleep without eating dinner. I was too tired to chew.

In what seemed an instant I sat bolt upright to the sound of a freight train—literally a freight train—roaring down train tracks that apparently ran about six inches from my right ear. The ground shook. Pine needles fell from the trees. My kayak seemed to be vibrating and moving around on the ground below me. When I set up my campsite I assumed there were acres of vacant wooded land behind me. I never imagined train tracks would run so close to the water. Thank you, Henry Flagler. These were originally his tracks, laid down in the 1890s in a push toward his Royal Poinciana Hotel in Palm Beach.

I was disoriented. "I'm okay. I'm okay." I repeated it until the train passed.

Again, I took a deep breath of salt air and pine forest. Just like that I was asleep.

I woke sometime after dawn and was back on the water in about twenty minutes. The rush meant that I still hadn't eaten a full dinner for nearly two days. I had ten or more miles to the St. Lucie Inlet and was beginning to bonk from lack of food.

Bonking means the body has run out of fuel and it can't process what remains in the stomach or fat reserves fast enough to sustain a high level of physical exertion. I was rested and I had plenty of food in my boat. What I lacked was time to prepare and eat it. I decided to wait until I reached the spoil island north of the St. Lucie Inlet. I could have cooked my meal back where I spent the night. That might have been faster. For some reason I just wanted to get out of there.

I wasn't the only competitor in the Florida Challenge to run out of gas near Jupiter Island. Several days later, Pelican stumbled ashore at 1:00 A.M. seeking a convenient place to snooze for a few hours. Rather than the western (freight train) side of the Intracoastal, he landed on the posh eastern shore. He clambered up a rocky bank and discovered a patch of soft, cushy grass. It was so nice he decided to do without his tent and sleeping bag.

He spread some of his damp clothing over the bushes to dry. Then he lay down on the grass, using his life jacket as a pillow.

His peaceful slumber was soon interrupted by a storm. It was one of those violent Florida storms with lateral, pounding rain. Pelican sensed something wasn't quite right about this storm. The blasts of rain fell in regular intervals, sweeping across him and stopping, then sweeping across him again. Pelican opened his eyes and could see the stars and the half moon above him in a cloudless sky. "After about the third dousing, I realized it was a sprinkler system," he says. "I was on a golf course."

That wasn't just any golf course, it was the Jupiter Island Club. The horror. Riffraff on the back nine.

Pelican didn't care, but he didn't want to get wet, either. He gathered his damp clothes and got back in his boat.

Stuart

I was grateful that my few hours of sleep near Jupiter had gone without interruption. But now, paddling toward Stuart I was really hungry. When I reached the spoil island I stopped to eat dinner and call my mom to arrange for her to meet me at the checkpoint at Sebastian Inlet. I was about fifty miles south of the inlet and intended to get there that night.

I asked for two roast beef sandwiches, three packages of Lenders blueberry bagels, a package of snow peas, some fresh orange juice, and a New York strip steak from Outback Steakhouse. "Don't try to keep the steak warm. It'll dry out. Just get it and let it get cold. Believe me, I'll eat it."

I told her I'd give her a call a little later in the day when I could tell her more precisely my arrival time at Sebastian Inlet. My mom and dad live in the Stuart area and it takes about ninety minutes to drive up to Sebastian. I didn't want her to get there too soon and have to wait around.

Now that I'd made my resupply arrangements for that evening, it was up to me to actually get to the checkpoint. My night in the woods with the freight train hadn't left me with the greatest night's sleep. At least now I'd had a meal and set up the prospect of an even better meal that night in Sebastian. Ordering the steak is one of the smartest things I did during the Florida Challenge. It gave me a reason to paddle hard all day. I could already smell the smoky savor of that steak. I could hear it sizzling on the grill.

With expectations of an extraordinary dining experience, I headed north, up the Indian River. The wind blew from the southeast at ten to fifteen. I raised my sail and paddled under the Stuart

Causeway. I knew this section of the river, having paddled here often. It is usually a long, boring ten-mile slog all the way to Fort Pierce. The river is wide and there's not much to see.

The wind couldn't change the view, but it did speed my trip. I soon found myself riding line after line of moderate waves rolling northward. When a kayak catches up to waves in this way the boat shoots forward. A paddler can use the energy of the waves to ease the strain of paddling and increase the speed of the boat. The technique is called surfing because it involves the same physical forces as catching and riding waves with a surfboard.

I flew up the Indian River, surfing quickly under the Jensen Beach Causeway, past the nuclear power plant, under the bridge at Fort Pierce, and down a long line of spoil islands beside the dredged channel. At 4:30 P.M. I stopped at a small island just south of Vero Beach. I phoned in my position to Linda: N + 27°36'58.08", W - 80°21'41.22".

I was about twenty miles south of Sebastian and feeling pretty good. I told Linda I'd be at Sebastian checkpoint at eight or nine in the evening. Usually just hearing her voice is a big emotional boost. This time it made me miss her even more. I paddled past Vero Beach, thinking of her the whole way.

It should be a ceremony. It doesn't have to be in a church, but that would be nice. I'd like to see you in a white satin dress walking down the aisle. I'd like to see that. The ring. The cake.

That would be great. You're not going to want the dress, are you? That's okay. It's up to you. Whatever you want. Believe me.

We could elope. Take off for Vegas. No, not Vegas. That wouldn't be good at all.

We've been together for a while now. A lot of marriages don't last as long. But we don't live in the same city. I don't want to do the long-distance relationship and be married. I guess it depends on what's important. Is it the relationship. Or the being together.

Maybe both. Or maybe that's the secret.

I don't know. It still feels new to me. I see you for two weeks in Washington and then I'm gone two weeks in Florida, then I see you again in Washington. It keeps the romance going. It really makes me appreciate our time together—to make the most of it. There's no time to take each other for granted.

That's the death of marriage, or any relationship, taking each other for granted. I suppose a little deprivation can be a good thing.

But I wish you were here. I really wish you were here right now. Or I was there with you—in a pair of dry pants. Oh yes. Dry pants.

Vero

Vero Beach is a quiet seaside community with a pristine shoreline and many well-heeled residents. This is where the Los Angeles Dodgers conducted spring training for nearly sixty years in a place called Dodgertown. It also is the location of an unusual hotel: the Driftwood Inn.

In 1935 the beachfront building was constructed as a family retreat out of sea-swept timbers and other flotsam that washed up on the beach. Owner and mastermind Waldo Sexton did not rely on blueprints. He shouted his vision to the befuddled carpenters who dutifully sawed and hammered in accord with his instructions. Years later, the building was expanded and converted into an inn.

A citrus grower, a dairyman, a developer, and a town father, Sexton acquired a number of impressive titles. In his heart he was a savior of discarded treasures. When a once-great dynasty fell into financial hard times, he'd arrive at the Palm Beach estate just prior to the wrecking ball looking to salvage a few relics of that age of opulence. He decorated the Driftwood Inn with an assortment of 250 bells, from ships, schools, churches, and even Flagler's East Coast Railway. When the Palm Beach estate Playa Riente was demolished in 1957, Sexton obtained four panels of relief sculpture that had been positioned above doorways in the mansion. They became part of the hotel. One depicts Spanish explorers arriving in Florida. The Driftwood Inn also features perhaps the only surviving piece salvaged from Flagler's Royal Poinciana Hotel in Palm Beach—a section of porch railing.

Vero Beach exudes a laid-back old-Florida feeling. As much as I would have liked exploring Waldo's legend, I had an important date at Sebastian Inlet—with a steak.

I reached the Route 510 Bridge at Wabasso Island just as the sun set. It got dark fast. I still had my sail up and kept up a pretty good pace. As usual I stayed to the east of the channel.

Good thing.

About fifteen minutes beyond the bridge a poorly lit boat zoomed past in the channel. As he passed I heard his engine slow. He circled around and came back. That's when I saw the words "Marine Police" painted on the side of the hull. I'd heard stories about police officers ordering WaterTribe challengers off the water late at night, telling them that they shouldn't be out in the dark in such small boats. Of course, I had the required navigation lights. I was wearing a reflective vest, and I was completely comfortable paddling at night in my boat. The only thing that made me nervous was the prospect of a large, fast motorboat zipping through the darkness in my general direction. That, or being hassled by a Marine Police officer.

I stopped paddling as the officer's boat pulled alongside.

"You okay?" he asked.

When he asked it I decided I'd better try to sound as optimistic and happy as I could. I didn't want him to think I was tired or in need of assistance. I certainly didn't want him to raise questions about my being out on the water after dark in a sea kayak.

"I'm great," I said. "And thanks for stopping to check. I really appreciate that."

When I heard the words come out of my mouth it surprised me. Then I realized that's exactly the right approach. I'd just given him a compliment—I think. If he really was concerned about my well-being, I'd answered that too with an upbeat response.

"Okay, then." That's all he said. Just "Okay, then." He turned his boat around, throttled up, and sped off toward the Route 510 Bridge.

To be completely honest I was a little confused about my whereabouts. I expected to see the lights of Sebastian State Park by now. There was nothing but dark horizon to my right. I could see lights straight ahead and some lights to my left, way off in the distance. They were in the wrong direction. I needed to go northeast. Instead I kept moving northwest toward the lights straight ahead. I wasn't so much lost as I was tired and a little confused.

I could see the outline of an uninhabited mangrove island to my northeast, about two o'clock off my bow. But I couldn't understand what it was doing there. It should have been open water. I'd paddled here once before—during the day. It didn't look anything like this during the day. The reality is, it never does. I can paddle up and down the same river ten times in daylight, then do it once in the dark and it will be transformed into a completely different waterway.

I knew Sebastian State Park was somewhere northeast of my current position. But the mangrove islands made it appear there was nothing there. I did the only thing I could: I aimed for the lights straight ahead.

Then I experienced one of those magical moments that happens in long journeys—a sight that made me want to stop and just drink it all in, a sight that made all the hours and days of hard, thankless slogging suddenly worth it. I rounded the corner of a long, dark mangrove island and the wide, expanse of the Indian River opened in front of me. Campfires blazing in two perfect lines extended up both sides of the Intracoastal like a giant, illuminated airport runway. A bonfire roared on each of the spoil islands that bordered the dredged channel. The double line of fires stretched for miles up the river. I'd forgotten. This was Saturday night and camping on spoil islands in the Indian River is a favorite activity on weekends here.

I paddled to the first island with a fire and staggered ashore into the orange glow. I didn't think of it at the time but I must have scared the crap out those campers. Here they were enjoying the serenity of a warm, dark Florida night. Suddenly a sweat-stained and unwashed version of Swamp Boy comes trudging out of the dark water, kayak in tow.

"Do you know where Sebastian Inlet is?" I asked.

A middle-aged man in a baseball hat met me halfway between the beach and his campfire. He had this look on his face like I was holding a gun on his pet poodle. It was beyond worried and well on the way to terrified. I stayed near the beach, noticing his body language, and asked my question again. "Do you know where Sebastian Inlet is?"

He pointed into the darkness. "It's right over there."

I walked to the east side of the island, avoiding his campfire and campsite. I cupped my hands around my eyes. Small lights glistened about two miles to the northeast. Sure enough, Sebastian Inlet.

"Thank you. Thank you very much," I called out, offering an appreciative wave to the camper. He sort of waved back, reluctantly, as if any gesture might encourage me to stay. He watched me disappear into the night.

Sebastian Inlet

I arrived at 8:35 P.M. Saturday at the concrete boat ramp on the west side of Sebastian Inlet State Park. A WaterTribe member named Porky manned the checkpoint. He spotted me paddling in. He stood on shore, waving. I was amazed he could see me, but I sure was grateful to receive such a friendly greeting.

Porky filled me in on race details. Manitou Cruiser arrived in the afternoon and left that evening. I was seven hours behind him and probably a day and a half behind Wizard. He arrived at 10:40 P.M. Friday night and left a few hours later.

Sebastian Inlet was a great location for a checkpoint, but the state park was a terrible venue for all the essential activities associated with checkpoints.

There was a small campground about a half mile from the boat ramp, but it offered only a few campsites and they were so popular among RV drivers that to secure a site I needed to make a reservation pretty much the second week after I was born. There was no place to

camp—at least not legally. This made Sebastian Inlet more a temporary rest stop, a place to pause, sign the logbook, stock up on supplies, and keep going.

I was exhausted by the time I got to the park and I really didn't
relish the idea of having to get back into my boat to find a safe place
to sleep. For one thing it was Saturday night and the nearby spoil islands were jammed with campers. It would have been particularly
cruel for me to return to that first island where I'd asked directions
to Sebastian. My reappearance would really freak that guy out.

But the main issue was exhaustion. I just wanted a dry place
where I could fall down on the ground and get a few hours of sleep.
At that point the Sebastian Inlet parking lot looked pretty soft and
cozy. Had it not been for the regular patrols by park rangers, I might
have just curled up beside the curb.

I wasn't the only challenger to face this issue. Several days later,
Doooobrd arrived at Sebastian. He pulled his sea kayak up on shore
and promptly fell sound asleep on the concrete slab under a picnic
table.

Before I could even consider sleep, I had several essential checkpoint chores to perform. Porky had my container of supplies in his
truck. From that, I extracted charts for the next leg up the Florida
coast to Amelia Island. I deposited my old charts in my resupply bin
and then took out five pre-organized dinners and various other supplies of food and fresh batteries.

I gathered up my dirty clothes, retrieved a fistful of quarters and
some laundry detergent from my supply container and headed off
to a washing machine at the nearby campground. Good thing the
washing machine was positioned a few quick steps from the showers.
When you pack light like a backpacker there's no room for a bath-
robe or even a bath towel. I glanced sheepishly around the campsite.

All was quiet. I quickly slipped out of my paddling clothes, all of them, dumped them with the other dirty clothes into the churning washer and headed for the shower.

While my clothes went round and round, I took a slow, hot, steamy, luxurious, mind-numbingly wonderful shower. I'd had that refreshing little spritz in that men's room on Peanut Island near Palm Beach. But this was the first genuine shower since Key Largo.

Wasn't Key Largo only a few days ago? It seemed like a month. This was the eighth day of the race. I was almost halfway around Florida. *Almost halfway around! Is that possible? How could I get this far in only eight days?* I couldn't even remember the start of the challenge.

Then a terrible thought came to me. What if this was all a dream. What if I wake up back at Placida on that horrible first night of the race with my left arm dangling at my side like an elephant's trunk. It was all a dream. Just a dream. Going exactly the wrong way in Everglades National Park. The night in the mud at Twisty Mile. That magnificent Miami cityscape rising out of Biscayne Bay like Dorothy's first vision of Oz. Drifting through the condo canyons of Hollywood in the predawn dark. Searching for Jupiter with my mind lost in outer space. Talk about horror. What if it had all been a dream?

It wasn't. I focused on the funnel of muddy water swirling down the shower drain. It is hard to understand how one can get that dirty. And there aren't words enough to describe that wonderful feeling of sudden cleanliness. Prolonged deprivation has its rewards. After a little over a week of the Florida Challenge, I learned all over again how to appreciate the little stuff; the imagined scent of a savory steak, a clean shirt still warm out of the clothes dryer, a cascade of hot water running over my head to that place between my shoulders where it felt like someone had lodged a butcher's knife.

As I stood in the shower, all kinds of aches and pains began to flare up. Strange how when I begin to enjoy a few minor comforts, a little softness of civilization, my mind drops all its defenses, all that metaphysical armor, and I am suddenly a prisoner of sore, fatigued muscles. I never felt this kind of discomfort when I was alone in a remote place in my boat on the water. Not once. But bask in the glow of a few electric lights, add some hot water and the prospect of a juicy steak, and what do I get? Ouch. Ouch. Ouch.

My friend Matt "Sore Shoulders" Coiro, and his girlfriend, Stephanie, arrived. Or that might have just been a dream. Who knows? At some point, my mom and sister, Carolyn, showed up with the steak and other requested items from the grocery store. The New York strip steak from Outback Steakhouse was indescribable. It came in a white Styrofoam carton. I ate the entire salad with tangy tomato dressing. Then I started on the steak. It was cold, but it was, without a doubt, the most delicious steak I have ever eaten. After a week of dehydrated meals, that steak made my eyes water. It made my knees weak.

After dinner, I loaded new food supplies into the front hatch of the kayak. That's when I discovered that the very specific grocery list I'd given my mom earlier in the day hadn't been followed with any precision. Instead of two roast beef sandwiches, I was presented with two turkey subs. Instead of three packages of Lenders blueberry bagels, I was presented with three packages of Pepperidge Farms bagels. Now, you might ask, what's the difference? A bagel is a bagel is a bagel. On one level you would be correct. But these Pepperidge Farms bagels were huge. They were the size of those lifesaving rings they hang up near public swimming pools. They weren't just bagels, they were *giant* bagels. When you are spending a month living in a kayak, cargo space is a precious thing. One of the reasons I asked for Lenders bagels is that I knew how big they were and I knew they would fit into my fully loaded front hatch and emerge days later still resembling bagels. The *giant* bagels didn't fit. But I wasn't about to be defeated. I carefully positioned them in the hatch with the other supplies using the same technique as artillerymen during the Civil War when they jammed that long pole down the barrel of a canon to ensure a snug fit.

Around 11:00 P.M., I closed up my hatches, hugged my mom and Carolyn, and pushed off to find a camp spot somewhere out in the river.

Paddling across the dark water toward the spoil islands I thought about the extreme level of my exhaustion. All I needed were two trees for my hammock and the chance to get some sleep. I headed for the first island I saw.

I came ashore on the east side, looking for some deep water that would make launching in the morning a little easier. I saw a possible campsite but decided to check around on the west side. The water was shallow. There was no breeze. I got out of my boat and waded around the island about fifteen feet offshore. That's when I noticed a Kruger canoe pulled up on the beach and a small tent. I recognized both.

I stopped right there in the water. I was afraid I might be making too much noise. I didn't want to wake him up.

"Warren, is that you?" It was Manitou.

"I can't believe I caught up to you." I said. "I figured you'd be at Fort Clinch by now."

I wanted to camp around a point to the west, but now that Manitou was up I asked him if he'd mind if I camped in a grove of trees near his site. I kind of regretted waking him up and tipping him off to my presence. It would have been better to let him think I was far behind him. Now, he would break camp early in the morning and really set a pace to Fort Clinch.

As I lay back in my hammock I decided I wouldn't worry about Manitou. I knew he'd leave early and I had no desire to try to keep up with him. I needed a good night's rest and I wasn't about to short-change myself here.

Just before dawn I woke and heard Manitou preparing to leave. I briefly—very briefly—considered getting up and making a race out of it. Just as suddenly I was asleep again. By the time I woke up the second time, the sun was up and Mantiou was long gone. Not even a sail on the horizon. But I felt great. I'd accomplished all I needed to accomplish at the Sebastian checkpoint. I'd even had the steak. Oh yes. The steak.

Physically, I was holding up pretty well. My shoulders were sore, but strong. My left arm grew stronger each day. The third and fourth toes on my right foot had gone completely numb.

If there was one emerging significant physical problem it was my butt. I used two cushions to soften my kayak seat and help stave off numbness. But let's face it, human butt cheeks aren't intended to take this kind of punishment. They are intended to help keep your pants up, not to cushion your hip bones from twenty hours of stress and pressure.

I hate to mention this, but it's not just the sitting. Constant wetness can add a certain tint and odor to the problem. Yes, I know. I'm sorry. You will be pleased to know that I did not document this issue with actual photographs. You'll just have to take my word for it. By day nine—and this is no exaggeration—the Florida Challenge became a real pain in the butt.

PART IV

Halfway and Not Even Dead . . . Yet:
Sebastian Inlet to Amelia Island,
200 Miles

Sunday: Day Nine

The word for this day: boring.

The day consisted of eating two turkey subs piece by piece while paddle-sailing past Melbourne and Cocoa Beach. This section of the Indian River was wide and uninteresting and just seemed to go on forever as a series of long paddles between bridges. I passed under the bridge at Melbourne and discovered the Eau Gallie Bridge five miles away. Once under the Eau Gallie Bridge I found myself looking at the Pineda Bridge—again five miles away. I paddled under that bridge and there on the horizon—ten miles away—stood the Hubert Humphrey Bridge.

One high point of the day was paddling past Cocoa, a place made famous by an astronaut, Major Tony Nelson, who once lived there in the 1960s with someone named Jeannie, who wore a hot little genie costume, lived in a bottle, and could make stuff disappear by nodding her head really fast. They even made a TV show out of it. I couldn't help wondering where they lived.

Oh, I almost forgot to mention, after the bridge at Cocoa, there was the Bennett Bridge, three miles north, followed by eight miles to the NASA Causeway, and, finally, seven miles to the bridge at Titusville.

Paddling the Indian River was so boring it made me yearn for a chance to retake the SATs. I started counting individual drops of water on my forward deck. After that, I enjoyed watching them evaporate. Fascinating. Then something inexplicable happened. It happened on the approach to Titusville just before the NASA Causeway. I sliced across the water at about four miles an hour in a pretty good tailwind, an easy and relaxed cruising speed under those conditions. I wasn't pushing hard. I just kept the boat moving steadily through these wide, dull sections of the river. Near Bellwood I felt the kayak surge forward. It started moving noticeably faster. It was unmistakable. I wasn't pulling any harder on the paddle. I perceived no gust of wind or boat wake that might push me forward. I wondered if there were dolphins or sea turtles or manatees under the boat boosting my speed. Maybe I'd become the beneficiary of an underwater current of some sort.

The first time, I dismissed it.

That didn't just happen.

Of course it happened.

No. No. I just imagined it.

An hour later, it happened again.

I suppose you imagined that, too?

Maybe.

Idiot.

What about that. Did you imagine that?

The boat started moving faster. It seemed to be moving on its own. Speeding up. I felt it several times that afternoon. I studied my surroundings for an explanation. Maybe it was a bull shark, pushing me out to deeper water for a picnic. Oh goody. Or Jeannie toying with me. There's an explanation.

Whatever it was I could see no physical reason for it, but it always had the same effect on me. I picked up my pace. I paddled a little harder.

The next time it happened, this strange idea popped into my head. It arrived as a question: Am I supposed to win this race?

I kept paddling. You can't make a big deal out of every inexplicable thing. I mean, if I kept track of all the crazy ideas that sprang into my muddled mind during the Florida Challenge I'd probably have enough material for an entire book. Crazy things are popping into my head all the time. Hallucinations. Misperceptions. Weird stuff. Maybe it was the lingering effects of earlier sleep deprivation, or loneliness, or maybe it really was dolphins. Here's the thing. Who cared? At that point I assumed Wizard was at least two days ahead of me with Manitou Cruiser fast in his wake. In contrast, look at me, far behind and probably falling even farther behind. It was not my goal to win the race—my goal was to *survive* the race. That didn't have anything to do with Wizard or Manitou, or any of the other challengers. It was up to me to decide how far and how fast to go. More important, it was up to me to discover how far and how fast I could go. To me, the Florida Challenge was a race against myself. So it didn't make sense, this question: Am I supposed to win this race?

Stealth Camping

The problem with competing in a nonstructured, expedition-style race is that, night to night, you have no idea whether you will find a decent place to camp for a few hours. In this way competing in the Florida Challenge is a little like being homeless. You never know where you'll be or what you'll encounter once you get there.

A big part of my strategy for moving long distances in a sea kayak is to always try to pick a known camp spot fifty, sixty, or seventy miles away and then paddle hard to get there. This is generally a better approach than heading off into the dark unknown with a sense of dread about what might be in store. If you know where you are going and are looking forward to reaching your destination, you will paddle harder and arrive sooner.

My strategy works well in south Florida where I am familiar with plenty of safe places to camp. I know my options. But once I pushed north of Melbourne, I was entering waters I'd never paddled. Of course, I'd studied the charts for possible campsites, but a paper map can be deceiving.

One of Chief's innovations for WaterTribe adventure races is a concept he calls "stealth camping." The basic idea is that it doesn't matter where you camp as long as you arrive in the dark, stay for only a few hours, and leave before first light.

Some WaterTribe members have snoozed soundly on patio lawn furniture, in waterfront houses under construction, as well as in the cushioned cockpits of moored sailboats. One WaterTribe member, named SnoreBringGator, once strung his hammock beneath the Naples fishing pier. It didn't work out so well. He kept being jarred awake by the disorienting sound of footsteps on the boardwalk a few feet above his head. Chief appropriated a waterside playground for a quick nap. He strung his hammock between the swing set and the jungle gym. Sometime in the night, a police officer arrived with a flashlight. The patrolman scanned the edges of the playground but never thought to look in the center where Chief remained hidden in the shadows.

One longtime WaterTriber tells the story of braving serious security to catch a few hours' sleep in the bushes at Steven Spielberg's gulf-front mansion in Naples. After a nice snooze, he left an impressive calling card, a massive pile of steaming crap near the edge of Mr. Spielberg's manicured lawn. Close encounters of the *fourth* kind.

I don't want to leave a false impression. Stealth camping means more than just not being seen. It also means leaving no trace of one's presence. The pile of crap was left at the bottom of a foot-deep hole, carefully covered up, and smoothed over. Eventually even the footprints washed away. That's stealth camping.

At 8:35 P.M., I pulled my kayak up onto a boat ramp on the Titusville Causeway near Cape Canaveral and phoned in my position report to Linda.

I'd been paddling less than thirteen hours since leaving the spoil island near Sebastian Inlet. Not a very productive day. But the wind picked up and I was having trouble seeing the channel markers. I didn't want to get stuck in the middle of nowhere, hoping Steven Spielberg had a place up here somewhere.

I decided to turn in early and camped on a spoil island about a half mile north of the causeway. Once in my hammock, I lay back, listening to the wind in the trees and the sound of a distant train. I woke several times to check the ground under the hammock. It appeared the tide had risen and that water now completely covered the area of my camp. Fortunately I'd rigged the hammock high enough that the water would not reach me. I'd tied my boat to a tree, so I did not worry about the kayak floating away. Not that it would. There was no water under my hammock or in my campsite. It was an illusion.

This happened almost every night. I wouldn't call it a hallucination, more a kind of waking dream. I would look out from the hammock and be sure water surrounded me, but at the same time I knew it was not real. I haven't sought a professional opinion (or professional help), but my theory is that since I spent virtually all my time on the water, my mind retained that watery landscape even at night when I was trying to restore myself physically and mentally for the next day's journey.

It didn't happen just once a night, it often happened several times in the same night. I'd wake up, see the water, go back to sleep, wake up again, see the water, tell myself that the tide had not come up, go back to sleep, wake up, see the water, and go back to sleep. That's what happened at Titusville. Who knew what it meant. Maybe I was pushing too hard. The last time I woke up it was already dawn.

The Open Door

What makes the Florida Challenge particularly difficult isn't that it involves paddling twelve hundred miles around the state. Anybody can cover that distance in a sea kayak in calm conditions on flat water. What puts the *challenge* in the Florida Challenge is the thirty-day deadline. When you have to travel at least forty miles a day, every day, you cannot afford to wait on shore for a storm to pass or to rest up for a few days before attempting a difficult, wide crossing. You can't afford the luxury of camping for eight or ten or twelve hours. There isn't enough sunlight in a day to avoid nighttime travel. That ticking clock keeps you on the water, pressing forward, forcing you to do the best you can to endure whatever is thrown your way.

It isn't just the dangers of weather, sea conditions, wildlife, or potential encounters with boats and propellers. There's also the inevitable sleep deprivation and physical strain of round-the-clock paddling. What is most difficult is the accumulation of all these things. At some point, if you push long enough and hard enough you reach a precipice.

That's when the real exploration begins. When those muscles at the exact center of my upper back between my shoulders are screaming with pain; when I wake in my hammock with my hands swollen and all ten fingers seized up and locked into ugly, immobile claws; when my butt becomes one gigantic throbbing bruise; when my skin, constantly sodden with seawater, begins to itch incessantly; when my mind is so clouded from lack of sleep that I see phantoms in every shadow; that's when the race begins. That's when the real challenge starts.

Everyday I paddled until I felt I had nothing left, that I'd gone as far as I could go. After dragging my boat ashore at night, I'd double over, trying to work the kinks out of my cramped, aching body. Some nights when I stopped I didn't know if I'd be able to continue. I never knew for certain that I'd have enough to go even one more day, sometimes even one more mile. I would close my eyes and think, *At least I made it this far.*

But somehow after a hot meal and a few hours of sleep I got back in the boat and kept going. The act of taking down my hammock and repacking the boat helped restore suppleness to my stiff and swollen fingers. Reclining in the hammock eased the stabbing pain in my upper back. Wearing dry camp clothes relieved the itchy skin. Even just a few hours of sleep restored my mind to a state of clear thought, at least for a while.

I was amazed. Day after day after day problems would arise, but so would solutions. Obstacles, barriers, discouragement gave way to wide vistas, gentle seas, and inspiration. Through it all I held to a simple goal: just keep moving forward. There is power in perpetual motion, a kind of momentum that extends beyond the force necessary to propel a kayak across the water. Somehow I got this crazy idea that I was part of a larger effort, the beneficiary of a giant unseen hand with a finger firmly on the stern of my kayak, pushing.

The farther around Florida I progressed, the more I surrendered to the idea that I was not alone. At some point I began asking permission to keep going. I began listening for guidance about when and how to go.

None of this is physical. It is attitude, perspective, expectation, intuition. It caused me to think about the race in a different way. It was not my purpose to force myself around the course to finish the race—or win the race. Instead I had to trust that my journey would be revealed hour by hour, minute by minute, and that everything I might want or need would somehow be supplied.

I began to think of the race route as a series of doors. As I approached each hazard, I attempted to assess all the potential dangers. Then I asked a question: Is the door open?

If the door was open, my expectation was that even if conditions weren't ideal I'd have the strength and anything else I needed to get safely through. If, on the other hand, the door was closed, some other necessary course of action would become clear. I'd find a place to rest, or eat, or sleep. But the important point is that it was not my choice to make. The correct choice would be revealed. The key was asking permission first and being obedient to the answer. Even when I didn't like the answer. Especially when I didn't like the answer.

Crossing Mosquito Lagoon

Why did I sleep so late? That was bad. I should have left earlier. I should have left at four or five.

Don't even start with that. You needed the rest.

God, it is hot. What happened to the breeze? Where's the wind. Drink.

That tastes good. Don't drink too much. You can die from drinking too much. Can't die from thirst. You never hear of it. Probably because the only people who die from thirst are never found. They just shrivel up and spontaneously combust. Poof.

It's too hot. I gotta open this spray skirt and dry out. Damn that itches. I can't stand it. Don't scratch. Don't scratch. Damn.

Oh, yes. Yes. Yes. Yes. I'm going to scratch until I bleed.

Manitou must have passed by here last night. He's probably at Daytona by now. Or Flagler. Why did I sleep so late?

Is my back hatch full of water? Am I sinking? Why is this boat so heavy?

Paddle. Come on. Paddle.

Manatee

This was one of those days that sailors recognize as signaling a significant change in the weather. In the morning it was calm and hot and so still that I would have welcomed a headwind just to cool me down a little. Imagine that, a headwind. No kayaker *ever* wants a headwind. But it was hot. Too hot.

I kept up a reasonable pace through the Mosquito Lagoon, just north of Cape Canaveral. The lagoon is so shallow in places even sea kayakers must stay close to the dredged channel. This is not hard to do in the daylight. The channel is clearly marked. But it can present problems at night, as Sandy Bottom learned when she paddled through these parts about a week later. Like me, she had trouble finding the channel markers during a moonless night. At one point she came dangerously close to being run over by a barge and a tugboat as she unknowingly paddled down the center of the channel.

That was only the beginning of her travails. At 4:45 A.M. Sandy Bottom was still on the move, paddling alone in near total darkness at the north end of Mosquito Lagoon. Spooked by her earlier close encounter with the barge, she stayed west of the Intracoastal Waterway—well outside the channel—paddling in about three feet of water. But even that carried risks. It was a quiet night with no indication that anyone or anything was around. Then, *whoosh*. The sea under her boat exploded upward as if she'd hit a mine.

"It was frightening. The back of my boat was lifted at least two feet out of the water," she said, recalling the experience. "The next thing I knew, my boat was upside down."

She had startled a sleeping manatee. When the manatee panicked, its powerful tail launched a giant mushroom of seawater skyward. Sandy Bottom and her fully loaded expedition canoe also went skyward and flipped in midair.

Now, capsized in the black water, her world had suddenly transformed from warm, dry boat into cold, wet catastrophe. But unlike the fleeing manatee, Sandy Bottom did not panic. She methodically checked and gathered her gear, then walked her boat through the shallows to a nearby island where she pumped it out and changed into warm, dry clothes. Within two hours, she was back in her boat and heading north.

That wasn't the only soggy encounter with Florida's beloved sea cows. A week earlier, Wizard startled two manatees at dawn in the shallows west of Sebastian Inlet. It happened as he sailed very slowly in about two feet of calm water. He felt his boat, *Enigma,* gently ride up on something.

The water exploded. Two large tails threw a wall of water that reached halfway up *Enigma*'s sail and drenched Wizard's normally bone-dry cockpit. The same thing happened to Wizard again that night with two manatees north of Merritt Island.

Wizard thought it might be mating season. If so, he'd been sailing his boat through the sea cow equivalent of a bedroom.

I don't consider manatees dangerous. They are truly gentle giants, but when they want to move quickly they can throw a tremendous amount of water into the air.

I'd had a similar experience near Vero Beach while on a training paddle prior to the race. This one involved a mother and a calf. They were in about three feet of water and about ten feet from an island. Their strong tails and the upwelling of water did not flip my boat, but it easily might have. A substantial wave of water hit me full force in the face and chest. This happened in the middle of the afternoon on a hot day without warning in a peaceful section of the Indian

River. This is not to suggest manatees are in any way a menace. I'm sure the mother and calf were as frightened as I was.

The episode provided important information. Sometimes while crossing shallow areas I intentionally tapped the edge of the kayak cockpit with the shaft of my paddle every few strokes to send out a warning through the water to any sleeping manatees. I wanted to avoid boat-swamping encounters.

Manatees are nine to ten feet long and weigh about a thousand pounds. They are members of the order Sirenia and are said to be the mermaids of seafaring legend. Christopher Columbus wrote in his 1493 ship log of spotting mermaids off the coast of what is now the Dominican Republic. Historians say they were almost certainly manatees. Columbus observed that these "sirens" of the sea were "not as beautiful as they are represented."

Seeing a manatee in local waters is one of the treasures of Florida. This is the only place in the United States where the marine mammals can be seen year-round. But because they are large and lumbering they are frequently struck by motorboats. The collisions leave propeller scars on their backs. Some are fatal.

Survival is by no means guaranteed. In the 1970s, manatees were fast on their way to extinction. It wasn't until state and federal biologists took active measures that the Florida manatee began to make a comeback.

Manatees reproduce slowly, with one calf born every three to five years. Their habitat—shallow sea grass beds—is shrinking and under siege from urban pollution. They face significant mortality rates from being struck by motorboats, maimed by propellers, poisoned by red tides, or caught for an extended period in cold conditions. Manatees cannot survive in water colder than 68 degrees Fahrenheit.

Marine biologists in Florida use this need for warm water to help gauge the health of the manatee population. Each winter, during a prolonged period of cold, the scientists take to the skies and conduct an aerial survey of places the sea cows are known to congregate to stay warm. They include natural springs that flow at a constant 72 degrees year-round and the warm-water effluent at power plants. In 2006, scientists counted 3,113 manatees. That same year they recovered 416 dead animals.

Although manatees feed on sea grass and other aquatic vegetation and pose no danger to man, they have become an object of controversy in Florida. On one side are conservationists and naturalists who are fighting to preserve Florida's coastal habitat as a safe haven for manatees and other wildlife. On the other side are developers who want to build more condos, marinas, and bulkheads that will allow fast and easy recreational access for larger numbers of boaters. Many fishermen and pleasure boaters complain that special no-wake manatee protection zones are an unnecessary inconvenience. It is a matter of perspective. Kayakers, like me, appreciate the no-wake zones. They are peaceful sanctuaries where the water is free of speeding, noisy, smelly motorboats. In a way, manatee protection zones are also kayak protection zones. Since 1990, 2,500 signs have been erected in Florida waterways establishing slow-wake or no-wake zones to protect manatees. These zones are important, just like the fifteen-mile-per-hour traffic zones outside schools. But I never hear drivers complain that school zones should be done away with. Young children can't always get out of the way of a speeding car, or even see it coming. They need special help. Manatee zones are the same. They are a small price to pay to help guarantee the survival of a fascinating animal.

A few years ago a manatee made national headlines when it attempted its own version of the Florida Challenge, but on a much grander scale. Most manatees stay in Florida waters all year, but one was spotted in 2006 off the coast of Cape Cod. It was considered a new record for northern travel by a manatee.

Manatees don't swim very fast. They cruise at about three to five miles an hour and spend sixteen hours a day eating or sleeping. Although their cruising speed is similar to my own, manatee travel habits are almost the exact inverse of my travel schedule. While I spent four to six hours sleeping and eighteen to twenty hours cruising, manatees only cruise about eight hours before stopping to sleep and eat.

The 2006 manatee wasn't the first to head up the east coast. It is not uncommon for some manatees to extend their northern range up the coast during the warm summer months. But they are not a common sight outside Florida.

In 1995, a manatee named Chessie made it to Rhode Island before turning around in cold seas. That manatee had acquired his name a year earlier while exploring the Chesapeake Bay in the fall of 1994. Scientists believed he was lost and confused and were worried that a sudden cold snap might leave him too far north to make it safely back to Florida's warm waters. The Coast Guard captured him and flew him south. Researchers released him near the Kennedy Space Center with a satellite-tracking tag attached to his tail.

The following summer, manatee experts were thrilled as Chessie started back up the east coast toward the Chesapeake. But he didn't stop there—he continued north to Rhode Island before turning back toward Florida.

When a manatee was spotted in 2006 in the Hudson River and later off Rhode Island and Cape Cod, scientists were hopeful that it might be Chessie. But close examination determined it was a new explorer.

Researchers aren't sure why some manatees travel so far from their warm-water range in Florida. Some experts suspect they may be looking for a reasonably attractive mate. Others say manatees can be curious. Perhaps they were just exploring. I have my own theory. I like to think that at some point Chessie swam over to a large group of manatees grazing on a lush sea grass bed in Florida and announced his intention to see New England that summer.

Now, this may not be exactly how it happened, but I suspect it's pretty close. The other manatees suddenly stopped eating the sea grass, just froze in midmunch. If manatees have the ability to look incredulous, that's the look they directed toward Chessie at that moment. Sea cows are generally too polite and gentle to do anything malicious, but they must have all been thinking the same thing. "New England? Waddaya, crazy?"

Daytona

Six bridges. That's how I knew I was at Daytona Beach. Once I'd counted to six I was past Daytona and already someplace else. Paddling through downtown Daytona I found myself thinking about years past. It had been decades since I'd last been here.

Now there were glass-and-steel office buildings, high-rise condos, and plenty of traffic—the hustle-bustle of a small, but growing resort city. This was not the Daytona Beach I visited as a kid to see my grandfather. Back then it was a quiet town—not even a city—with ranch-style homes shaded by coconut palms and large oak trees. It was a peaceful place, except during the Daytona 500 stock car race and biker week. Then—for an endurable period—it went just a little bonkers. But that was okay, too.

Visiting my grandfather was one of the treasures of my child-hood. There was something about him. I just liked being with him. Even just being in the same room with him.

He was never rich. Like others of his generation he survived the Great Depression. He and his wife, Marie, had done it together with four children—six mouths to feed. A hard decade of struggle. They worked together and survived. Then, just as the economy and the country were on the mend in the mid-1940s, Marie passed away. Warren Pearce found himself a single father raising four children. He had a son graduating from high school who was headed into the army air corps, one of the most dangerous branches of military ser-vice in World War II. That alone would have tied the average parent into emotional knots. He also had three daughters, two who were barely teenagers. My mother was thirteen when her mom died.

It is easy looking back through the years to discount the uncer-tainty, the doubts, the fear he must have felt. It is easy when you know how the story ends to ignore how difficult it must have been along the way. Maybe he wouldn't even acknowledge the struggle. Maybe he would just shrug and set up the board for another game of chess. "Your move," he'd say.

My grandfather was a chess champion. Not just one of those clock pounders who wow you with fast moves. Sure, he could do that. But you could tie a bandana over his eyes and he'd still beat you in thirty moves. His most valuable piece? The knight.

He preferred the knight because of all the chess pieces the knight operates with the most stealth. Up two, over one. Back one, over two. Over two, back one. There are eight separate moves for a knight po-sitioned near the center of a chessboard. This was an essential part of his strategy. Control the center of the board and you control the game, he'd tell me. Get those knights out fast and into the battle.

Don't put them in the center of the board and just let them sit. To be effective, they must be in constant motion, working in tandem while fully protected by other pieces. He valued his knights more than any other pieces on the chessboard.

Many chess competitors use their queen as a primary source of attack. My grandfather was different. He preferred to attack with his knights in coordinated slashing assaults. His queen played an essential role. She provided protection from a fortified position. She served as the anchor—the center of power—that facilitated the daring moves of the knights.

If I had the chance now, I would ask him: Where did you find the strength and courage to keep moving? In many ways it is the obstacles that define the man. How far you walked is not nearly as revealing as how far you crawled.

This is the thing about my grandfather: He lived his life like a knight near the center of the chessboard, but with no queen for protection. To play chess that way is to exist on a razor's edge, always in the midst of a dangerous place, always surviving by cunning and perpetual motion. As a traveling salesman he never made a lot of money, just enough to keep going. He was an excellent salesman, but it wasn't his love. He did it to survive and to help his children grow strong enough to survive as well.

Chess isn't a game of luck. It is, at bottom, ruthless—like life. You pay a price for mistakes. You have to do the best with what you've got left. There are setbacks. There is pain. But that doesn't mean the game isn't worth playing—and winning.

My grandfather was a chess champion. That's what I remember about him—the champion part. Every time he set up the chessboard, he was showing me something important. He was showing me what it takes to be a champion.

For me, Daytona will always be more than just six bridges. It is only a few miles of water through the city, but it took me back nearly forty years. As I paddled under those bridges, one after another, I thought how nice it would be to see him again, even if just for a moment. I didn't scan every bridge or scout out every spot along the shore, but I looked, searched. I like to think he was up there on the bank somewhere standing in the shade of a coconut palm cheering me on.

This'll Be the Day That I Die

By the time I passed under the sixth bridge at Ormond Beach I'd reached the limit of my endurance. If I had a gas gauge somewhere on my body, the warning light for empty would be glowing bright red.

The sun shone low on the horizon somewhere off my left shoulder. My least favorite time to paddle a boat is just after sunset. It's that period of confusion that happens as my eyes attempt to adjust to the dark. If it is cloudy or there is no moon sometimes I get a sensation of paddling into total darkness, like I am floating right off the edge of the world into nothing.

There is a gloom that comes with being alone at the end of a long day with many miles yet to paddle and no clear idea of when or where I will spend the night or even if I will find a decent and safe place to sleep. The last thing I want is to sleep sitting up in the boat again—not after that long night in the mud in Florida Bay.

If there had been a vacant spoil island within sight at that moment I would have pulled over and drifted off to sleep for eight to ten weeks. I'm sure of it.

I'd seen the chart. Concrete bulkheads lined the shore for as far as I could see. That meant no place to land and no place to camp unless I wanted to risk stringing my hammock between two palm trees in someone's backyard. It's always an option. Just my luck, I'd pick a yard with guard dogs. The owners would deliberately wait until I'd closed my eyes and was in the midst of that unbelievably wonderful sensation of descending into a deep sleep. The door would fling open. Maybe I could snore through it. The growling, snarling, perhaps even the bared fangs. Guard dogs won't attack a dead man. I think.

I knew I must find a place to stop, but I told myself to keep going. *You can do it. Just keep moving.*

This is one of those moments in the race I will long remember. Grappling with complete and merciless exhaustion and pathetic emotions—a little sad, a little lonely—as darkness shrouded the Atlantic coast of Florida. My light seemed to be going out too.

I see cars heading home. I see houses with lights on, people returning from work. I imagine families gathering for dinner, sitting around a table in seats that are dry and homes that are warm and well lit. I begin to wonder why I am doing this. Is it worth it?

At the same time, I tried to anticipate the potential hazards of the night. Each night is different. Each night has its own personality to be endured or enjoyed. But as the sun goes down it brings a sense of foreboding, a dread. Like maybe I am headed into a darkness from which I may never emerge. It is a confrontation with all that is unknowable—and it is most unsettling when that last light is gone and the darkness grips the boat—and me in it.

It passes—the funk, the disconcerting desire for light. Once through the transition, the night becomes a fabulous place. Rather than embracing me, I embrace it. That's when the magic happens.

It came just after the Granada Bridge at Ormond Beach. The wind had dropped to a mere puff. I drifted outside the channel, studying the chart for a possible campsite. I'd used a red marker to circle two potential stopping points. But I couldn't be sure they were suitable for hassle-free camping without seeing them. I didn't know how much longer I could keep going. Then I remembered the radio. *Maybe there'll be something on the radio.*

As my thumb pushed the dial it stopped momentarily at 99.7 FM. Almost immediately, a DJ announced: "You are listening to 99.7—The Hog." He had the same kind of unnaturally deep and overexpressive voice as that guy who narrated movie previews. "In a world ruled by soggy underpants, a lone kayaker stuggles to find a dry spot to sleep . . ."

"The Hog," I thought. "Probably country and western."

Wrong. The Hog is pretty much the best classic rock radio station anywhere in the Western Hemisphere. It just so happened I was within range of its transmitters.

It started with "Midnight Rider" by the Allman Brothers. The music moved through my headphones and into my ears and from my head down to my back, shoulders, and arms. It radiated through me like the warmth of a hot shower. I started paddling—not just moving the paddle, but actually pulling.

Next came "Locomotive Breath" by Jethro Tull. I couldn't believe it. I hadn't heard the song since I was eighteen.

It was as if all the miles I had paddled that day and all the days before were being wiped away. I could feel my strength returning. I could feel my spirit building. The Band. The Moody Blues. The Beatles.

They played "Bohemian Rhapsody" by Queen. "Purple Haze" by Jimi Hendrix. By the time they got to Janis Joplin the water was flat and smooth like black ice and I tore a swath of white foam right through the middle of it. I have never experienced such a fast transformation from dead tired to overflowing with energy. I couldn't believe my ears. Each new song seemed even better than the one before.

I felt I could paddle all the way to Tampa nonstop. Nothing could stop me. I was flying. My boat knifed through a school of bait fish, and one leapt from the water and hit me in the chest. It flopped around on my spray skirt. I pushed him back into the water.

Then something amazing happened. I'd just traveled about eight miles in what felt like eight minutes. Up ahead, I saw a small drawbridge. The bridge was lit by an overhead streetlight. The area around the bridge remained dark and spooky. An odd thing to see, just the glow of a bridge framed by a circle of darkness. Nothing was visible around it, but I knew the Intracoastal went under that bridge—so that's where I went.

As I paddle closer, I see a fisherman near the bridge casting a large topwater plug for snook. About fifty yards out, The Hog goes silent. This isn't any ordinary silence. I'm not talking about the kind of silence you get when your radio batteries go dead. I have fresh batteries in the radio. No, this is a different kind of silence. It is the kind of silence you get just before the heavens open up to reveal all the secrets of the universe.

The radio crackles back to life. With no introduction, no warning, one of my all-time favorite songs begins to play:

"Long, long time ago . . ."

Now, understand this, in ten days I've paddled and sailed from Tampa to Daytona—much of it alone at night in my boat. I'm already talking to myself. I don't mean minor chitchat, either. These are complete conversations including raging debates over important stuff like whether I should eat another Snickers bar now or after I've covered fifteen more miles. Big, important stuff, like that.

So when this song comes on the radio I don't care who is around. I don't care who might overhear me. I don't care what they might think, because I am already as loony as a buffalo in a phone booth trying to make an airline reservation. I am going to sing. Damn it, I am going to put my singing voice on and strut my stuff all the way up the Intracoastal until the dolphins complain to the cops. To be completely honest, that's what happens when you are out by yourself too long. Something like hearing "American Pie" by Don McLean on the radio can push you completely over the edge.

For a long-distance sea kayaker this is just about as close to an out-of-body experience as you can get. In that split second, thirty-two years fell away. I was suddenly driving a tan 1969 Volkswagen Squareback with a blue and white G&S surfboard on the roof crossing the Sea Bright Bridge on my way to West End. There was a hurricane off the coast, blowing in huge waves. Anyone with a board and a pulse knew what to do. At Monmouth Beach I could see the waves crashing over the rocks. Over the rocks! And then this song comes on the radio. "American Pie."

It made the evening news. Reporters stood on the beach in front of TV cameras delivering the same old tired line about stupid surfers risking their lives to catch a few waves in a storm. What they didn't know, what they failed to inform their viewers, is that it only happens once in an entire lifetime. There is no surf in New Jersey. Just once—maybe, and if you aren't there when it happens, you'll never know.

"So bye-bye, Miss American pie . . ."

In a blink, I'm back in the boat, except not entirely. My arms are as strong as a teenaged surfer. My butt is no longer sore. If I am wet, it doesn't even matter.

I see that fisherman on the bridge in front of me. I see him draw back his spinning rod and launch a lure into the black water. He turns, directing a frightened eye in my direction as I emerge from the shadows into the glow of the illuminated bridge, bellowing out those sacred words, something about whiskey and rye.

He stops. Just freezes, like I'm an enforcer sent direct from hell to strike him off this mortal earth with a double bolt of lightning. But, no. No. That's not it.

What he doesn't know is that I don't care if he hears my flat-ass voice all crooked and out of tune. He can't hear the real music pumping from the radio through my ears and directly into some perfect place in my soul. All he hears is me, sounding like a sexually aroused walrus in competition with two other suitors for the sweet affections of a fetching she-walrus named Lulu. It ain't pretty. I admit it. And all he knows is that something is shooting out of the darkness at him, something yellow and painful to his ears. By the time that chorus is over I am paddling hard and fast enough to pull water-skiers. Not just one or two. I'm talking about the whole pyramid of water-skiing women from Weekie Watchie.

"Bye, bye, Miss American Pie . . ."

I am under the bridge, my voice echoing in the steel cavern. Then past the bridge, and headed into the darkness on the far side, moving forward with effortless, unstoppable momentum.

I glance back, smiling. The fisherman stopped fishing. His rod tip is in the water. His hands are at his sides. His eyes are wide and fixed on the boat while he kind of crouches for protection behind a concrete pillar. Maybe he's worried I'll come ashore to panhandle for mind-altering substances or fishing tackle. I don't care. I don't care. I don't care. Here's why. It was bliss, absolute perfection.

Leapfrog

Somewhere north of Flagler Beach, The Hog disappeared into a barely audible crackle. For several miles the signal faded in and out, toying with me. It offered hope of continued entertainment, but then that hope was gone, sucked into empty airwaves.

Soon I was at the outer edge of my endurance. I needed a place to stop, and soon. I scanned the shore for any kind of beach fronting on undeveloped land—preferably with two trees to support a hammock. It didn't even have to be dry land, just shallow enough to string my hammock up and tie the boat to a tree. There were too many houses, too many docks with floodlights.

I kept going.

Around 2:00 A.M. I spotted a spoil island in the shadows to the west. I checked the chart and was surprised to see I was just past Palm Coast. I knew the name from the exit on I-95. This was the first place I'd stop to fill up my gas tank when driving from Fort Lauderdale to Washington, D.C. The island had been used as a frequent campsite. It was high and roomy, but the trees were not close enough together to hold my hammock. I needed two trees about twelve feet apart. These trees were about thirty feet apart. I was so tired I could have just propped myself up against one of the trees and slept that way, but I knew if I could somehow get the hammock up I would sleep better. Good sleep would help me get through the next day, and the day after that. I wasn't interested in shortcuts. Any shortcut, I knew, would cost me later.

Think.

I walked through the campsite again, reexamining my options. I realized I didn't need two trees. In the center of the island was a large tree with thick branches that hung down about five feet off the ground. That's where I tied my hammock—between two branches from the same tree.

I was too tired to do anything but sleep. Had I tried to cook I might have burned myself, or burned a hole in the boat.

I fell immediately into a deep, deep sleep, then woke up. Glassy water covered the land below me. My kayak was tied to a tree. I closed my eyes, confident I was safe above the flood and my boat secure.

At dawn, a full meal of turkey tetrazzini. Rested and refueled, I pushed out into the water and started working the kinks out of my hands, arms, shoulders, and back. This was day eleven, a Tuesday.

The sun streamed through the trees east of the Intracoastal. The wind blew ten to fifteen from the southwest. I put up my sail and starting paddling and sailing north toward Matanzas Inlet and Crescent Beach.

After a few miles a motor yacht, *Luna,* pulled up slowly beside me. A woman watched from the deck as a man at the wheel yelled across the water: "Are you the same yellow kayak we passed at Haulover?"

"Yes, I am," I yelled back, still paddling.

"You were doing six miles per hour back there in the channel," he said. He was impressed. I could hear it in his voice.

I explained that I was in a race around Florida and was about a day behind the second-place boat and probably several days behind the race leader.

The captain of the *Luna* wished me luck and a good trip. He powered up a bit and pushed up the channel.

The encounter wasn't unusual. Traveling on the Intracoastal Waterway over a period of time, I began to recognize other boats. It's like long-distance driving on an interstate highway: a small group of cars and trucks travel at about the same speed and you find yourself playing a kind of leapfrog with them throughout the day. The same is true on the Intracoastal.

There is an entire community of yachts cruising slowly on the Intracoastal, going either north or south. I played leapfrog with several of them heading north. I'm sure they couldn't figure out how a sea kayak was able to catch and pass them repeatedly day after day. As I moved up Florida's east coast I could see the routine emerge. Most of these yacht captains spent the day cruising up the Intracoastal. At night they pulled into a marina, bought supplies, and maybe went out to a restaurant for a meal. The next morning around eight or nine o'clock they began cruising north on the Intracoastal again. At some point during the day, they'd come across this crazy guy in a yellow sea kayak paddling just outside the channel. And they would wonder: "Isn't that the same guy we passed yesterday?"

Maybe some of them did the math. Several of them shadowed me for an extended stretch of water, apparently trying to measure my cruising speed. From that they could calculate distances by earlier sightings. But here's the tricky part: the calculations would have left a huge question mark. To cover those kinds of distances—and to repeatedly pass some of them, as I was doing—would mean I was paddling fifteen, eighteen, twenty hours a day. Most yacht captains would likely think it impossible. I don't blame them. I would have thought so too, if I wasn't in the process of doing it.

St. Augustine

As I passed Fort Matanzas, the wind began swirling and gusting to twenty. It was difficult to counteract the buffeting of my sail, so I took it down and just paddled. It brought an immediate feeling of security. I knew, no matter what, I could always take down the sail, just paddle, and still make decent progress. I also knew that when the wind acts this way it means a storm is coming.

By the time I reached the Route 206 Bridge at Crescent Beach, it started blowing hard. I needed to concentrate on getting to St. Augustine and points farther north, fast.

On my chart it looked like a straight shot up the channel through a wide salt marsh. A quick and easy trip. I could almost see St. Augustine, just up there around that bend.

North of the bridge, two sailboats motored past me. The boats disappeared up ahead in the grass. I watched their masts turn almost due west for what seemed miles through the wide marshland. Then I watched in dismay as the masts came back toward me almost due east, then turned west again, then east, then west, then east. This was a warning. Rather than the straight shot depicted on my chart, the channel followed a serpentine route through the marsh. It doubled my estimated time of arrival at St. Augustine.

When I finally arrived, the city looked tempting. Brightly colored buildings, the old fort—it is a historic jewel of a city. I'm ashamed to admit I've never actually stopped there. I've driven through many times, usually with a surfboard on the roof of my car, but never bothered to stop to look around. I would have loved stopping for some hot food and genuine rest in a waterside motel room. But I could feel the wind picking up, thick and moist. It smelled like big weather. Whatever it was, I wanted to be farther north and away from civilization in a place where I might be able to camp for the night, if necessary, when the storm hit.

I paddled straight through the city, through moorings crowded with sleek sailboats and luxury yachts. East of the Bridge of Lions a flotilla of dredge barges blocked the channel. I kept a careful eye on a tug steaming back and forth between the north shore and a barge. The outgoing tide swept me quickly through on the strong pull toward the inlet and the Atlantic Ocean. A fast trip, until I turned north to paddle up the Tolomato River.

My speed dropped immediately from a fast, easy swoosh into a white-knuckled slog. I might have been going one mile an hour, maybe two. I bucked the tide, fighting the inevitable. This is when strategy and intelligent tactics can make a difference. I could paddle to shore and rest, or I could plant my feet firmly on the foot pegs and pull hard on each stroke to keep up steady progress. There wasn't much debate. It would have been sacrilege to stop so early in the day.

The sky to the northwest darkened into the color of a three-day-old bruise, all purple and bluish black. The ugly, menacing sky issued a warning. "Surrender Dorothy!" No, that wasn't it. Turn back now. That was the warning. Get off the water. This is going to be nasty.

I promised myself that the strong tidal pull would ease substantially around that next bend in the river. Or maybe the tide would turn around soon and give me a push. Under normal circumstances I would have stopped and found shelter, but I just didn't want to wait around and sit there watching that storm hit. To me, stopping that early in the afternoon would have been like jutting my face out in anticipation of a sucker punch. That's just not happening. Not today.

The banks of the Tolomato River are unlike anything I encountered in the southern half of Florida. Gone were the ubiquitous mangrove roots clinging to the muck like desperate fingers. Gone were the lush and tangled branches, the green impenetrable jungle along the shores. Gone were the white sand beaches. Now I found myself paddling through a kind of savannah, a vast grassland of moist earth and black muck bathed in a saltwater ooze and scented with the stink of brine and decay. Beyond the water and grass, way off in the distance, pine forests rose as a kind of fence on the western edge of the grass, a monument to the existence of firm dry land. In between were islands of fern and pine, but only a few, and none were close enough to open water to suggest an easy landing and launch. Still too early to think about camping, yet camping was all I thought about.

I wondered about the grass, whether it would be dry and solid enough to sleep on. From a distance it looked comfortable, even mattresslike. But when I edged over close to test the landing options, the mosquitoes found me and began to organize into regiments, battalions, and divisions to launch an all-out assault on my blood supply.

These aren't ordinary mosquitoes; they are Florida mosquitoes. Florida mosquitoes are known for their large size and aggressive behavior. Mosquitoes in other parts of the United States are puny. They buzz around and make a nuisance of themselves. Florida mosquitoes are different. Imagine a blue jay wielding a milkshake straw. I guess this is just a long way of saying it would be impossible to try to pull my boat up into the grass to get a good night's sleep. Without two trees to hang my hammock and the ability to deploy its protective mosquito netting, I'd be little more than an open trough of blood for the dining enjoyment of pretty much every flying bloodsucker from Daytona to Jacksonville. As much as I support efforts to preserve wild Florida, I wasn't prepared to become a human plasma version of a V8 cocktail drink.

Right about the time I realized I'd have trouble finding a place to camp, the storm hit. Someone somewhere just flipped the switch marked STORM.

Boom!

It happened about five miles up the Tolomato, near the entrance to the Guana River. A band of black clouds raced across the sky. The wind and rain were one, completely mixed together. The river was maybe seventy-five-yards across but the force of the wind was strong enough to whip up significant waves and chop. I had just emerged around a bend and was fully exposed in open water. The force of the squall pushed my kayak backward and I had to paddle at full strength to get to the sheltered side of the river behind a three-foot bank of mud and grass. This was not easy. I dug the paddle into the water and pulled. The bow surged forward. But between each stroke the wind pushed me back. I increased my pace. I pulled harder. I reminded myself to hold the paddle tight.

The rain pounded my face at thirty miles an hour. In gusts, I had trouble breathing. I could see a motorboat to my north near the entrance to the Guana River. He appeared to be watching to see if I needed help. I appreciated the concern, but hoped he wouldn't put himself in any danger to try to help me. When he saw me reach the somewhat sheltered side of the river and hunker down to try to get out of the slashing rain, he motored east up the Guana and disappeared. It felt like the sky was crashing into the earth with no regard for those of us caught in between. Nonetheless, I felt safe and secure behind that little mud bank. There were a few times the gusts felt strong enough that had I been out in the open river they might have picked my entire boat up—with me in it—and flung us way back into the grass. I wondered how long the storm would last. I didn't want to stay there any longer than necessary. I could see a possible

campsite just north of the Guana River entrance. But this was still
the middle of the day and way too early to stop. I started munching
on a bagel and a few strips of beef jerky.

When the wind cut down to about twenty, I continued upriver.
Soon the sky lightened and the wind dropped to a breeze and a gentle
rain.

With each bend, the river grew more remote and beautiful. No
houses. No roads. Just salt marsh and trees in the distance. When it
finally stopped raining I pulled up on a beach that looked like an
old homestead. The chart said it had a name: Shell Bluff Landing. It
looked like a pretty good spot to camp, except for a prominently
displayed sign that announced: NO CAMPING. Other than the sign, it
was perfect. I got out my cell phone and called Linda. I reported my
position as: N + 30° 0' 55.38", W - 81°20' 45.36".

"I'm north of St. Augustine, but not very far north in the river," I
said. "I came through a storm. There was no thunder and lightning,
but plenty of horizontal rain with wind gusts. It rained enough to
wash the salt out of my shirt."

It was the equivalent of a shower, the first washing I'd had since
that glorious hot shower at Sebastian Inlet.

Linda asked my plans for the night. I told her I didn't know yet
but that there was no way I'd get to the next checkpoint at Amelia
Island that night. The checkpoint was at Fort Clinch, at the north
end of Amelia Island and about twenty miles north of Jacksonville. I
wasn't close enough to even begin thinking about the checkpoint. I
still had to get to Jacksonville and I still had to find a place to sleep.

It felt great to stand up straight and use my legs on dry land. It
was wonderful to hear Linda's voice. As we chatted on the phone I
could feel the temperature falling. It was a kind of nudge, a warning.
Don't get too comfortable.

"I've got to go," I told her. "I've got to get moving."

I had no idea how cold it might get.

I was somewhere between St. Augustine and Jacksonville and moving north at a steady pace. Things were looking up, but I still had this nagging feeling. Something was wrong. Then I realized what was wrong. It was the day of the week. Tuesday. Exactly a week earlier I'd spent that cold, uncomfortable night sitting up in my boat in the mud in Florida Bay looking across the flat at Manitou Cruiser. Was it really only a week ago? Here it was Tuesday again and I had no clue where I might spend the night. Could it be possible that this might once again become a horrible night spent sitting up in the boat, fending off the cold?

That was the problem with this section of the state. I'd never paddled here before. The marsh grass was completely different from the mangrove islands in south Florida. The river banks near Jacksonville are muddy and slippery, unlike the stable sandy bottom down south. It complicated finding a safe and decent place to sleep. My eyes scanned the shoreline for campsites. I saw a few areas that might work, but it was too early to stop.

I arrived at a dredged canal that ran about ten miles, connecting the Tolomato River with Jacksonville's Pablo Creek. The creek cuts through the center of another wide salt marsh and eventually joins the St. Johns River. Before the race I tried to imagine what might happen when I arrived at Jacksonville. I assumed I'd arrive at night. I was worried about this exact scenario. I'd be tired and a little delirious from exhaustion and sleep deprivation.

A few weeks before the race I called two kayak shops in the Jacksonville area and asked for campsite suggestions. The first person I asked didn't understand my question. She indicated there were many places to camp. But she couldn't pinpoint any. It was hard to explain that I needed exact directions, that I really was going to be there, and that I would desperately need a place to camp. What I couldn't convey was the idea that I'd probably be trying to find this place at 3:00 A.M. in raging wind and rain with a sleep deprivation IQ of about 5.

I called a second kayak shop. He wasn't much better. I studied the chart and visited Internet satellite websites to try to identify decent landing beaches. I circled possible camping areas using a thick red marker. I also circled a potential emergency stopping point, a boat ramp near the Beach Boulevard Bridge in Jacksonville Beach. If I needed it, at least I could get off the water and maybe hunker down in the parking lot for a few hours. Other than that I didn't have the slightest idea what I'd do or what might happen when I got to Jacksonville.

Walking in Grizzly Country

When my son was ten years old, I took him hiking in Glacier National Park in Montana. The park exists as a kind of transition point between earth and heaven. Consider it near-heaven, or a kind of training ground for those on their way. At least that's how I think of it. Most hikers agree with me.

At every turn, in every direction, the scenery is worthy of a postcard. These aren't the cheap 25-cent postcards, either. They are the kind of postcards that are too beautiful to scuff up in the mail, the kind I might frame and hang on the wall just to show people that such a place really does exist.

The air is crisp, clear. The higher mountains in late summer are still streaked with snow. The lakes are a bright green-blue. Tiny alpine flowers—yellows, reds, blues—carpet the valleys.

We walked over the continental divide from Many Glacier Lake through Swiftcurrent Pass to spend the night in a backcountry lodge. The lodge had thick stone walls and we were advised not to wander around outside after dark. There are grizzly bears.

We saw a bull moose on the walk in. There were deer, squirrels, chipmunks. The next day along the Highline Trail we saw mountain goats and bighorn sheep. But foremost in my mind was the king of these mountains, the grizzly bear.

Jason carried his own pack, to which I'd tied a bear bell. It actually looked and sounded more like a sleigh bell, but I guess if the marketing folks had called it a sleigh bell hikers wouldn't buy them. The concept behind bear bells is that hikers way out in the backcountry should make a nonnatural sound—like the metallic ring of a bell—to alert the abundant population of bears to the presence of humans. Grizzly bears don't like surprises. The only thing worse than truckin' around some bend in the trail and startling a grizzly bear is truckin' around a bend in the trail and startling a grizzly sow and her cubs.

There is a debate about bells. Some folks call them dinner bells.

Some hikers walk through the wilderness calling out every few minutes—"Hey bear! Hey bear!" Banging pots and pans might accomplish the same thing. But all that racket destroys one of the key attractions of the park: listening to the sound of the wind, the gurgling water in a brook, or the pounding of my heart as I stand on a precipice of the jagged spine of North America. The bell is a compromise, not as noisy as pots and pans and yelling, but not as dangerous as walking quietly through the woods.

Making noise isn't the only strategy. One popular hiker's tale goes like this: Two guys are walking together through grizzly country. One of them is reading a book about grizzly bears. "It says here, grizzlies can run thirty-five-miles per hour. I don't think either one of us can outrun a grizzly. What do you think we should do if a bear is about to attack?"

Without hesitation, the other, more experienced hiker says he'd run like the wind.

"But there's no way any man can outrun a grizzly," the hiker with the book says.

"I don't have to outrun the grizzly," the more experienced hiker replies. "Just you."

The problem with this strategy is that I would never leave Jason. Never. Instead, I bought a big can of pepper spray/bear repellant and I had Jason practice balling himself up into a fetal position on the ground with his hands protecting the back of his neck.

"We're going to pretend we are dead," I explained. "We are not going to look the bear in the eye. We are going to get down on the ground and play possum. If necessary, I'll use the bear spray. If I do, and the bear retreats, we'll get up and move quickly and quietly away before the spray wears off. If I can't get up, you go and get help. Don't look the bear in the eye. Don't turn around. Just get help."

I watched Jason closely to gauge his reaction. My son's eyes were large and round. But he listened carefully.

"Do you still want to go?" I asked.

This is one of those moments when you get a preview of the kind of man he'll become. "Yeah," he said. "Let's go."

I tied a bell to his pack, and instead of "Hey bear, hey bear," we resolved to do a lot of singing. We concentrated mostly on the classics— "Just sit right back and you'll hear a tale, a tale of a fateful trip . . ." and

"This is the story of a man named Jed, a poor mountaineer, barely kept his family fed . . ."

I had never been to Glacier National Park. Most of my hiking took place east of the Mississippi, where there are no grizzlies and the local black bears tend to be skittish. This idea of walking in grizzly country was new to me. In preparation I did some reading about bears.

Grizzly bears can grow to seven feet tall while standing on their back legs. Adult males can reach eight hundred pounds. Sure enough, they can chase down a meal at thirty-five-miles an hour. When they catch it, they deploy saberlike claws and a bone-crushing bite. Everything I needed to know about grizzly bear behavior was summed up in the bear's scientific name: *Ursus horribilus.*

Grizzly bears eat both plants and meat. Their diet includes grass, roots, berries, fish, and both small and large mammals. There are an estimated thirty thousand grizzlies in Alaska, but fewer than twelve hundred in the lower forty-eight. Glacier National Park is one of the few remaining pockets with viable grizzly populations and it is one of the best places to see them in the wild.

We hiked over the continental divide to the backcountry lodge. It took most of the day. When we arrived a park ranger had set up a telescope near the shelter. It was aimed down into a valley a couple of miles away, where a grizzly bear was chasing a marmot. Huge chunks of earth were flung up into the air behind the bear. He thrust his head into the hole and then dug some more. This was just exactly the way I'd prefer to see a grizzly in the wild—from about two miles away.

The next morning I woke up early. I told Jason I wanted to walk up to the top of a nearby ridge above the tree line and look down at the glacier on the other side before breakfast. He stayed in bed. I walked quickly about a mile up the trail and then climbed directly up the steep slope. When I reached the top of the ridge I looked down into a high mountain valley coated with snow and ice. There was even snow near the top edge of the ridge. I enjoyed the bite of the cold wind on my face. Then I looked down into the snow at my feet. There I saw the unmistakable track of a large bear. It had moved from south to north near the top of the ridge, and the track was fresh. I turned and could see the lodge below me about two miles away. I thought, "Oh great, I'm out here with a bear." I looked around and suddenly felt a deep sense of helplessness, like I had fallen out of a plane, plunging toward earth without a parachute. I started walking back toward the lodge, thinking about what I'd do if that bear caught my scent in the wind, circled around, and confronted me on the trail.

"Just sit right back and you'll hear a tale . . ."

When I got back to the lodge Jason was still asleep.

We left the lodge after breakfast and hiked to the Going-to-the-Sun Road. Along the way there are a few places where a careless step might involve falling several hundred feet. Jason is a good hiker. He's careful. Smart.

"Pay attention," I'd tell him. "Pay attention here."

About a mile from the end of the trail we met a group of hikers headed in the opposite direction. Among them was a boy about Jason's age. His dad had tied a piece of clothesline around the kid's chest and tied the other end to himself. These weren't rock climbers or mountain climbers. It was a piece of cotton rope used to dry clothes.

After they passed, Jason told me he was glad I didn't do that to him. He was glad I just let him walk it himself, even the parts high up on the cliffs. The dangerous parts.

I've thought about that. Life is going to be dangerous. But you can't give power to every little thing that might go wrong. Life lived well means pushing the fear away, demonstrating its powerlessness. It is knowing that singing the *Gilligan's Island* theme song in grizzly country is better than carrying a rifle. A life lived well is understanding that just because we could die by falling off a mountain or by being attacked by a grizzly bear doesn't mean we should be afraid of walking on the mountain.

There is a disconnect between modern American life and the natural world. Man is the most dangerous animal, with his ability to think, reason, and plan. But the greater challenge isn't to fight the natural world; it is to find one's place in it. Human beings are not intended to walk the earth as omnipotent gods demanding that all other forms of life bow down. If the world is a perfectly balanced system, the place for man is as part of that balance, not as the one who determines the balance. We are not the creator; we are part of the creation. To think otherwise is the worst kind of sacrilege. To me the most important lesson in Glacier National Park is humility. It is achieving a kind of grace in a place of terror. Or at least trying. That's what it means to walk in grizzly country. All that great scenery, the snow-streaked mountains and fresh air, that's just extra.

The day after our hike, we took a boat tour of St. Mary Lake. At the beginning of the tour the guide asked if anyone on the boat had seen wildlife in Glacier National Park. Jason sat in the last seat at the back of the boat. His hand shot up.

"What did you see," the guide asked. I could tell from the tone of her voice that she expected a story about chipmunks, or deer, or maybe a mountain goat.

"Grizzly bear," Jason said, proudly. The boat was full, maybe twenty tourists. All twenty heads turned immediately in amazement. I was sitting next to him, smiling. That's my boy. That's *my* boy.

Terrible Tuesday

It was dark. No moon. No stars. Just black on black on black.

A cold wind blew fifteen steady from the north. That spot between my shoulders began to tighten and ache. I had just passed under the Route 202 Bridge and felt I'd slid down into an endless cavern of shadows. There were lights off in the distance all around me, but they were no use for navigation. They were confusing, making the shadows bigger and darker. Green lights. Red lights. Headlights. Floodlights. Airplane lights. Traffic lights.

Then, bam! A wave broke over the bow. Where'd that come from?

I ran a soggy sleeve across my face and blinked several times to clear my vision. I can't see, at least not clearly. No depth perception. Just darkness and lights. Lights everywhere—but no light to help me see where I am, or where I'm going.

Somewhere in front of me is a single blinking green light marking the edge of the Intracoastal Waterway. Night navigation becomes a game of follow the lights. Green to green to green. If the channel is heavily used at night and well marked, I can follow a clear trail of green-red, green-red, green-red. But I was in some backwater near Jacksonville Beach, and the channel seemed to be moving around in front of me, playing defense. At one point I aimed at a clearly visible green light and paddled directly toward it for a few minutes until it turned red. Instead of a channel marker, I'd navigated to a traffic light on a nearby road. In my exhaustion, I found myself fighting a losing battle to stay on course and ward off the growing barrage of hallucinations.

The steady wind drove the temperature into a chilling freefall, and my worries about finding a place to camp began to multiply. Would this be another terrible Tuesday? I felt as if I was trapped in an episode of the *Twilight Zone*. I half expected Rod Serling to step out of the shadows to deliver his usual melodramatic monologue.

"A solitary kayaker, alone in the night, racing around Florida. He thinks he's on the trip of a lifetime. Instead, he finds himself a prisoner, not of the tides or the wind, but of a day of the week. Caught in the grip of the Terrible Tuesdays, he is about to run aground on the shoals of . . . the Twilight Zone." Cue up that bone-chilling *Twilight Zone* music.

Here I am near Jacksonville with a similar cold north wind and no place to tie my hammock. That's when I noticed my back deck light had burned out. It sat suction-cupped to the deck behind me, just beyond my reach. I needed to find a way to install fresh batteries.

I'd marked a boat ramp on the chart for a possible emergency stop, so I decided to pull in there, change the batteries, put on a jacket, and get something to eat. I arrived at about 11:00 P.M.

The last time I had stood on my feet and legs was six hours earlier calling in my position to Linda on the Tolomato River. It felt good to stretch my legs, but just as I stood up straight I noticed two police cars speeding into the parking lot and heading toward the boat ramp. My heart sank. A week earlier kayakers competing in the Everglades Challenge had been questioned by police officers in boats near Sanibel Island. Some law enforcement types hold the view that anyone who does something in the least bit unusual or different *must* be up to no good.

What I wanted to avoid was the hassle of having to explain to the police why a grown man kayaks through Jacksonville in the middle of a cold and windy night. I also wanted to avoid any possibility of having to spend the night in a Jacksonville jail.

But something didn't make sense. Why would they send two deputy sheriffs in speeding cars to question a kayaker? A little extreme, don't you think? Perhaps Jacksonville had experienced a wave of criminal paddlers and was in no mood to tolerate any funny business.

I decided to use the ostrich approach. I put my head down. I pretended they weren't there. I turned toward my boat, opened the front hatch, bent over, and tried to look busy. The police cruisers zipped past the boat ramp and stopped about twenty yards away near a white Volvo sedan—the only car parked in the paved lot. What happened next was like a movie. They got out of their cars and hunched down into defensive positions like there might be some shooting. They moved slowly toward the car, training a flashlight beam into the area near the steering wheel. I tried to act like I wasn't watching. I didn't want to draw attention to myself. But I mean, geez. I even looked for a protected spot to dive if bullets started flying.

Then one of the deputy sheriffs noticed me. He started walking over. I braced for what was coming.

"Is this your car?" he asked.

Having seen what I'd just witnessed, even if it was my car I'd have to have been an absolute idiot to admit ownership. Whoever owned the car must have done something pretty serious.

"I just got here," I said, looking up at the deputy. His gun was not drawn. "I don't know anything about that car."

He turned around and joined the other deputy shining the flashlight into and around the passenger compartment.

I tried to speed up my reorganization in the front hatch. I'd already changed the batteries in my deck light. I had my jacket on. But I still needed to move some food into the cockpit and top off my Gatorade supply. "Come on, come on." I worked as fast as I could. I just wanted to get back on the water. Then I heard it, from somewhere behind me.

"What are you doing out here?"

I turned and saw both deputies standing above me. They looked at me, sizing me up. I could see them checking out the boat, trying to figure this out. I knew I had to say something.

I hesitated.

If I told them the truth they might think I was certifiably insane and not let me go back out on the water. It is difficult to explain to someone who can't conceive of traveling alone at night in a kayak even in nice weather. Of course, it *is* completely nuts. Everyone knows that. But that doesn't mean it isn't worth doing.

"You don't have to answer," the deputy said. I noticed there were now three deputies standing on the bulkhead. I'm thinking, "Oh, great. They called for backup. I'm toast."

"Actually, I'm in a race," I told them. "It's a race around Florida. We started on March 4 in Tampa."

"Tampa," one of the deputies said. "You came all the way from Tampa?"

"Tampa, down to the Keys, and then up the east coast of Florida. I spent last night at Palm Coast."

"Wow," one of them said.

"You must have really strong biceps," the other said.

"I do now," I said, laughing and trying to be agreeable. "I still have a ways to go. I'm heading up the St. Marys River and down the Suwannee and then back to Tampa."

"Damn," the deputy said.

We talked a little more. One finally said, "Good luck." That was my cue. I got into the boat and pushed off. Paddling back out into the cold darkness, I was glad to be on my way. Those guys were obviously investigating something fairly serious. They had work to do and it did not offend them that I was involved in an activity that some public safety officials might consider unsafe.

Later, I learned that the Jacksonville sheriff's office was investigating the murder of a twenty-three-year-old nursing student named Sarah Whitlock. Her body had been discovered four days earlier, stabbed thirty-one times. The national media were on the story and the sheriff's office felt pressure to solve the crime.

Four days after my boat ramp encounter, investigators charged seventeen-year-old Kimothy Simmons with the murder. News reports said he allegedly posed as a police officer to gain entry to Sarah Whitlock's apartment. The crime had frightened the city's residents. A killer posing as a cop. Simmons was arrested a week after the murder during the carjacking of two other women. Two years later he was convicted of first-degree murder and sentenced to life in prison.

Although Jacksonville is a city, it retains many of the charms of a country town. People are friendly and these kinds of gruesome murders aren't supposed to happen.

I'm not sure the deputy sheriffs I met on March 14 were involved in that investigation. But every cop in the city was on edge because of the unsolved murder. I didn't ask them about the white Volvo. I was just grateful that they didn't hassle me.

About a mile into the darkness I again began to worry about finding a place to camp. I had considered asking the deputies, but I was afraid they might tell me camping is illegal within city limits. I'd rather take my chances on a few hours' sleep in blissful ignorance of the law than spend a restless night in fear of imminent arrest.

At that point I'd been on the water more than ten days, covering over sixty miles a day. The relentless pace came at a cost. Since the first night of the race I'd been unable to feel the three center toes on my right foot. When I was dry, my butt ached mercilessly from the constant pressure of sitting in the boat. When I was wet it itched like a million mosquito bites. The lack of sound sleep made it impossible at times to think and reason clearly. My memory shrank. My judgment disappeared in an ever-thickening haze of uncertainty. Did I mention that my memory shrank? Eventually, my ability to control my thoughts and emotions slipped away as I felt myself sliding toward anger and frustration.

This slow-motion disaster wasn't a complete surprise. I had prepared for this. I knew when I arrived in Jacksonville I'd be dead tired. I had used a red marker to circle possible campsites on my chart. The problem was that I'd never paddled here before and the islands that looked like promising camp spots on my chart turned out to be surrounded by mosquito-infested marsh grass. Most would be underwater at high tide. One island after another—rejected.

I continued paddling north, looking for a place to sleep. I stopped just past the Atlantic Boulevard Bridge at a spoil island with a small beach exposed by the falling tide. But there were no trees for a hammock and I noticed that the beach would be completely submerged when the tide came in. I felt my frustration mounting. I wanted a safe place to eat a hot meal and sleep, not a potential disaster site. Is that asking too much? Everything was going wrong.

I moved north toward the outline of another island. Again, it was just wet sand that would be under water at high tide.

The frustration built and built, until it boiled over. "Shit. Shit. Shit."

I saw no other land and no trees where I could tie up my hammock. "What am I supposed to do now?"

I gave up. I pushed my boat up onto the wet sand maybe fifteen feet from the water's edge and attempted to doze off while sitting up in my kayak. This is what happened exactly a week earlier. I knew it. I just knew it. Terrible Tuesday.

Sleep

I dropped off for about an hour. When I awoke, I'd had enough. I was beyond frustrated. This was pathetic. I pushed off, determined to find a better place to get some real sleep.

I stopped at the next island and again it was just wet sand, no dry land or trees, but there was also a ridge of shells close to the high-tide mark. I gave up my search for a decent campsite. I got out my backpacker air mattress, the waterproof tarp, my sleeping bag, a pair of thick socks, a fleece sweatshirt, and a fleece ski cap. The tide was low and still running out. I knew it would turn around quickly and cover the shell mound. There were no trees, not even a large rock to tie the boat and prevent it from drifting away. I tied a line from the bow of the boat to my wrist. Then I lay down and fell fast asleep on the softest shell mound anywhere in the state of Florida. I think at that point I could have easily dozed off naked on a bed of broken glass and rusty nails.

I slept for a few hours, but it was nothing really satisfying, more like passing out on a urine-soaked bus station bathroom floor. I kept waking up to check the level of the tide. Everything was wrong. Everything was out of kilter. I was mad. Mad at the world for having tides. Mad at the water for not cooperating. Mad at myself for failing to locate a better place to sleep.

It was only a matter of time before the tide rose high enough to sweep across the entire shell island. I didn't want to get soaked, particularly not in this cold weather. With the arrival of the front the temperature had dropped down into the upper 40s. I was warm enough in my sleeping bag, but if I got suddenly dunked by the tide and everything got wet, that could put me in serious danger of hypothermia.

Finally, I just got tired of waking up. I packed the boat and shoved off. The incoming tide cut my forward progress down to a hair above zip. I understood immediately what a big mistake I'd made by stopping on the shell island. Had I not been so sleep-deprived, had I not lost my ability to think rationally, I might have understood the need to keep paddling with the tide until I encountered the tide shift. That way I would have maximized my help from the tides, catching up on my sleep instead of fighting the swift current. If I'd known of a suitable camp spot up ahead I could have paddled with the falling tide to that spot. Instead, I squandered the chance. If I had only kept paddling instead of stopping on the shell mound, the tide would have pulled me right out into the St. Johns River.

Now the tide ran in hard, which meant I had to paddle against it. More proof of the general conspiracy underway to crush me. "Fuck you," I said to the tide. "Fuck the world."

I could see a bridge up ahead crossing the Intracoastal, a big, high-rise, well-lit bridge. The sight of the bridge came as a real shock. I couldn't remember seeing such a bridge on my Jacksonville chart. I stopped paddling and pulled out my chart. In the bright beam of the headlamp my finger traced my route, and sure enough it showed no bridge between the Atlantic Avenue Bridge and the St. Johns River. I knew I'd passed under Atlantic Avenue because the bridge had a large green sign that announces that fact. But what the heck was this. This bridge wasn't like the others I'd seen. The others were standard drawbridges that required a bridge tender to stay in a little office and raise the bridge for sailboats. This bridge in front of me was built high enough to accommodate sailboats.

Had I been well rested and thinking clearly I might have figured it out. All the newly built bridges along the Intracoastal Waterway are flyover bridges. This must be a new bridge, built since my chart was printed. Unfortunately there weren't enough circuits connected in my brain to reason this out. I just told myself to keep going and try to ignore the ghost bridge.

After about an hour of fighting the current, I reached the bridge and discovered the most beautiful island with an open sandy beach and a grove of trees from which I could have easily hung my hammock if I had just kept going . . . This island was only a mile or two past the wretched collection of shells and sand on which I had tried to sleep, but now I was back in the boat and too stubborn to stop.

I crossed the St. Johns River at dawn. The Intracoastal crosses the river and continues north through a tributary called Sisters Creek. I expected the entrance to be well marked and easy to find. Wrong.

Once in the full flow of the St. Johns, I drifted quickly and missed the entrance. I ended up about a half mile upriver, trying to find a creek that didn't seem to exist. I paddled back and forth across the same quarter mile, stopping twice on a sandy shoal pretty much just to scratch my head in bewilderment. Finally, I noticed a drawbridge and some channel markers.

Up a Creek

The Intracoastal Waterway follows Sisters Creek through the forty-six-thousand-acre Timucuan Preserve, a national wildlife sanctuary of pristine wetlands and islands watered by meandering tidal creeks. Sisters Creek is more than just a creek, it is wide and deep enough to carry Intracoastal Waterway boat traffic. Studying the charts before the race, Sisters Creek looked secluded and wild with beautiful scenery and plenty of animal life. It looked like the kind of place I would go with my kayak for an enjoyable weekend paddle. But by the time I reached the boat ramp near the entrance to the creek I was in no mood for sightseeing.

I pulled up at the ramp, ate two bagels and some beef jerky for breakfast, and then started paddling up Sisters Creek. The tide ran against me (of course). Once I paddled past the drawbridge, the landscape opened into a wide salt marsh as far as I could see. The view was spectacular, but the wide vista also meant there was nothing to block the wind. It blew hard from the north, about twenty with higher gusts. The tide played its part and seemed to ratchet up a few notches. I had to work hard just to hold my place in the water. I couldn't build up any speed. I measured my forward progress in feet and inches rather than miles. If I'd been on flat water on a calm day I'd have been moving at about six miles an hour. Instead, I might have been moving at one or two.

To sustain this level of effort all day would be difficult. I realized I'd made a mistake back at the boat ramp. Instead of taking a few minutes to cook and eat a hot noodle meal, I cut a corner and chomped down a few bagels. They are a great source of carbs, but not as effective in the long run as a cooked meal with fruit and vegetables. Having carried that food in the boat I should have eaten it—if for no other reason than it is more valuable as burnable energy in my stomach than as dead weight in the front hatch.

To my west, about ten miles away, stood the twin cooling towers of the St. Johns River power plant. For hours those white concrete towers lingered on the horizon as an annoying monument to my sluggish progress.

I wasn't the only one struggling. A few miles up the creek I glanced to my left and saw a four-foot alligator swimming parallel to me. Like me, he fought both the current and the wind-driven chop. We traveled at about the same speed. I couldn't see where he wanted to go, but it looked like he was challenging me to a race.

You think I'm scared. Do I look scared? Let's see what you got, Mr. Gator.

Eventually I pulled ahead of him. I looked back in amazement. He kept coming. I'd never seen anything like that. Most gators avoid boats. This gator was a competitor. I liked his spirit. I guess they grow them different in north Florida.

There is a word for this, the twelfth day of the race. That word is "slog." There is nothing redeeming, nothing pleasant about fighting the wind and the tide to make modest progress when there is still a long way to go. Earlier I had checked my GPS and discovered

I was only twenty-five miles from the checkpoint at Fort Clinch. I tried to guess how far I'd come since then. I figured five, maybe six. I thought about getting my GPS out and checking. I didn't. As soon as I stopped paddling I would have been quickly pushed back in the wrong direction by the wind and tide. I couldn't bring myself to surrender even a foot of hard-fought progress for the sake of a GPS reading.

There's another reason I avoided the GPS. As Sisters Creek began to wend its way through the grassland, I realized that the GPS had measured my distance to the checkpoint at twenty-five miles as the crow flies. Once I entered the marsh I realized that could mean fifty miles of creek channel meandering like a lazy snake through the marsh grass. With the headwind and counter tides, it amounted to a trifecta of spirit-crushing bad news. My only choice was to hunker down and suffer.

I Do

Why would anyone want to marry me anyway. What if I get to Tampa and she says, "No thank you."

It's not like I'm a great catch or something. Let's review. As a newspaper reporter I don't make much money, and what little money I had saved was cut in half in the divorce. I don't drive a fancy car. I don't have a souped-up boat. My boat doesn't even have a motor—or a seat for a second person. My hair is in a perpetual state of retreat. I can't dance. Sometimes I eat with my mouth open. Sometimes I slurp when drinking a can of Coke. And, above all, I'm a guy. That means sometimes I like to

walk around in my boxers and scratch myself while belching out an ex-
traspecial rendition of Jingle Bells. *I'm pretty much the complete pack-*
age. Which makes me wonder why Linda would say, "I do."

There are three hundred reasons she might say no. Maybe even three
thousand reasons. I can think of three reasons she might say yes. First, I
know I can make her laugh. Second, I love her with all my heart. Third,
she knows that I love her with all my heart.

Fort Clinch

Around 4:00 P.M. I passed Fernandina Beach and pulled up at
the checkpoint at the state park campsite near Fort Clinch. I found
the orange lockbox and signed in. The logbook showed that Manitou
Cruiser had arrived at the checkpoint at 1:00 A.M. I thought back to
1:00 A.M. I had been at Jacksonville somewhere near that phantom
bridge, somewhere near that shell island. Also in the lockbox was a
note from Chief explaining he had rented Campsite 33.

I used my cell phone to call my parents, who agreed to drive up
to help with logistics at the checkpoint. Then I attached my lightweight wheels and pulled the boat across the beach and up the road
to the campsite. As the sun went down so did the temperature. I was
grateful to be off the water. It felt good to stand up and relieve the
pressure on my throbbing butt.

Checkpoints are critical to surviving the Florida Challenge. The
rules say that racers are barred from having any in-person contact
with family members or friends at any point between checkpoints. It
would be a violation of the rules to have a friend or family member

meet me along the way with fresh food or water or provide a place to sleep. There is no problem with someone standing on the shore cheering and taking photographs, but along the racecourse I am expected to be on my own.

Checkpoints are different. Family members can bring food and drive me to a restaurant, even take me to a hotel for the night. The cost of such luxury is lost time. It is a calculation one makes.

I was prepared to camp at Fort Clinch. As the sun went down and the temperature dropped, my father suggested that I rent a hotel room. I considered it, and eventually decided the shower and soft bed would be worth the extra time it would take. I'd gotten pretty badly beaten up over the past twenty-four hours and could use a little pampering. I organized my boat and then separated out my dirty clothes. What followed in the next few hours was a study in logistical efficiency. First, we went to a laundromat where all my paddling clothes were put into a washing machine. While the washer churned, we drove to the hotel where I took a quick shower, then went to the supermarket where I picked up fresh vegetables, more bagels, sandwiches, and Snickers bars for the next leg of the race. We returned to finish the laundry. Next we went to Sonny's, a barbecue place, where I ate a half rack of babyback ribs and took one trip to the salad bar. Then we drove back to the hotel.

I'm not sure when I lay down on the bed, but exactly one nanosecond later I woke up. It was just before dawn. Time to go. This was probably the purest, deepest sleep of my life. I felt terrific, ready to go. It is a beautiful thing, the restorative power of a few hours of sound sleep.

Another shower—sheer bliss. I stuffed down as much of the lobby breakfast food as I could hold. Then it was a short drive back to Campsite 33.

Predawn temperatures were in the 40s. I could see my breath. Each puff hung in the still air. The relentless north wind of the prior day had blown itself out and covered the region in cold air.

Chief was at the campsite. He delivered some sad news. There-AndBackAgain had dropped out of the race somewhere near Stuart. He'd spent a lot of time paddling into a ferocious headwind and finally decided it just wasn't fun anymore. Of all the challengers, TABA was, for me, the most inspiring. He has a spirit I admire. To attempt the challenge with no legs just made all my own fears and concerns seem so trivial. I had hoped that when I turned the corner at Key Largo and started paddling north TABA would be in the same neighborhood. I had hoped that just as I'd done with Manitou Cruiser, we might paddle up the east coast together. It didn't happen.

As the sun rose, the chilly morning air warmed quickly. I organized my food and repacked all my clean clothes. I replaced the old charts with new charts for the next leg of the race. I sealed up my hatches and double-checked to make sure I wasn't leaving any key piece of gear behind. Then, at about 7:30 A.M., I wheeled my boat down to the water's edge and squinted in the general direction of the St. Marys River.

I knew Wizard was somewhere on the portage, and maybe already headed down the Suwannee. I figured my leisurely checkpoint stop had given Manitou Cruiser a pretty good lead too. I assumed he'd probably start the portage sometime later that day. I wasn't thinking about catching them. All I wanted was to get up the river. That meant catching the tide and staying smart. For the first time in the race I was about to turn west and head across northern Florida to the Gulf of Mexico. The weather conditions were perfect—sunny, cool but not cold, with a slight breeze. I had enjoyed the deepest, soundest sleep since probably several weeks before the beginning of the race. I was ready to go.

As I paddled away from shore I tried to think of everything that happened earlier in the race as mere preparation, two weeks of training. This next section would be the most difficult stage of the race. The real challenge was only just beginning.

PART V

Go West:
Amelia Island to Cedar Key,
380 Miles

Paring Up

With Wizard, Manitou, and Sharkchow in the lead, and three other boats already out of the race, the four remaining challengers found themselves catching and passing each other frequently. In the same way that I had run into Manitou at unexpected moments, Sandy Bottom and Dr. Kayak kept crossing paths. The same thing happened to Pelican and Doooobrd. "From Sebastian to the finish, we were always within a couple of hours of each other," Doooobrd said.

Sometimes the company was helpful; two sleep-deprived minds are better than one. Or maybe not. Later in the race, Pelican and Doooobrd would spend an hour paddling in the wrong direction up the Santa Fe River in a dense fog before realizing they were no longer traveling downstream on the Suwannee.

Dr. Kayak and Sandy Bottom cruised together on and off throughout the race despite different goals during the trip. Sandy Bottom wanted to get to the next checkpoint as fast as possible. Dr. Kayak was anxious for another meal. "He would be scanning the shoreline for golden arches," she said.

Their collaboration ultimately proved important if for no other reason than to provide a witness. In one of their most harrowing adventures, Dr. Kayak and Sandy Bottom found themselves four miles offshore in the predawn darkness paddling frantically to avoid the spotlight of a fast-approaching shrimp trawler.

"He kept turning toward us, so we turned ninety-degrees away, but that damn shrimp boat was following us," Sandy Bottom said. "This went on for a half hour. We were paddling in circles trying to get away from the shrimp boat."

Already exhausted, now they were in a mad sprint to try to outrun the grim reaper. When they could paddle no more they sank down in their boats and braced for the collision. They listened to the approaching engine. Then from somewhere across the dark water came this, "Are you guys okay? Do you need any help?"

Sandy Bottom couldn't believe her ears. "The shrimp boat captain had been chasing us because he thought we needed help."

Nowiminflorida, Nowimingeorgia

I remember as a kid—I was maybe eight years old—sitting in the backseat of the family car driving from New Jersey to Florida for vacation. When we drew near the Florida-Georgia border my attention was riveted on the mileage signs announcing the distance remaining before reaching Florida. There was one important ritual that had to be performed. At the exact spot where you leave Georgia and enter Florida it's necessary to say out loud as fast as possible: "Now-I'm-in-Georgia, now-I'm-in-Florida." It is eight words (ten without the contractions), but to do it right is to say it as if it is only two words with a brief pause in between.

It has since become a time-honored tradition in recognition of that special moment of arrival in Florida. Driving down from the northeast, the ritual always happened on a bridge. Long before the I-95 Bridge, it was the Route 17 Bridge, just south of Kingsland, Georgia. Whichever road, there were signs announcing the accomplishment. We would cheer in the car. Not just me, everyone in the car would cry out. Even my sister.

That's not the only thing. While all this excitement was happening I would also be looking out the side window and down below the bridge at the sinister dark water that marked the border between Georgia and Florida. I didn't know the name of the river, but sometimes I'd see a boat navigating the serpentine course of the main channel through wide vistas of marsh grass. The river meandered in loop after loop from the west where it emerged from stands of dead trees draped with Spanish moss, trunks and branches sun-bleached white as bone. I was sure the slow dark water held menacing secrets of unimaginable evil.

The next several miles of the car trip were consumed with thoughts of what it would be like taking a boat up that river. This was no ordinary river. Anyone with an ounce of common sense could see it was a river of no return. Going up that river would be a journey across black water into a junglelike marsh coated with a thick layer of slime and muck, farting out deadly swamp gas, and populated by poisonous snakes with red eyes and an entire colony of murderous bank robbers with Samsonite luggage stuffed full of unmarked bills. Even if I made it past the bank robbers, I was sure alligators would tip over the boat and chomp off my arms and then my legs so I couldn't swim anymore and then when I sank to the bottom the red-eyed snakes and earthworms would eat my eyeballs so that even if I could swim I wouldn't be able to see the right way to go. I'd just keep bumping into the same log. Over and over again. Damned log. Which raised a question. Once I was already dead and the snapping turtles starting eating the delectable meat on my neck, would my head float up to the surface and then drift downstream like a cork, or would it just sink to the bottom and stay stuck in the mud for a million and a half years and eventually turn into motor oil? And, if so, which brand would it be? Shell? Texaco?

Now was my chance to answer at least some of these important questions. Now was my chance to explore the St. Marys and follow it far into the backcountry. Now was my chance to do exactly what I'd first thought of doing as an eight-year-old kid in the backseat of the family Chrysler.

When I launched into Cumberland Sound near the Atlantic Ocean it was midtide. This was absolutely the perfect time to go. Some WaterTribe challengers were under the mistaken belief that the most advantageous way to start up the St. Marys River was to leave Fort Clinch at low tide. But that is a bad idea. The best strategy is to try to ride the incoming tide as far upriver as possible. If I began at dead low tide at the Atlantic Ocean I would quickly outrun any incoming tide and eventually even outrun the slack tide. When that happens I would be paddling against the current. Who wants to do that?

I learned this from paddling a canoe in and around Chokoloskee and Everglades National Park in southwest Florida. I would ride the tide out to the Gulf of Mexico, fish for sea trout on the falling tide, and then ride the incoming tide back to my car. The tides work the same on Florida's east coast. I had also consulted my friend Marty "Salty Frog" Sullivan, who warned me about leaving Fort Clinch when the tide was too low. Years earlier he'd competed in Chief's first cross-Florida race, so he knew what he was talking about. He knew the way from Fort Clinch to Cedar Key. More important, he knew a few mistakes to avoid.

There was another reason I liked the midtide plan. Low tide arrived at about 4:00 A.M. Midtide came at about 7:00 A.M.—a much more civilized time to begin a journey. Leaving at seven o'clock would allow me to sleep a little longer and not feel like an indolent slothful laggard for doing it. And I'd be improving my efficiency up the river later in the day, right?

Once on the water, my first goal was to avoid taking a wrong turn on the approach to the St. Marys. The marshy area near Point Peter includes numerous tidal creeks that branch off the St. Marys leading nowhere. I needed to find the main channel and stay in it. Normally this would be relatively easy, but I had been unable to locate a good map of the river. All I had was a squiggly line on a sheet of paper printed off a tourist webpage on the Internet and a corner of my waterproof chart number 44. The Internet map showed no real detail; I used it for mileage. I marked river miles at each point where a road crossed the river. It would help me keep track of my progress. The only detailed map of the river was chart number 44, and all it showed was the place where the St. Marys emptied into Cumberland Sound. It didn't even extend far enough upriver to show the location of the town of St. Marys.

When I arrived at what I assumed was the entrance to the river I decided to follow the widest water. In addition, I'd stay in the strongest current on the theory that a side channel leading nowhere would not pull in a significant amount of water.

Heading upriver I found and passed St. Marys, the scenic little town for which the river is named. It looked like an idyllic painting, adorned in the brilliant morning light with white brick buildings, lazy Sunday afternoon porches, picket fences, and Victorian inns shaded by giant magnolias and live oaks. The town's waterfront featured shrimp trawlers, sailboats, and motor yachts. St. Marys claims to be the second oldest town in the United States, after St. Augustine. It is also a place Aaron Burr is reported to have hid out briefly after his lethal duel with Alexander Hamilton. The town looked to be a nice place to stop for a tasty meal, except I wasn't hungry and it would have delayed my mission to get upriver as fast as possible. I paddled on.

Just past St. Marys, the cry of the seagulls and the sound of the breeze in the grass was replaced by the distant whine of tractor-trailer tires crossing the I-95 Bridge. I could see the bridge just to the west across the grassland. It seemed so close, and would be close if I could walk or paddle straight to it, but I-95 was still hours away following the long loops and sharp bends in the river channel.

The strategy to leave at midtide worked perfectly. I rode the surge of incoming tide all the way to the interstate highway. That's where I stopped to eat lunch. In the excitement of launching earlier that morning, I forgot to move my food for the day from the front hatch into the cockpit. Under normal circumstances this would pose no particular difficulty. I'd simply paddle to shore, get out of the boat, retrieve the food, and eat lunch. That idea was quickly rejected when I got a good look at the water in the St. Marys River. The tannin that leaches into the river stains the water. In some rivers I've paddled the water is the color of Coca-Cola. Here the St. Marys runs in shades of crimson. It is a natural occurrence, but to me it looked like an alligator had just chewed a man's leg off.

No way I'm sticking my foot down in that, I thought. Instead, I performed a kind of intra-kayak ballet, carefully balancing as I rose up out of my seat in the narrow, wobbly boat. I leaned and crawled up over the deck to open the front hatch. I'd never attempted this particular maneuver before—for good reason. It was nuts—an engraved invitation to flip the boat. I told myself to concentrate. Move slowly. No sudden actions. Whatever you do, don't flip the boat. Of course it didn't help that at this exact moment I imagined a bevy of hungry gators nestled below in the muck, just waiting for dinner to be served.

Alligators have a kind of prehistoric way of hunting. They don't actually try to bleed or crush their prey to death. What they can't swallow whole, they drown. Their powerful jaws are designed to drag a large mammal—like a man—under water where he can't breathe. Then comes the really interesting part. Gators don't always eat large prey right away. They carry their food back to a den in the muck and roots where the fresh meat remains for days or weeks to bloat and rot and otherwise achieve an alligator's sense of delicious.

I heard a story once about a man snatched and drowned by a gator. Mercifully, he passed out quickly. When he regained consciousness he found himself in a dark muddy gator den, just above the waterline. I like to think he clawed his way out of there and saved himself before that gator came back. I don't even know if that story is true, but I'm hoping the only way we know is because that guy survived to tell the tale.

I snatched the food out of the front hatch amid this death-defying, delicate contortion—two roast beef sandwiches, some Cheez-Its, a few bagels, and some beef jerky. I resealed the front hatch and enjoyed my sandwich as I watched traffic zip past on the highway. Then I took up my paddle and started moving. I could hear the familiar gurgle once again at my bow, but my thoughts were up on that bridge behind me. I imagined a kid sitting in the backseat of the family sedan celebrating his arrival in Florida and looking down from I-95 to see a lone kayak paddling through blood-red water up a menacing river of no return.

Marriage Is Wonderful

It is nice to be loved. It is nice to be appreciated. However, at some point you have to get married. I mean, that's just the way things are. Right?

Why can't we just love each other? Why can't we just feel what we feel for as long as we feel it? If the relationship is strong, that's the reward. A piece of paper isn't going to change that. A ceremony in a church or at city hall or some tacky chapel in Las Vegas isn't going to change that. If there is a sacred bond between two people, it is a bond between two people that they have made sacred. Let it alone. Just let it be what it is.

If our relationship, if our love, survives through the winter and many winters, why tinker with the design? Some say marriage is the best place, the most noble place to be. Marriage is wonderful, they say. I know something about marriage from personal experience. Wonderful isn't the right word.

Love is wonderful. Love is noble. Marriage is a context in which love can take place—but there is no guarantee.

This thing we have is too important to mess up. I don't want to lose it by being careless. I don't want to lose the essence of it by doing something for the sake of appearance.

It isn't that I want to preserve my ability to walk away at any moment. Only a fool thinks that is freedom. It isn't that I don't trust you. It's that I like the idea that you have the opportunity to walk away from me at any moment. You have the freedom to do as you like. You have the freedom to hurt me. Yet you don't. You have the freedom to leave me at any moment. Yet you don't. There is an edge to the relationship that helps feed the fire. I can't imagine not being with you. I would rather spend one day and one night in the hot glow of that fire than a lifetime in a cold marriage. Because at the end of my life, at the very end, I could think back and know that at least I'd had that one day and one night. That would be enough. More than enough.

Target Practice

It felt good to pass under I-95, establishing solid proof of my westward progress toward the Gulf of Mexico. Psychologically it was a good moment. I had slept the sleep of the dead in that hotel bed and arisen a much younger, stronger man in the morning. My two showers, one in the evening and one the next morning, had managed to hose the mud and other crud from my body. Again, a vortex of grime swirled down the drain near my feet as the steaming water helped loosen the tense muscles in my back and arms. I had been enveloped in a nasty halo of stink and stench, a reek not unlike a curb in New York City's Times Square. At one point, I smelled so bad songbirds fell from the sky. It is astounding what fifteen minutes in a steamy shower can do. I slowly, slowly rejoined civilization.

Now, here I was, a new man, heading up the St. Marys. I felt ready. My spirit was so high I had to keep telling myself to slow down and set a relaxed, easy pace. I still had a long way to go.

Unlike any other part of the race, here I ran up the river. At some point I would outrun the rising tide from the ocean and start paddling against the seaward flow of the river itself. I didn't know what to expect, how fast the river might be draining, how narrow it might get between downed trees, and whether there might be confusing forks in the waterway that could take me far off course and deep into Georgia to some dead-end backwater swamp. I'd traced the course of the river many times with my best map to try to anticipate obstacles the river might offer up, but I wouldn't really know until I arrived on the water. Whatever it would be, I wanted to be prepared. That meant I needed to be efficient and conserve as much energy as possible so that when the time came to paddle hard or to swim out of a dangerous situation, I'd have enough left in my arms to get the job done.

As I moved farther west, the river seemed to widen. Why would it widen? Aren't rivers supposed to get narrower the closer you get to the source? Did I take a wrong turn? Every few miles I stopped paddling just to test the flow of the river.

A bank of clouds passed over, producing a brief shower. Long sections of the river are remote, with thick junglelike vegetation growing to the water's edge. In other areas there are houses with docks—and dogs. For some reason the sound of a paddle in the water holds a special level of annoyance for dogs. Those that could, ran to the bank and let loose with noisy barking. Others confined inside a house or shed did their best to make their presence known.

Just before I shoved off from Fort Clinch, during the final moments of my packing, Chief warned me to watch out for a place way up in the backcountry where, he said, the locals take target practice across the river. "Be careful up there," he said, smiling his sly smile. Apparently, they sit somewhere up on the northern bank in Georgia and shoot at stuff in Florida on the southern bank. "Be careful," he repeated. What Chief didn't reveal is whether they will stop shooting long enough for a kayak to glide past. What if they decide to turn the river itself into a shooting gallery? How much authority would my protestations carry way out here?

I'm talking about people who live in places called Cabbage Bend and Flea Hill. Does anyone honestly believe that someone who calls Flea Hill home is going to care what I think about how he conducts target practice?

All of this was mere speculation, just groundless fear based on a few offhand comments from the ever-mischievous Chief. Then I started to hear gunfire. *Oh crap.* The farther west I paddled the louder it got.

There wasn't really much I could do other than keep paddling and hope for the best. The houses this far back in the woods were either weekend hunting shacks or just flat-out country poor. It made me think of that movie *Deliverance* and all the terrible things that befell a group of four men on a canoe trip down a river in northern Georgia. When I signed up for the Florida Challenge, sodomy was not on my list of potential experiences.

Deliverance is fiction, I kept telling myself, just fiction. My own experience is that folks in rural areas may be a bit suspicious of strangers, but once they have an idea who you are they are the best people on earth. Given the choice I'd rather live in a country town with real country people than in a city where basically everyone assumes everyone else is a murderous thug. I tell myself that crime rates are much higher in cities. Then I also recall that for some reason the most horrific crimes almost always seem to happen in the Deep South, in rural areas with names that sound like Cabbage Bend and Flea Hill.

Finally, I reached a place where I could almost hear the bullets whizzing through the air. A house with peeling white paint sat up on a hill above the river. From somewhere behind the house came a fairly steady crackle of gunfire. It was too much shooting for a hunter. I was grateful for that, but I worried that whoever it was might look over and see a seventeen-foot yellow and white target moving up the river. With one or two well-placed shots he could obtain a bonus round of practice shots at my lifeless body and boat as they both floated back down the river.

I decided not to linger. When I tasted that fine bouquet of fear rising in my throat, I felt motivated to paddle fast, but quietly. When the need arises I can make the kayak move. There is no way I can outpace a bullet, but I was prepared, if necessary, to give it a try. I'm not suggesting I'm Superman or anything, but there was a wake behind my boat as I rounded that bend, and that wake stayed behind my boat for another mile.

About four in the afternoon I stopped briefly to talk to a man sitting in his backyard fishing with a cane pole. He had a nice modern house and a neatly organized lawn. He even had a nice shiny fiberglass bass boat tied up at the dock. Yet on this day he preferred sitting under a shade tree with a cane pole in his hand. Sometimes, it seems, the best kind of fishing is the kind you did when you were a kid.

"Where you goin'?" he asked.

"I'm headed to St. George. The bridge at St. George."

He told me I was six hours from Traders Hill. That would put me at Traders Hill at around 10:00 P.M. Then he added, from Traders Hill to St. George is a ten-hour trip going against the current. It's about thirty miles, he said.

I was astonished at the precision of his estimates. How could he know how long it would take to paddle—against the current—to these places?

If he estimates I'd be at Traders Hill by ten o'clock, I'd probably make it by eight, I thought, hopefully. I did not express this opinion to the fisherman, but I did ask him how well he knew the river.

He told me he once ran a canoe livery business on the St. Marys. He knew every twist and turn.

Sixteen hours still to go? I hoped he was wrong. I hoped he based his estimates on someone paddling a canoe, not a kayak. Nonetheless, the encounter was important. It helped me prepare for what lay ahead.

Once the sun set I discovered a hazard of river travel at night. Generally at night I turn on a battery-operated light on the deck behind me. Rather than trying to affix a headlight to the boat to illuminate the river, I prefer to keep my lights off and use my own night vision to scout out the water ahead. The paddling was easy and fast. I just tried to stay clear of obvious snags, overhanging branches, or downed trees near the bank. The problem was, everything was black. The water, the sky, the surrounding trees. Around 9:30 P.M. I ran the kayak way up on a submerged log.

It is hard enough to see a foot or so below the surface of the dark water during a bright, sunny day, but it is impossible to see anything at night. I had been moving fast. I slid all the way across the log until it reached just below my thighs. Then the boat stopped and I immediately felt the hull flex from the weight of the boat against the log. For a moment I balanced like a teeter-totter. The bow tipped down. Then the stern tipped down. It was dark, so dark that all of this took place by feel. I saw nothing. I knew that I was a split second away from disaster. Two terrible things could happen. First, the hull could crack under the weight of the loaded boat, stranding me out in a remote and muddy section of the river with no obvious place to land. Second, the log could flip the boat over and spill much of my gear into the black current, sending both me and my boat down into the dark unknown, again with no obvious place to land.

This was the reason why I had been conserving my strength earlier. I summoned every bit of power available and used my paddle to push large waves of white water back in the direction of the log. The boat rocked and then listed to the right. I used a constant, hard, left-right-left-right back paddle to push the boat off the log. It slid into the river.

Drifting backward in the current, I took a long, deep breath in recognition of a huge disaster that had just been averted. I realized I'd need to change my tactics. I needed a bright light, bright enough to see potential submerged logs.

I had a small bright flashlight that usually hung around my neck for use in checking out possible landing spots. I had never used it for long periods. This qualified as an emergency. I needed to keep going.

The St. Marys River is a beautiful river during the day, but at night it is a scary place. Every sound triggers the imagination. It wasn't too bad having that little flashlight beaming out across the water. The downside is that small bright lights don't last very long. The batteries gave out before I reached Traders Hill.

When that happened I went back to my old tactic of relying on night vision, but I slowed down. Just as predicted by the fisherman, I reached Traders Hill at about 10:00 P.M. I considered camping in the parking lot there. It is an open area and there is a launch ramp that would make for an easy exit from the river. The launch ramp also meant that others might arrive in the middle of the night, either coming off the water or from the nearby highway. I didn't want to worry about intruders, I just wanted to eat a big meal and get some sleep. I paddled for another half hour before I came upon a large white sandbank with a grove of trees nearby that seemed perfect for a hammock. I pulled up carefully beside the sandbar and was able to step onto the dry sand without getting my feet wet.

With the boat pulled high onto the sand and tied to a tree, I ate a dinner of beef stroganoff, mandarin oranges, and fresh snap peas. Then I climbed into my hammock.

A Good Long Ways

I was up at 4:30 A.M., broke camp within fifteen minutes, and wolfed down a couple of bagels while paddling. I pushed hard against a steady current. At times I had to resort to using my hands to claw through branches of downed trees, always aware of the moving water and the danger of allowing my boat to turn sideways. If the kayak broached in these conditions and then got pinned up against a downed tree, the force of the water would soon push the upriver side of my cockpit down into the water. The power of moving water is deceptive—and deadly. If my boat was dragged under, the pressure of the rushing water might pin me into my seat where I would remain underwater and lifeless until some fisherman or the next Florida Challenge participant found me.

The current in the river was stronger than I'd anticipated. There were many more downed trees than I had imagined. The river between Traders Hill and St. George was all back and forth with very little straight ahead.

This is where that fisherman's advice the day before about the ten-hour trip from Traders Hill became extremely valuable. It helped me take the hardships of the upper St. Marys in stride. The difficulty of this leg of the race had me puzzled. Everyone who competed in the Cross-Florida Challenge a few years earlier had talked of the difficulty of the portage. No one complained about paddling up the St. Marys. The portage must be even harder than this, I thought.

At several points the current ran strong through a narrow passage between downed trees. I wondered how Wizard had gotten his sailboat up the river. With no ability to sail, he'd have to either scull, or use his oar to pole the boat forward. He couldn't do that for thirty miles—not against this current. Either that or he'd have to get out of his boat and drag it up river. He couldn't do that either. Could he?

I paddled out of the predawn black and into a beautiful morning. A gray mist swept through the trees and across the water. The sandbanks seemed to glow as I glided through the woods. The river alternated between silent flat water and gurgling flow through choke points and tangled branches and tree trunks. As I moved upstream I kept scanning the bank, identifying great places to hang my hammock. I vowed to come back sometime when I wasn't in a hurry.

Just after sunrise, I came upon three turkey vultures standing wing to wing in a perfect row on a sandbank on the Georgia side of the river. As I paddled past, their heads swiveled in unison toward me. I knew what they were thinking. Breakfast. It made me wonder just how bad I must look and smell.

"Sorry, boys, not today." I actually said it out loud. They did not fly away or show any concern that I might alter my course and come after them. They knew their place in the food chain. They just stood there acting all superior, waiting for me to die. Damn vultures.

———

Sometimes I just can't stand being apart.

But I don't know, maybe that's part of why the attraction is so strong. I always want what I can't have. Then when I have it, I've got it. The desire disappears. Or diminishes. I don't want it to diminish. I don't want it to change at all.

Here's the thing. I'm afraid if we go ahead and get married everything will change. I'll move in with you in Washington. Then I'd be around all the time. You'd be around all the time. We'd stop counting the minutes. We'd stop planning. We'd stop being lovers.

I think I'd rather count the minutes. I've never had a relationship like this. There's part of me that says don't fix it. Don't even try.

But then, sometimes, I just can't stand being apart.

———

By midafternoon I was anxious to be done with the St. Marys. The river just didn't want to end. I even broke my usual rule. I don't like to consult my GPS unless it is necessary to avoid getting lost. In other words I don't use the GPS to estimate my time of arrival—I only use it for navigation. But I broke the rule somewhere in the jungle surrounding the St. Marys. It said six miles and I thought, six miles isn't so far. The problem with using a GPS on a river like the St. Marys is that it measured the distance in a straight line. I wasn't traveling in a straight line. The river is a series of twists and turns.

I came upon a man fishing in a canoe. He could have been the twin brother of Lawton Chiles, the late Florida senator and governor. He wore a straw hat and had the look of someone who had grown up discovering all the best places to cast a line in the St. Marys.

"How far is it to the bridge at St. George," I asked.

He turned and looked up river, as if the answer was written somewhere up in the branches. He gave the question some thought. "A good long ways," he said.

I nodded and groaned. "Thanks," I said.

Further upstream I encountered another boat. It was a man fishing with a young boy in a rowboat with a small motor. They saw me paddling against the current. They kept fishing, but also kept an eye on my progress.

When I got up to them I asked: "How far is it to the bridge at St. George?"

"That's a good long ways," the man responded.

A good long ways isn't the most precise description of distance. I felt like the object of some conspiracy. Maybe everyone in this part of the country uses the term "a good long ways." If so, what does it mean? A mile? Ten miles? A hundred miles?

I didn't want to be rude and ask the question again. I couldn't exactly cross-examine the guy. How long would that be in miles, I wanted to ask. I didn't.

A good long ways? That sounds like I'll have to keep going until I get where I am going. How far might that be? That's easy. A good long ways.

I rounded about three bends in the river and then I heard the sound of tires on pavement. It was disorienting. It could have been falling water. Or the wind in the leaves. I picked up my pace a bit, turned a corner, and there over the river was the most beautiful span of concrete I had seen in a long time. The bridge. Just a little ways beyond it I found the boat ramp. I'd made it to St. George and the start of the portage.

By the time I pulled my boat onto the ramp, the man and the boy came motoring up.

"How many snakes did you see?" the man asked.

"Snakes?" I'd seen three alligators, but they were small and shy. They slid into the water long before I got anywhere near them. I wasn't looking for snakes.

"Water moccasins," the boy informed me.

"Water moccasins," I repeated, considering the implications of the words. Suddenly I realized that drowning may not have been my number one worry on the St. Marys. Water moccasins are famous for dropping out of overhanging branches into boats. I've heard plenty of stories where a paddler decided to take his chances with gators in the muddy water rather than share a ride in his canoe with a big fat water moccasin that had suddenly plopped down from above.

As I pulled my kayak up higher on the ramp, I chatted with the man. He was a local resident taking his grandson fishing. I mentioned that during the past two days I'd just paddled all the way from Fort Clinch on the Atlantic Ocean.

"Fort Clinch," the grandfather said. He chewed on the idea of it, gauging the distance, assessing the accomplishment. Then he said: "That's a good long ways."

I completed the ninety-mile run up the St. Marys River from the checkpoint in roughly thirty-three hours. When I set out from Fort Clinch early Thursday morning I did not know it might take that long.

I was lucky to have stopped and talked to that guy fishing on the lower part of the St. Marys. He estimated it would take me ten hours to paddle the thirty miles from Traders Hill to St. George. I was sure I could do it faster. We were both wrong. I covered the distance in about thirteen hours.

The Portage

Of all the daunting aspects of the Florida Challenge, none gave rise to more prerace jitters than the idea of walking forty miles on a rural highway through the Okefenokee Swamp while towing a seventeen-foot sea kayak behind me. It was also the one aspect of the trip likely to draw looks of disbelief from relatives, friends, and co-workers. They had a point.

State Road 94 between the St. Marys and the Suwannee is used extensively by logging trucks carrying mountain-sized loads of freshly cut timber to nearby paper mills. If one of those log truck drivers reached for a Tootsie Roll or a pinch of chewing tobacco at the wrong moment, *bam!* I'd be pancaked to a radiator screen, shoulder to shoulder with mangled moths and dragonflies.

I admit it, I was worried. Sure, I had practiced. I suppose you could even call it training, pulling the boat around a park a few times on the portage cart. I had tried to anticipate what might happen during the portage, to think through each mile in advance in order to prepare and brace for the punishment to come. But that just freaked me out. I mean, consider what I might encounter alone out there? I ran down the list—alligators, water moccasins, wild dogs. What really terrified me was the idea of meeting up with a drunk driver at about 120 miles an hour.

By the time I got off the St. Marys River and began the portage it was 4:30 P.M., Friday, March 17: Happy Hour on St. Patrick's Day. As if the locals in that part of rural Georgia needed a special reason to start drinking. They didn't, but they sure had one. Can you think of a better night to be out on a dark and narrow highway in the middle of a swamp towing 120 pounds of kayak and camping gear?

I wasn't the only one with worries on the portage. Earlier that day, one of Wizard's wheels blew out. By the time he noticed, the rubber tire had disintegrated. Just to put this into perspective, Wizard's boat weighed about three hundred pounds on wheels, but he had already towed it, while walking, at least twenty miles. He had planned for the possibility of a flat tire—he had packed a spare tire tube and an air pump. What he hadn't anticipated was needing a spare rubber tire.

That's when Wizard did what he does best. He found the magic necessary to turn a bad situation into a slightly better situation. He used rope to replace the tube and tire on his wheel rim. He pressed on. Then, when the rope wore out, he cannibalized rubber from shredded truck tires littering the side of the highway, clamping the pieces into place. It wasn't pretty, but it rolled well enough to get him to the Suwannee River launch point at Fargo, Georgia.

Manitou Cruiser wasn't far behind, having carried a folding bicycle in his boat to breeze over the portage. And I wasn't too far behind Manitou.

There was an orange box at the boat ramp at the takeout point on the St. Marys. I signed in, noting my arrival time. Then I pulled my boat up to a level spot near the woods to reorganize for the portage.

I immediately struck up a conversation with a guy camped near the ramp. He'd been there for several days. He told me all about Chief and Wizard. What really got my attention is when he told me that Manitou had just left about two hours earlier. Two *hours* earlier? He said a local news reporter had interviewed Manitou about the race. I asked him again. I thought I might not have heard it right. Manitou had been there only two hours earlier?

My feet had to dry out a bit before I could put on my socks and running shoes. I changed my clothes from damp paddling garb to my dry walking duds. I assembled the kayak portage cart and tied a small backpack to the front of the boat so I would be pulling the boat with the shoulder straps of the backpack. Then I searched the woods for a sturdy stick to use as a handle to keep the bow of the boat from banging into my back.

My portage strategy was to walk about ten miles west of St. George to find a peaceful place to sleep in the woods. I wanted to get to sleep early so I could wake up after midnight to cover as much of the dangerous road during the deserted predawn hours as possible.

I was not looking forward to this portage. State Road 94, which runs from St. George to Fargo, is a two-lane road with a fifty-five-mile-an-hour speed limit. There is no shoulder on the highway. Not even a whiff of shoulder. It is tar and then grass.

I managed to get on the road within a half hour. It felt wonderful to be walking and stretching my legs after two weeks of sitting on my now extraordinarily tender and sore butt.

Once in St. George, about a half mile from the river, I stopped at a gas station/supermarket. I bought some bananas and three large Snickers bars. You might think that towing a kayak along a country highway would attract a bit of attention. But not much happens in St. George. These folks still remember Chief's first Cross-Florida Challenge, and Wizard and Manitou had already come through recently, so when I showed up with my kayak, they didn't look twice at me.

"The race," the clerk in the store said, as if I passed through every third Wednesday.

"The race," I nodded.

Outside in the parking lot, a local kid, maybe ten or twelve years old, walked up to me. He pointed down at the tires on my portage cart.

When I assembled the cart and positioned the boat over the wheels, they looked a little soft, a bit underinflated. The cart rolled fine, but the wheels ballooned out like radial tires on a car. They needed air. The kid saw it and said it. "You need air," he told me. "There's a pump right over there."

Here was an engraved invitation. All I had to do was say, "Okay. Yes, I need air."

Did I do that? No. Why? Because sometimes I just do stupid things and this was one of those times.

I wasn't paying attention. I told the kid the tires were fine. And then I started off down the road. A few miles down the road I realized the kid was right. I needed air in my tires. By then it was too late: the next gas station was at the end of the portage at Fargo.

I walked facing traffic. That way I could see the cars coming. Once I got outside St. George the road shot out straight ahead and seemed to go on forever. I had plenty of warning of an approaching car. If no other car came from behind I would cross over to the other side of the highway to let the approaching car zip by. If there were two cars coming from opposition directions at the same time I would try to assess the intent of the approaching car, and if it seemed the driver would not slow down or make an effort to avoid me I'd veer off the road onto the grass.

This system worked pretty well. When the sun went down, the traffic dropped to maybe a car every few minutes. Around 10:00 P.M. near Moniac I noticed a grove of pine trees. I followed a dirt road into the grove, pulled my boat behind the trees, and covered it with my dark green tarp. I strung the hammock up and plopped down inside it.

I had been up since 4:30 A.M. on the St. Marys and was now fully prepared to enjoy a few hours of sleep. I lay back, listening to my own steady breathing and a lone cricket. I closed my eyes and fell asleep.

In the very next instant, a 747 jumbo jet roared out of the dark sky and ploughed through the trees in a tangle of screeching twisted metal. I braced for the impact. I could feel the entire planet trembling at the magnitude of the unfolding tragedy. At any moment trees and earth and huge pieces of the plane would rip through the little pine grove and erase any hint of my puny existence from the face of the earth. My eyes wide, I sat bolt upright in the hammock, arms and legs splayed out and rigid for stability, waiting to be consumed in a massive, roiling wave of flaming jet fuel.

Where's the fireball?

Anyone whose been to the movies in the past twenty years knows well the fine points of aviation catastrophes. I can't say I was disappointed at the lack of a fireball, but in those few nanoseconds swaying in my hammock the distinct absence of blazing, boiling fury left me perplexed, flummoxed.

What? No fireball?

I clung to the fading prospect of instant immolation, that my last moments of life would be spent suspended between two trees at the center of a hellish ball of molten death like some badly overcooked rotisserie chicken.

Slowly, gradually, I realized my mistake. A jumbo jet had not crashed into my peaceful little pine forest. The roar, the shaking earth, were the work of a big, fast freight train. I couldn't see the train, but I could feel the wind from it. The thunder of the engine filled the forest. The tip-off was a metallic rhythm embedded in the boom and rumble—a clearly distinct *click-clack, click-clack, click-clack.*

This was the second time I'd selected a campsite only feet away from train tracks. Unlike the other camp, these tracks were busier. Four trains passed that night. I didn't care. Once I knew I wasn't camped on the tracks and that there would be no fireball, I immediately fell back to sleep after each train.

I broke camp at 2:30 A.M. and started walking west through the dark, my sea kayak in tow. The road was so straight and flat I could see an approaching car miles away. A car passed about once every half hour.

I stopped on a bridge at about 3:30 A.M. and fired up my propane stove to cook up a healthy portion of turkey tetrazzini. I slurped down two cups of mandarin oranges and a few fistfuls of snow peas waiting for the hot meal to cool enough to eat. I'm not sure how well balanced these meals were, but I like to think that the different food groups kept my fuel level higher than if I had tried to exist on Power-Bars and one of those fortified athletic sludge drinks.

Among my secret nutritional weapons are Snickers bars. Hikers on the Appalachian Trail swear by the regenerative power of the bars. That might be true, but I liked them because they were chocolaty delicious and offered an excellent reward for arriving at some distant destination. It helped get places faster, this idea that once I'd arrived I could break out another Snickers bar.

Food may sound like an indulgence, but when you spend the entire day and most of the night paddling or towing a kayak, you ignore it at your peril. Food is fuel. To keep moving in the Florida Challenge it was necessary to think like a man with a shovel in a steamship boilerroom. You have to keep shoveling in the coal in regular increments to keep the fire burning hot. It is far better to have four or five small meals spread out over a day than one big feast.

Everyone in the Florida Challenge knew this from experience, but no two racers approached food in the same way. Each challenger had a favorite food and a little secret formula, his or her own mixture of rocket fuel. Dexter "ThereAndBackAgain" Colvin is said to have cruised down the Everglades coast fueled by a ready supply of Diet Coke and menthol cigarettes. Near the start of the portage, Donald "Doooobrd" Polakovics walked into the local grocery store to make a critical purchase. Then he crouched by his kayak in front of the store and wolfed down two cans of Beefaroni—cold. Leon "Dr. Kayak" Mathis took a more civilized approach to Florida Challenge cuisine. He developed a keen eye for waterside dining opportunities. There were those two Cuban sandwiches with garlic, onions, and roast pork (Chokoloskee), a vanilla milkshake from Dairy Queen (Fort Lauderdale), and a western omelet and grits (Boynton Beach).

"It bragged on the menu that they were the best grits in the world, and they were," he told me later, laughing. "I had to get another order."

Just before Pelican began his forty-mile portage, he pulled into Rhonda's Café. He had a bike and figured he'd have a good meal and hopefully get some better weather before towing his boat to the Suwannee. It was 11:00 A.M., cold and raining. "Can I get some breakfast?" asked Pelican.

"Sorry. We're serving lunch now."

The lunch special was fried pork chops. That sounded about as appetizing to Pelican as deep-fried Hostess Twinkies.

"Lunch?"

"Lunch!"

Pelican thought for a moment. "Can you fry me up a couple of eggs and can I have ham with them and some wheat toast and home fries, a side of sausage and some cereal?"

Robin, the waitress, wrote it all down as a legitimate lunch order.

"As long as I didn't call it breakfast I could have it," Pelican said. When the food arrived, he arrayed the plates around him like a conductor directing a symphony orchestra. He spent three exquisite hours at Rhonda's.

"Food is more important than anything else," Pelican told me. "It is right up there with sleep."

A truck zoomed past as I ate my hot dinner on that bridge out in the middle of the swamp. One truck. I wondered what the driver must have thought, seeing me emerge from the darkness in the glow of his headlights—a spoonful of tetrazzini aimed toward my mouth and a sea kayak parked nearby on the bridge.

After the meal, I picked up my pace. I had wondered what it would be like walking out here alone, and dreaded the idea of it. My reaction surprised me. It felt outstanding. The night was so peaceful. There was no moon. As I walked I turned off all my lights and used the light from the stars to follow the road. I thought I should be afraid, but I wasn't. Not at all. I didn't know why. I just wasn't. It was the most liberating feeling.

As long as I walked alone, I felt safe. Once a pair of headlights appeared several miles away, I began to tense up. The idea of a drunk driver frightened me. The darkness right and left and my solitary place in it, that was comforting.

At some point that dark morning, I passed an agricultural inspection station at the Florida-Georgia border. As I approached, I saw the quasi police car and I was a little concerned that the officer might detain me or take me into custody for kayaking in a no-kayaking zone.

As I got up to the inspection station with its floodlights trained on the highway I saw the officer sitting inside. He looked up and saw me. I gave him a friendly wave. He waved back. That was it. He'd probably seen Wizard a day or two earlier, and Manitou. I was just confirming the trend. Whatever it was I was grateful to just keep moving down the road without having to answer any questions.

Just after dawn I pulled over to the side of the road to enjoy a Snickers bar. That's when I noticed a bicyclist on the road behind me. Odd for someone to ride a bicycle out here on such a remote highway. It must be an intrepid European tourist. A few minutes later the tourist called out: "Hey, Warren, is that you?"

Manitou Cruiser peddled up on his fold-up bike, towing his boat behind. He had a pretty good rig, he could complete the portage at six or seven miles an hour rather than the three miles an hour I was probably averaging. To do it he had to lug that bicycle in his boat the whole way around the state. There is no way a bike would fit in my kayak. Even if it did, there is no way I would tolerate the extra weight. By my way of thinking, averaging three miles an hour across the portage was not far from my on-water paddling average. All I needed for the portage was a cart, a small backpack tied to the bow of the kayak, and a pair of running shoes.

Manitou was surprised to see me, but not nearly as surprised as I was to see him—behind me. At some point I had passed him. That meant that I had actually been in second place in the race and didn't even know it. I assumed that Manitou would use his bicycle to ride all forty miles of the portage in one effort straight through to the

Suwannee River. I didn't give it a lot of thought. I just assumed both he and Wizard were already on the Suwannee.

Manitou and I walked together for a mile or so. He explained that just before he reached Moniac a car had brushed him at high speed. It unnerved him a bit, the close encounter with several thousand pounds of speeding automobile. Perhaps this was a good time to stop and get some sleep, he decided. He camped on the north side of the highway just before Moniac. I told him I had walked until about 10:00 P.M. and camped on the south side of the highway just before Moniac. I suspect it was a lot like that spoil island near Sebastian Inlet. If I had yelled out, "Manitou, where are you?" he probably would have heard me across the road and answered, "Hey, Warren, is that you?"

I bet we were camped within a quarter mile of each other.

Eventually Manitou mounted his bike and steadily pulled away toward Fargo. Farther up the road I met Chief. He had a video camera going and asked me how I felt, stuff like that. I didn't really think about it but watching the video later I noticed that I never actually stopped walking as I talked to him. I just kept going. As I headed down the road, Chief yelled out a question. He wanted to know if I thought I could catch Manitou.

"I doubt it," I said, truthfully. "But I'll give it my best." I wasn't being modest, just realistic. He had a bike. I assumed he would be able to cover the twenty or so miles to the Suwannee River in half the time it would take me to walk that distance. He'd get a pretty good head start down the Suwannee.

There were mileage signs on the road, so I knew how much farther I needed to walk. As the sun rose higher in the sky the day grew warmer. Mile after mile, the constant tug of the towed kayak began to take a toll. The muscles on the lower right side of my back were sore. My legs were sore. Even my feet were kind of sore. This is when I needed the kayak cart tires fully filled. Even though the tires still had more than enough air to roll, properly inflated tires would have made it much easier to pull the cart. This was when I paid the price for ignoring the excellent advice from that kid back in St. George.

As I started counting down the last ten miles, I discovered a deep and enduring truth. Here it is. A thirty-mile portage is a lot easier than a forty-mile portage. The first thirty miles had been fine, even enjoyable. It was great to be able to stretch my legs. Wonderful not to have to sit in a wet boat. Fabulous to actually be 75 percent finished with this portion of the challenge that had been the object of so many of my prerace worries. But those last ten miles were some of the toughest of the trip.

Peddling

Remember that trip to Harpers Ferry? Sixty miles by bicycle. Sixty miles. We got a little ways out on the C & O canal path from Washington and I began to wonder if I'd made a mistake. What if you couldn't do it? What if you got tired? What if you became delirious and rode your bike off the path and over a cliff into the Potomac?

But I was the one limping at Harpers Ferry. I was the one with the hand on my lower back and my eyes closed tight.

Here's the thing: You aren't the fastest on a bike, but you have guts. You have the courage to try things that only some crazy guy would try. Then when you are in the midst of it, you find a way to get through. You do not complain about the heat, or the dust, or anything. Instead, you notice the wide views of the river, the blades of sunlight slicing through the tall branches, the line of six black turtles on a log in the canal and how they plop into the water as we roll past.

I don't have to say, "Look." I don't have to say it, because you've already seen it. I guess that's the definition of a perfect companion— someone who sees it and appreciates it at exactly the moment you do.

Chasing Manitou

By the time I drew close to Fargo the temperature had soared into the upper 80s. My legs started to cramp up. Rather than stop to eat another hot meal I kept alternating between bagels and Snickers bars. In retrospect it would have been smarter to stop for about twenty minutes somewhere between mile thirty and mile thirty-five to eat another high-carb backpacker meal. I was anxious to finish the portage. Believe it or not, I was even anxious to get back into the boat. I began looking forward to paddling with the current on the Suwannee.

My plan was to launch on the Suwannee sometime that afternoon. I'd paddle fifty miles downriver to Big Shoals, the only Class 3 rapids in Florida. I'd portage around the rapids, and then camp on the far side of the portage that night. The next day I'd try to camp somewhere just north of Branford, which was about a hundred miles downriver. The following day I'd make the trip down to Fanning Springs and a motel I'd discovered on the banks of the Suwannee— the Suwannee Gables Motel. The idea was to enjoy a little taste of luxury—a hot shower, a real bed, some real food—for six or eight hours before pushing off for the final fifty-mile trip to the check-point at Cedar Key.

This was a big part of my race strategy: find destinations desirable enough to inspire me to paddle hard to get there. It meant having to plan three days in advance to improve my chances of arriving at that motel with enough time to make the most of the stay. It was great strategy and good motivation. It gave me a reason to keep walking on the portage, a reason to keep moving downriver on the Suwannee. In short, it was something to look forward to. I started daydreaming about the Suwannee Gables Motel. Just the *idea* of a hot shower. Just the *idea* of a big restaurant meal. Just the *idea* of sleeping in a real bed.

When I reached the edge of Fargo, two teens pulled up in a pickup truck and asked what in the world I was doing.

I didn't like it. Not a bit.

They slowed down to take a close look at the spectacle of a grown man towing a kayak down the highway.

A million scenarios race through my mind, all of them bad. One involves a barrage of rocks. I imagine being chased down the dusty shoulder of the road by a careening, tire-spinning pickup truck with two joyful teens hooting and swearing and thoroughly enjoying themselves. I hear the unmistakable sound of a tire iron whirling through the humid Okefenokee air. Ha ha! Missed. Then I turn and notice a tire iron embedded in the hull of my kayak.

"What are you doing?" the teen on the passenger side asked, trying to suppress a laugh.

I explained I was in a race around Florida and that I was in third place behind a guy just up ahead. I told them that we'd started in Tampa a few weeks earlier and were headed back to Tampa.

"Tampa," the teen said. "Damn."

I was a little worried when they pulled up in the truck. Actually, they turned out to be nice guys. They offered to put my boat in the back of the truck and give me a ride to the river. I explained the rule that I had to walk the forty miles myself. They nodded in agreement with the rule. They wished me luck. I told them to have a good day. They made a U-turn and headed back toward Fargo and the Suwannee. About ten minutes later, they came back.

The teen on the passenger side leaned out his window. There was an urgency in his voice. He sounded excited. "You are about to catch that guy in front of you," he said.

"What do you mean," I asked, looking at the road ahead, unable to see the Suwannee.

"He's still there at the river."

Fargo: Gateway to the Suwannee

Sure enough, when I reached the bridge over the Suwannee River at Fargo I looked down at the boat ramp and there he was. Manitou had spread his gear out on the grass. He was taking his time, carefully repacking for the trip down the Suwannee. With no wind on the river he had stowed his mast and outriggers. Now he was simply an expedition canoe running downstream.

I felt a great boost seeing him, a boost not necessarily for catching up to him, but just to have some company, even for a few minutes.

He helped me lift my boat over the wooden guardrail near the river. He agreed to watch my stuff while I searched for a source of clean drinking water and used the men's room at the nearby visitor's center. Air conditioning. I'd forgotten that they had invented that. The clean, cool men's room was a blissful moment of pure luxury. An actual sit-down toilet. Being able to scrub my face and neck with soap *and* hot water. I used about 60 million paper towels to dry off. Just being dry. Unbelievable. Wonderful. Unfortunately, the feeling didn't last.

My legs started to cramp up. Even worse, I started feeling weak. The portage was catching up to my body. These were the first signs of bonking. I needed food, and I needed it soon. I also wanted to get on the water as fast as possible. I'd eat lunch while drifting down the river. That was my plan.

Back at the boat ramp, I sat down to rest for fifteen seconds. Big mistake. My legs froze. I hadn't eaten a real meal since 4:00 A.M., but now I was sore and tired and just about out of gas. In contrast, Manitou had stopped at Karen's Okefenokee Café at the edge of Fargo and devoured two complete breakfasts before arriving at the boat ramp. Four eggs (over easy), four pieces of toast, a mountain of hash browns, and, by his own estimate, at least a pound of bacon. "It was awesome," he told me. He was tanked up and ready to paddle, while I still had to repack my boat and get something to eat.

It wasn't just a food stop at the Okefenokee Café. The kitchen was visible from the restaurant. Manitou talked to Karen while she cooked. He told her about the race and how far he'd come across the water. Then out of the blue she says: "You must have a lot of time to talk to God out there."

"Yes, I do," Manitou replied.

Her husband ran the auto mechanic shop next door. She had two kids and a mother to care for. Life in rural Georgia wasn't all water lilies and roses. "I'll pray for your family," Manitou told her. And he did.

———

A Boy Scout troop arrived at the launch ramp and prepared to leave for a weeklong canoe-camping trip down the Suwannee. The boys were interested in the race and how far we'd already come. The Scout leaders, on the other hand, thought we were nuts. One said it would be completely insane to try to paddle a small boat all the way around Florida.

There wasn't much I could say in response, except, I disagree. These dads no doubt felt some trepidation about spending a week in a canoe paddling down the Suwannee. During the race Manitou and I were covering their entire weeklong distance in less than a single day.

I said none of this out loud. I felt happy for the dads taking the boys on the trip, sharing the experience. I even felt a little jealous of them being able to meander down the beautiful and mysterious Suwannee rather than having to race down it.

After filling my water bottles, I began reorganizing my boat as Manitou dragged his boat to the river's edge and prepared to leave.

The Scouts launched first, an armada of zig-zagging, swerving, crashing canoes. They resembled more a bumper-car ride than a camping expedition. Eventually most of the canoes straightened out and the Scouts proceeded downriver.

Manitou left shortly after them. Unlike me, he had a stomach full of good food and a boat primed for river travel. When he paddled away from shore I was surprised at how hard he pulled on each stroke and how fast his boat knifed through the water. In less than a minute he disappeared around a bend.

I felt a twinge of loneliness and a renewed sense of urgency.

Then, when I took off my running shoes, I discovered that I had blisters on the inside of each of my big toes. They were, in fact, huge. They looked like I'd sprouted an extra toe off each big toe. I've done a lot of hiking and I never develop blisters. I suppose this was different. It was the first time I'd walked forty miles with a kayak.

My miscalculation was that after more than two weeks of paddling my feet had swollen, making my running shoes too small. Combine that with a pair of thick socks and bingo! big blisters where my toes rubbed together.

They didn't hurt. If I'd felt them during the portage I would have stopped and tried to correct the situation. Now it was too late. The portage was over—that was the good news. The bad news was that I needed to take a few precautions to prevent the blisters from popping. I still had many miles to go to reach Tampa and the last thing I needed was an open wound to worry about while wading through stagnant, polluted swampland. I decided to keep my shoes off and paddle in bare feet to dry the blisters out and let them heal a bit.

I launched into the Suwannee about an hour after Manitou. Unlike Manitou my paddle stroke was tentative and weak. I needed to eat. I let the boat drift and began to eat. A bagel. Beef jerky. A granola bar. I just kept wolfing it down between long slurps of Gatorade. Finally, I turned to one of the most important emergency food items in my boat—Cheez-Its. The little orange square crackers aren't exactly health food, but under certain conditions they can save your life. They are loaded with salt and fat. I've discovered through experience that several handfuls of Cheez-Its can help speed recovery. Cheez-Its are a salt delivery system. If I am running out of energy because of poor nutrition or overexertion, I've probably been working too hard. I've sweated away too much salt. Cheez-Its can help put it back.

Today was day fifteen—just over two weeks into the race—and

the three front-runners, Wizard, Manitou Cruiser, and I, Shark-chow, were all on the Suwannee. Wizard had been out front, and at times way out front, for most of the race. Now all three of us were relatively close together.

As he predicted, this was not an easy stage for Wizard. The combination of the strong current and downed trees in the St. Marys River and his tire problems on the portage allowed Manitou and me to draw within striking distance of him.

I could tell from Manitou's purposeful paddling when leaving Fargo that his plan was to pass Wizard that evening, if possible. As for me, I knew that on the upper part of the Suwannee my boat would be faster than both Wizard and Manitou. Fast and efficient paddling would be important. My plan had been to try to paddle to Big Shoals and camp for the night on the back side of the portage, but now, after the forty-mile portage, I didn't feel physically up to it.

As the afternoon shadows extended across the river, my strength and confidence began to return. My arms went to work again. There was a small but steady wave of white water at my bow. I began to glide, almost fly, through the timeless beauty of the upper Suwannee with its towering cypress trees and huge, umbrella-like live oaks draped with wisps of Spanish moss. Soon I was back up to my usual speed. This was by no means a lonely wilderness. Folks were camped on the sandbanks that accumulate at each significant turn in the river and many of them seemed to know about the race.

"He's about an hour ahead," one fellow called out from the front of a tent. His two young sons watched me cruise past.

Not everyone was honest about it. There was a guy with a big, toothy grin driving a ridiculous red ski boat up and down the river. He wore mirror sunglasses, the kind that were popular with Elvis and certain truckers back in the 1960s. This guy was a genuine countrified jerk. He would position his boat directly behind me so I could hear him coming but couldn't see him. Then he would zip back and forth, up and down the river. Every time he arrived I'd have to scramble to get my spray skirt attached over my cockpit to prevent being swamped by his wake.

I didn't know where Wizard might be, but I had originally assumed he had already completed the portage around Big Shoals. I hadn't thought of catching up to him, at least not that day. Then I began to get such varied reports about Wizard and Manitou from campers on the shore that I didn't know what to believe.

At one point the jerk in the red ski boat came zooming back upriver and yelled over to me, "They are both about five minutes ahead."

I politely thanked him for the information, but I was certain he was lying. I was also sure he probably got a real thrill out of the deception. If he could convince me that Wizard and Manitou were only five minutes away, maybe I'd kick into high gear and paddle like hell to try to catch them. It takes a special kind of wit to see the humor in tricking somebody in the middle of an endurance race into a meaningless sprint. I'm sure I was a disappointment to him. I wouldn't sprint even if they were five minutes ahead. My plan for the next two days was to move as quickly and efficiently as possible downriver to reach the Suwannee Gables Motel, where I'd enjoy a giant restaurant meal and a hot shower. If I passed Wizard and Manitou on the way, even better.

A few miles farther south I received word from campers that both a white canoe and a sailboat were about an hour ahead. I took this as encouraging news. For the first time I began to think that I might pass both Manitou and Wizard before reaching Big Shoals. The Cheez-Its had done their job.

When I caught up to the Boy Scouts, they were busy setting up their tents on an elevated and shady campsite about ten feet above the river. I waved. A few waved back. They had just spent the afternoon traveling in fully loaded and relatively slow canoes. I doubt they'd ever seen how fast a sea kayak can move on flat water. I don't know my speed at the time, but the whole troop stopped what they were doing. They stood still and watched me go. One of them said, "Gosh."

I don't mean to give a false impression. I was tired. I'd started the day just after 2:00 A.M. in that little grove of pine trees near the railroad tracks. I'd walked the rest of the portage, bonked, and then recovered. Two weeks into the monthlong Florida Challenge and I'm already on the Suwannee. Life is good. I'm tired, but I'm also feeling pretty strong, strong enough. That had me moving fast down the river.

Then something bad happened. The sun went down and darkness fell all around me like a thick black blanket. I knew my location—somewhere just north of the Route 6 Bridge, but with no moon even the slightest contours of water and land were blotted out. I could not see my own hand in front of my face.

That's when I heard it, the sound of rushing water.

I had just come up the St. Marys River, occasionally pulling my way through, around, and under fallen trees. Anyone who has spent time paddling boats on fast-flowing rivers knows that a downed tree extending across the surface of the water is a formidable hazard. The tree trunk can push the water down into a funnel of concentrated force. If a boat hits the tree, and the boat turns and flips, the paddler may be sucked down under the tree and pinned by the power of the flow against the capsized boat or submerged branches. You can't swim against it. And a tired paddler may lack the strength necessary to pull himself free. In short, it's a death trap.

When a tree has fallen into moving water the river current makes a certain sound. It is a sound as important to a downriver paddler as a car horn is to a big-city pedestrian. That's the sound I heard in the black void somewhere up ahead of me on the river. Unlike the St. Marys, I now ran with the current, which meant that if for some reason I stopped paddling, the flow of the river would pull me into the tree trunk and branches instead of pushing me away from it. There was no room for error.

I back-paddled to stop my forward progress. Then I stared into the black nothingness to try to use whatever night vision I could muster to see what made that sound of rushing water. I saw nothing in the river. No downed tree. Nothing. It was so dark I couldn't even see the surface of the water.

I backed up and got out my brightest flashlight. Then I made a slow and controlled approach toward the sound of the rushing water. When I reached it I shone the light straight ahead, then to the right, and then to the left. I back-paddled to maintain my position against the current and then repeated the action.

I saw nothing.

Again, I retreated upriver. I considered my options. Should I just go for it, plunge into the darkness and see what happens? What if it's a waterfall? What if it's a downed tree? The boat could be pinned under the tree with me in it.

I turned my kayak around and started examining the shore for a place to camp, but I saw none in this section of the river. This was not going to be easy. Had there been a wide, sandy bank right there I would have immediately pulled over and camped. I knew I was getting close to both Wizard and Manitou. To camp now would foreclose the possibility not only of catching them but of getting to Big Shoals that night. There was another consideration, a more important consideration: camping now might complicate my plan to reach the Suwannee Gables Motel.

Two weeks before the race I traveled to northern Florida to scout as much of the race route as possible. I stopped at Sebastian Inlet, then drove up to Fort Clinch. I traced the route of the portage, and then followed the Suwannee. I was particularly concerned about finding a place to camp on the lower Suwannee. From everything I had read and heard, there were only a few tracts of dry land along the lower part of the river, and all of them were occupied by houses and businesses owned by armed citizens posting no-trespassing signs. Any wild or public lands were swamp. I needed a reasonably dry place to sleep on the lower Suwannee that would put me roughly a day's paddle from Cedar Key. That meant I needed a spot somewhere near Fanning Springs, give or take twenty miles. I drove to several spots along the river north of Fanning Springs. Nothing stood out as a sure-fire great destination, a place I'd look forward to arriving, a place worth paddling hard to reach.

On a whim, I drove south to Fanning Springs and followed State Road 19 across the river. There on the right-hand side of the road was one of those old-fashioned motor motels. I pulled into the Suwannee Gables Motel and immediately walked around to the back to look at the river. At the north end of the property I noticed a boat ramp—a slab of concrete tilted gently into the river. It was perfect. I could land at the ramp, ease myself out of the kayak, pull it up on shore, and then rent a room for the night. It got even better. Across the street was one of those mom-and-pop restaurants that draw folks from miles around. The crowded parking lot was testament enough that the food would be more than adequate for someone living on dehydrated back-packer meals and bagels. In addition, a convenience store sat a half block away. I checked my cell phone and discovered excellent cell phone reception.

All things considered, it was just about as perfect as perfect can get. This would be my destination. Getting to this spot would be my motivation, my goal, from the time I launched into the Suwannee River at Fargo. The intent was not only to arrive within two days, but to also arrive at the best possible time—something like eight o'clock at night. That is what gave purpose to my efforts on the river. I knew if I could get to that motel and enjoy good food and good sleep, it would be a relatively easy fifty-mile paddle the next day to the checkpoint at Cedar Key on the Gulf of Mexico. The one thing I did not want to do was spend a sleepless night sitting in my boat on a desolate section of the swampy lower Suwannee because I couldn't find a decent place to camp.

All of this swirled in my mind as I confronted the uncertainty and darkness before me. I needed to get downriver as far as possible to get into position the next night, which would then help set up my stay at the Suwannee Gables a night later. Once again, I paddled down into the blackness and shined my brightest flashlight into the void to identify the obstacle. Straight ahead, nothing. To the right, nothing. To the left, nothing.

If nothing is there, what is making that sound?

It's not worth it, I decided. I could break the boat and never make it to Tampa. I could break the boat and drown. Or I could camp now, eat a good meal, get some good sleep, and deal with this obstacle fresh and strong in the morning sunlight.

I asked a simple question: Is this door open or closed? In most cases, the door had been open. Now my challenge involved being obedient to the answer, even when I didn't like it—especially when I didn't like it. It meant falling farther behind Wizard and Manitou. It meant missing the chance to pass them and move into first place in the race.

At this moment in the race the most difficult thing wasn't to endure or fight off fatigue. The most difficult thing was to reject thoughts of what might have been and accept that the right place for me tonight was someplace upriver of this obstacle. I could not see any wisdom or any advantage in this course of action, but something told me to stop. So I did.

I had to backtrack about a half mile upriver to find a suitable place to hang my hammock. Rather than flat white sand, this section of the riverbank rose at steep angles from the water, and the few flat sections appeared slick with dark mud. I found two trees to keep my hammock out of the muck and a small, firm spot to stand.

I decided to try to justify my forced overnight exile on the bank by catching up on my journal writing. I opened the notebook. The last entry had been made a week earlier on the spoil island near Sebastian Inlet where I camped near Manitou. I wrote four sentences, closed my eyes, and fell sound asleep. I woke up once and noticed that the river had risen in the night and covered all the land under and around my hammock. No worries, I was safe and dry. I could see my boat where I'd tied it to a tree. I told myself it was only an illusion. Go back to sleep. All is well. I closed my eyes and drifted off again.

The Well

In the spring of 1980 I lived for a week in the Arabian desert with my friend Mohammed and his relatives. They treated me not only as an honored guest but as a member of the family.

We made the trip in the hottest season. By midday the temperature rose to well over 100 degrees. No electricity. No air conditioning. No running water. No plumbing. Mohammed's cousin granted special permission so that each morning I was allowed to use a few bowlfuls of water from the camel trough to wash. By 11:00 A.M. we were all asleep in whatever corner of shade we could find.

I'd imagined a sandy desert, like the Dahna or the Rub 'al-Khali—the Empty Quarter. Between the Asir Mountains and the Yemen border all is rock and dust and sky.

When I arrived with Mohammed word spread fast. Little children came from far away, beyond even the second line of black hills. They just stood there, staring wide-eyed at my blue eyes and light-colored skin. A brave boy with a fast smile poked my forearm and then checked the tip of his finger to see if anything had rubbed off.

They delighted in my eager acceptance of the bowl of camel's milk. That's how I told my first joke in Arabic. They handed me the bowl first, fresh and frothy from the camel. When I passed the bowl to my right they pointed at the white foam covering much of my beard and mustache.

"Old man," I said.

They laughed and laughed. Even the next day they called me Old Man and laughed.

They are desert people. The Arabic word is *bedu*. Many Saudis and urban Arabs think of the Bedouin as ignorant and dirty—Arabian hillbillies. To me they are the soul of Arabia. They are people who live on the extreme edge of nothing.

When I first arrived and looked around I couldn't understand why they lived in that place. They had camels, goats, and sheep, but not a blade of vegetation anywhere. It hadn't rained in two years. Each morning one of the boys would lead the animals out into the sun-parched hills to search for something to graze on. Each night he'd come back. The animals were thin, but alive. You could say the same about Mohammed's relatives.

It is no coincidence that Islam, Christianity, and Judaism trace their beginnings to episodes of survival in deserts. Who knows better than the *bedu* that life is no accident. They believe life is a gift from Allah, that Allah will provide all that is necessary. Not all that is wanted, only that which is necessary.

I am not a Muslim, but I admire their faith. I respect their discipline, their purity.

When I discovered they were digging a well, I insisted that I take my turn in the deep pit. The offer sparked considerable apprehension among the elders. Several of them were afraid that I might slip and fall while trying to climb down the rock wall to the bottom of the well. The truth is, it was slightly cooler down there and I didn't mind the risk. A debate broke out.

Finally they agreed to let me climb down, but they insisted that I tie a rope around my chest. I appreciated the gesture, but people in that part of Arabia are short and thin—not particularly well suited to support the full weight of a fleshy, thick-boned American. If I slipped and fell the twenty feet to the bottom of the pit, they'd soon be at the bottom of the pit as well. Nonetheless, my descent into the well became a community project. Everyone held tight to the rope for a few minutes until I was safely down. Once at the bottom, I worked hard, slamming a five-foot-long iron bar into the rock floor. We filled bucket after bucket with dusty chips and bone-dry gravel. We pried a few large rocks out.

After about an hour, I began to have doubts. I asked a question. "How do you know there is water down here?"

Mohammed's cousin just smiled, his face glowing with sweat in the dark pit. *"Inshallah,"* he said. God willing.

The next day, dark clouds rolled in from the Red Sea, 150 miles to the west. It poured rain for forty-five minutes.

A Place to Go

By 6:00 A.M. I could wait no longer. In the cold, predawn darkness, I shivered as I changed back into my damp paddling clothes. The temperature had plunged to the low 40s, creating a strong incentive to get moving and generate some warmth. Fog rose from the warm river like steam from a bowl of soup.

Soon the mystery would be revealed. Or would it? Paddling through the rising fog, a knife edge of fear pressed into my gut. What if by the time I arrived at the downed tree, the fog was so thick I still can't see it?

Whatever it was, Manitou and Wizard had made it through. I assumed both were now well beyond the rapids at Big Shoals and cruising merrily downriver toward the gulf. I thought of the Suwannee Gables Motel and my well-conceived plan to stop there. To do so, this would have to be one of my fastest, longest days of the race. I could not waste time.

With a steady curl of white water at my bow, I sliced through the mist and quickly discovered the menacing obstacle that had driven me back upriver the evening before. It was a riffle, a place where the river suddenly runs fast but shallow, causing turbulence at the surface. The river flowed wide with no downed trees, dangerous rocks, or other obstructions. I couldn't believe it. Instead of a death trap under a fallen tree, the sound I'd heard in the inky blackness had been shallow water. Nothing more. I stopped paddling and laughed as the kayak drifted with the current through the calf-deep stretch of the river.

My mind raced back to the night before. Perhaps I should have just plunged into the dark unknown. It cost me a chance to take the lead in the race. It complicated my strategy to reach the Suwannee Gables Motel.

But it did something else. It enabled me to recover from the portage after a long day that had started at 2:00 A.M. It allowed me to eat a good meal and enjoy some sound sleep. Perhaps most important, the episode provided strong motivation to make the most of this day. All doors stood wide open, and I was primed and ready to fly.

I reached the takeout at Big Shoals at 10:30 A.M. Big Shoals is the only significant white-water rapid in Florida. It rates a Class 3, suggesting a moderate level of difficulty for white-water paddlers. For most of its 235-mile course the Suwannee flows steadily but peacefully between limestone bluffs. The downstream current moves at about three miles an hour, but it can flow faster or slower depending on water levels in the upstream Okefenokee Swamp.

At Big Shoals the river narrows, pouring eighteen hundred cubic feet per second over a series of limestone ledges that form a rock stairway on the riverbed. The stairway is littered with a few large boulders. It is possible to run the rapids in a sea kayak. I considered it. It would save me the hour it takes to portage around the shoals, but an hour saved wasn't worth the risk of cracking my hull on a rock. In the grand scheme of things one hour for a portage is an acceptable price to pay for the certainty that I'd emerge on the far side of the rapids with a seaworthy boat capable of carrying me all the way back to the finish line in Tampa.

Having made that decision, now all I had to do was locate the takeout point just upriver from the rapids. I'd never paddled on the Suwannee and I worried about missing the takeout. The last thing I wanted to do was get sucked involuntarily into the rapids. The din of turbulent water up ahead gave the necessary warning. I angled over to the bank and found a clear spot leading to a path through the woods and around the shoals. That's where I found a note from Manitou. It was marked 11:50 P.M. "I'm camped at other end of portage. Manitou Cruiser." He had been at this spot at 11:50 P.M. the night before— eleven hours earlier. The one hour lead he took out of Fargo was suddenly multiplied by eleven. I knew Manitou was a strong river paddler, so I wasn't surprised to have fallen so far behind so quickly.

I told myself to stay efficient and try to get positioned to arrive at the Suwannee Gables Motel at the right time. To do it, I'd need to travel well beyond the Suwannee River State Park about fifty miles downriver, and, if possible, somewhere near Branford by the end of the day. That might be impossible. Branford was about 125 river miles from where I had camped that night and 100 miles from Big Shoals.

As predicted, it took an hour to assemble the kayak cart and tow my boat up the steep bank, through the woods, through a muddy creek, and then down the steep bank back to the river.

I launched the kayak amid large floating clumps of yellowish foam churned from the upstream rapids. The sound of rushing water filled my ears. It is a beautiful spot with white water cascading down through the shoals. The surrounding area is dark green and jungle-like, with stands of slash pine and a thick carpet of ferns and cabbage palm. A nice scene worthy of a day spent in reclined appreciation, maybe with a fishing pole. But not this day.

At 1:30 P.M. I rounded a bend just south of White Springs and saw a tiny white sail in the center of the river. A sailboat on the Suwannee? Then it hit me. "Wizard," I yelled. The word just emerged from me. I could barely contain my excitement.

Still a half mile upriver, my voice echoed across the high limestone banks. When he heard it, Wizard stood immediately in the cockpit. He turned and waved.

I paddled to him. "I can't believe I caught up to you." I never expected to see him anywhere along the course after Key Largo.

Manitou Cruiser had passed him the night before somewhere above Big Shoals. Wizard told me he completed the portage around the shoals at 10:30 A.M.—the exact moment I arrived to start the portage.

We talked about race strategy. I told him I still believed he was the most likely to win the Florida Challenge. Once back out on the Gulf of Mexico in the open wind, he'd easily catch and pass both Manitou and me.

Wizard wasn't so sure. The race would be decided by the weather, he said. A storm was forecast to move through the area within the next day. Much would depend on the strength and direction of the wind. A violent and dangerous storm could pin all three of us on shore for a day or two.

We didn't talk very long. "I suppose I should try to catch Mark," I said, referring to Manitou.

With that I increased my pace and pulled slowly away until Wizard's white sail disappeared behind a turn in the river.

I maintained a steady pace all day. It wasn't designed to catch and pass Manitou. The goal was to get far enough downriver to set up my arrival the next night at the Suwannee Gables Motel. Whatever happened in relation to Manitou would happen. I might see him, I might not, but what I really wanted, above all else, was to get to that motel.

Lights

Some boaters are comforted by lights. Streetlights on shore. Porch lights. Marina lights. The lights of other boats. The beacon of a lighthouse. Some folks position bright headlights on their bow like shining swords poised to do battle with the forces of darkness.

Not me. I kept a white light lit on the back deck of the kayak to prevent getting run over. Positioned about six inches above the deck and well behind me, the light did not interfere with the preservation of what little night vision I could manage. My preference is always to let my eyes adjust and rely on the small bit of available light to find my way. Sometimes it just meant staying close to the channel, or avoiding snags or submerged logs near shore.

At some point during the race I began to look forward to the darkness. I began to crave the most remote sections of the journey. Alone on the water I see the stars, I feel the undulation of the tide, the pull of the current. I hear the sound of each drip off my paddle. It becomes a form of music, notes plucked by unseen fingers in a celestial orchestra.

Why am I not afraid? I remember asking myself this question. Always alone, always wrapped in a thick blanket of darkness. I was amazed at how dark it could get. I loved it.

These were moments of triumph. Not just being free of fear—that was good enough. But I discovered something else. I discovered that when I was free of fear I was also free of pain.

It is one of the most remarkable things. Eliminate the fear and you eliminate the pain. It didn't matter how far I had traveled that day, how hard I had paddled. The ability to keep going did not reside in my muscles.

Unfortunately, this was not a permanent condition. All it took was a single lightbulb to wipe it away. One sign of civilization—even a suggestion of ease—and the aches and pains returned, the fatigue, all the heaviness of the remaining miles, thoughts of the other racers and where they might be, the dangers. Just one illuminated porch light on the shore would allow them to come rushing back.

It is difficult to describe, but let me try. I am cruising along with all systems running perfectly. No distractions. The paddling is effortless. I am flying. Then I face a reminder of all the comforts and luxuries of civilization, all the pampered contrivances I am denying myself. I fall back to earth. Rather than uplifting thoughts that help me glide over the water, my head is suddenly filled with limiting thoughts freighted with all the well-established facts of human experience. I can't go that far. I need rest. I must sleep. I am injured. I need more food. I might drown. I am going to die.

This is the daily struggle, a decision that must be made, moment by moment. Carry all that extra weight in my mind around the entire state of Florida, or instead pack light, travel fast, and be free.

Flying Dinosaurs

I passed Manitou Cruiser at about 9:30 P.M. just before reaching Suwannee River State Park. I wasn't even thinking about Manitou. I wanted to get to the park to sign the logbook at the checkpoint and then keep going. With near perfect conditions on the water, the miles clicked away. I used the light of the stars to keep the boat near the center of the river and away from any submerged trees or rocks. I rounded a bend and noticed a flashlight up on the bank. The person aimed the shining light directly at me. I'm thinking, why is this idiot shining that light on me. Then I heard: "Warren, is that you?"

I recognized Manitou Cruiser's voice. "Mark," I answered.

"I've already got my tent set up," he said

There was no way I could stop that early and still reach my motel the next night. As much as I wanted to stop and relax a bit and talk to Manitou, I couldn't. "I'm going to keep going," I said, pressing on into the darkness. I had just taken the lead position in the Florida Challenge, but there wasn't really any time to celebrate. If I wanted to make it to the motel in Fanning Springs I still needed to cover another thirty or forty miles that night. Sure, I was out front at the moment, but I didn't expect to stay in the lead for long.

When I reached the boat ramp at Suwannee River State Park I searched for the orange box containing the sign-in sheet. Chief had said he would place the box near a fence beside the ramp. I walked up the ramp and even partway up the road to the ranger station. No box. It felt great to stretch my legs, but I didn't really want to waste a lot of time here. I had to get farther south. I called Chief on my cell phone.

He asked immediately, "Where are you?"

"I'm at Suwannee River State Park."

"That's too fast," he said. "You can't be there yet."

"Well, I am."

When I explained that I couldn't locate the orange lockbox to sign in, he told me he'd decided to skip using the park as a checkpoint. "There is no lockbox there." That explained why I couldn't find one.

He asked about Manitou. I told him I'd just passed him camped on the bank a little ways back. Then I told him I expected to be in Cedar Key in two days.

I wished I'd been able to slip past Manitou without him seeing me, because now I knew he wouldn't sleep very long. He'd sleep a few hours, then get up and try to pass me and regain the lead. There wasn't anything I could do about that. I just knew that for my Suwannee Gables Motel strategy to work, I had to cover a lot of ground before I stopped to sleep.

There were several things about that late-night paddle down the Suwannee that made an impression. The wind died and it became so calm the water seemed to blend with the dark sky. I just kept moving between the two, making my own five-to-six-mile-an-hour breeze. At one point I sliced through sheets and sheets of gnats flying into my face. Blankets of gnats. More gnats than I could shake a fly swatter at. I had to close my eyes, my mouth, my nose, and just paddle on through. Bzzzzzzzzzz.

I eventually resorted to my radio to keep alert. The only program I could pick up clearly came from a country and western station in Valdosta, Georgia. They played Irish songs in a continued celebration of St. Patrick's Day. One song in particular almost stopped me dead in the water: Bing Crosby singing "Danny Boy." It came at such a beautiful time on the river, dark but peaceful. It brought tears to my eyes, which was a good thing because that helped wash some of those gnats out.

Other than the radio, I had a strong incentive to stay alert. Several days earlier while eating breakfast at a boat ramp near Jacksonville, I struck up a conversation with a north Florida fisherman. He asked me about the Florida Challenge and I told him where I'd been and where I was going. When he heard that I'd be paddling down the Suwannee he warned me to watch out for sturgeon.

"Sturgeon," I asked. "Why?"

"They jump completely out of the water," he said. "If you have a camera, get it ready." Then he added, as a kind of afterthought: "You might need a football helmet."

I've been hit in the arm by leaping mullet. They weigh a few pounds and such collisions could be dangerous if a mullet hit me in the head. Sturgeon can grow to eight feet long and weigh up to three hundred pounds. If they crashed into a person paddling a sea kayak the collision would likely be fatal. At a minimum it would smash the boat to pieces and rearrange a portion of someone's anatomy.

In May 2002, Lacy Redd, a school principal from Gainesville, Florida, was boating on the Suwannee with her husband and their three children when a six-foot, 130-pound sturgeon came flying out of the water. According to news accounts, it hit Lacy in the chest, knocking her unconscious and breaking three ribs. The fish also bent the boat's steering wheel.

Two months later, nineteen-year-old Danny Cordero and his girlfriend were knocked off his jet ski by a leaping sturgeon in the Suwannee. Danny lost some teeth. He was knocked unconscious and his girlfriend swam him to shore.

Such collisions happen a few times every year. There are only about three thousand sturgeon in the Suwannee. They are an endangered species. Any fishermen hooking the monstrous bottom-dwellers are required to set them free. The sturgeon, a relic of the dinosaur era, have reportedly been on Earth 200 million years. Each fish can live up to seventy years, scientists say. What scientists can't say, however, is why these giant fish jump. No one is sure why a fish that feeds and swims at the bottom of the river nonetheless is known to leap out of the water, producing a substantial splash.

I thought about what it would be like paddling while wearing a football helmet. Even that wouldn't be enough protection. Assuming I could survive the initial collision, there's no guarantee I wouldn't be knocked unconscious. At that point I'd be underwater. There would be no one to rescue me. That would be it. Race over.

That's the risk. I'd be lying if I didn't say it was on my mind, particularly as I got into the wider, deeper sections of the Suwannee. I could tell from a whoosh of water near the surface that several times I paddled near some very large fish—or gators. The water in the Suwannee is dark, and I couldn't see anything. I heard several significant splashes nearby during my three days on the river. Once, near the Route 751 Bridge, I saw something that looked like an alligator come shooting out of the water and then fall back in a giant splash. I'm pretty sure now it was a sturgeon, but the dark scales made me think first of an alligator. I was puzzled by the sight. It happened so quickly I thought I must not have seen it correctly, but I don't believe an alligator can come straight out of the water like that. Whatever it was, it was big and mean-looking—in a prehistoric kind of way, kind of like a dinosaur rocket.

Around 2:00 A.M. I stopped to sleep on a wide sandbank near Dowling Park. There were no trees near the water's edge to support my hammock, so I just dragged my boat up onto the dry sand and tied one side of my tarp to the deck of the boat and staked out the other side in the sand. I cooked a full meal and ate it as quickly as possible. Then I crawled under the tarp and went to sleep.

Two hours into my slumber, Manitou paddled around the sandy point, and saw my boat pulled up on the bank. He took great care not to make any noise that might wake me. He wasn't trying to be courteous, just stealthy. Although I didn't know it at the time in my deep sleep, the lead in the Florida Challenge had just changed again for the third time in two days. The race was only just beginning to heat up.

Day Sixteen: Neck and Neck Down the Suwannee

I woke before dawn and pushed into the river in less than twenty minutes. Passing Manitou the night before injected a new level of urgency. I spent four hours ashore—three and a half of them in a deep and peaceful sleep in the sand beside my beached kayak. Now, on the water again, I wondered if Manitou was still behind me. And what about Wizard?

I set a pace somewhere around five miles an hour. My plan involved more than simply staying ahead of Manitou. I wanted to spend that night at the Suwannee Gables Motel. To do it, I'd have to get to Branford (which was about halfway) as fast as possible. I couldn't take it easy. I had to push. The goal was more than simply getting to the Suwannee Gables. The goal involved getting there with enough time to eat and sleep, and then push on to catch the right tides to arrive at the Cedar Key checkpoint the following day.

I looked at the chart. I needed to cover seventy-five miles to the Suwannee Gables Motel. Seventy-five miles to a warm bed, good food, and a much-needed hot shower. To get there, I'd still have to overcome a few obstacles.

That morning, somewhere between Blue Spring and Telford Spring I noticed two teens about fifteen feet up on the left bank near a motor home parked in the woods. They crouched behind a tree like they were trying to hide. I could see them clearly. They stayed low near the base of the tree like soldiers positioning themselves to avoid being shot, using the tree as cover.

I kept up my pace running down the center of the river. I also kept an eye on the two boys, curious about their strange behavior. What were they up to, I wondered. The answer came in a few minutes. After I'd moved past them I heard a kind of repeating metallic sound. *Thwack. Thwack.* I wondered what might make such a noise. *Thwack.* I turned and scanned the bank for an indication. The two teens remained behind the tree. They'd rotated their position, keeping the tree between them and me. Odd, I thought.

Then I noticed a small splash about two feet from my rear hatch. I heard the distinct metallic sound again, three times. *Thwack. Thwack. Thwack.* I realized then the source of the noise, a BB rifle. They were maybe a hundred yards away at that point. Had they been better shots, I doubt they would have drawn blood or shot a hole in my boat. I know this much, it would have hurt if they'd hit me. There is a tremendous feeling of vulnerability paddling a kayak while being shot at from someone on shore. I thought about landing my boat and doubling back to confront the shooters. In the end I figured they were just kids, and I had a motel to get to.

An hour later, I noticed a familiar white canoe on the river ahead. When I called out, "Hey, Mark," Manitou turned, saw me, and started paddling furiously. I think I had just ruined his morning. He tried to outrun me, paddling with short, strong canoe-racing strokes, but I knew that wouldn't work. He couldn't outrun a kayak traveling downriver—at least not this kayak. When he saw me steadily gaining, he slowed down to a more relaxed pace. I pulled up next to him and we paddled together, talking for a while.

He explained how he had been especially quiet passing me as I slept on the beach. He also explained how I had been able to make up a twelve-hour deficit the day before to catch and pass him by that night. Manitou said he miscalculated when he packed his boat at Fort Clinch. He thought he would be able to resupply his boat at the Suwannee River launch at Fargo. Chief refused to allow him to resupply. The race rules only permit a resupply at the checkpoint at Cedar Key on the Gulf of Mexico, not before. Manitou had to get off the river and hitchhike to a store—a Walmart—to buy more food.

The fourth leg of the Florida Challenge is, by far, the most difficult and the longest of the five legs of the race. As I listened to Manitou's tale of woe I began taking a mental inventory of my own food supplies. With a potentially dangerous weather front approaching and the prospect of high winds and perhaps rain, I knew that I might have to wait on land for a day or more for conditions to ease. Did I have enough food to cover such an emergency?

A few miles upriver from Branford I pulled ahead of Manitou, trying to create some distance between us. My intended destination was a convenience store close to a boat ramp in a public park just after the bridge at Branford. If I could get to Branford fast enough, I might be able to buy the necessary supplies to cover the possibility of being stranded somewhere by a storm. My plan was to get in and out of the store and back on the water before Manitou arrived.

I glided into the boat ramp at Branford. A family sitting nearby in the shade agreed to watch my boat while I jogged up to the convenience store to shop. The store clerk eyed me suspiciously as I dashed from aisle to aisle in my squishy paddling booties, leaving a trail of wet footprints throughout the store. I'm sure she thought I was some exotic form of homeless person. I grabbed pretty much anything I thought might work—a loaf of bread, Snickers bars, trail mix, granola bars, Slim Jims, Gatorade, and drinking water. It wasn't exactly the most nutritious food. Certainly not gourmet. However, in an emergency it would keep me from getting too hungry. My little Branford shopping spree is notable for another reason: it is the first time I've had a convenience store bill totaling more than $30.

I ran back to my boat with two plastic grocery bags and arrived just in time to see Manitou land his canoe beside my kayak. He needed water and asked if I would watch his boat while he went up to the convenience store.

"No problem," I said.

When Manitou returned from the store, he had another request. He had left his weather radio in his resupply bin with Chief and under the rules he would not be able to recover it until the next checkpoint at Cedar Key. This was a significant mistake because a large weather system was headed toward the region. The wind had already picked up. Manitou asked if he could listen to my weather radio. I agreed. We listened together. The report called for southwest winds blowing to twenty for the next two days, followed by strong north winds for the rest of the week.

"Sounds like a sailor's forecast," I said. With his large sail and daggerboards, Manitou would be able to use the north winds to zoom the final 120 miles from Cedar Key to Tampa. In contrast, this forecast was not exactly the kind of weather one would want paddling a kayak. I, too, had a sail on my kayak, but much smaller than Manitou's.

While I might be able to outpace him on the Suwannee, there would be no way I could keep up with him, or Wizard, out in the wind-swept Gulf of Mexico.

Manitou announced that he planned to stay a while at the park at Branford. I wished him well and pushed off into the river. I went about a mile downriver and around a bend thinking about the weather forecast and how it might affect my Suwannee Gables plan. I pulled over on a sandy beach and called in my daily GPS position report to Linda. Then I used my cell phone to call the Suwannee Gables Motel. I used a credit card to make a guaranteed reservation for a room that night. I checked my watch: 2:00 P.M. I was still forty miles upriver from the motel. If I traveled at five miles an hour nonstop it would take me eight hours to get there, arriving at 10:00 P.M.

Although the river's current flowed with me, I would have to battle a stiff headwind, and I could feel the wind building. The motel clerk who took the reservation was very kind but somewhat puzzled at my inability to give her an estimated time of arrival. "I'm coming by kayak on the river. I'm forty miles away and don't know what the river conditions will be this evening. I may not get in until very late."

She said I could arrive at any time. If I was not there by 10:00 P.M. when the motel office closed for the night, she'd put my key under the mat in front of my reserved room. She told me the room number—105. I wrote it down in large numbers on my Suwannee River map, knowing that by the time I arrived I'd probably be too tired to remember and might even have trouble reading it.

Making the confirmed reservation was all I needed. Talk about incentive to paddle. I started paddling and kept paddling. I was not worried about leaping sturgeon, or BB guns, or running out of food. I knew I had a warm bed, a shower, a real toilet, and some real food in a restaurant waiting for me. It gave me a reason to paddle hard. And I did.

I had programmed the motel's longitude and latitude coordinates into my GPS. I had actually stood on the boat ramp a few weeks earlier and read off the coordinates to make doubly sure. This helped counter the many doubts that bombarded me during my prolonged push down the river. Every possible mistake popped into my mind. Did she get the reservation? Did she say room 105 or 104? What if I entered the wrong coordinates into my GPS? How hard will the wind blow? Will it rain? I would have none of it. My mission was simple and clear. Get to that motel and get there now.

I stopped and ate some bagels and Cheez-Its along the way, but just long enough to refuel. By the time I drew close to Fanning Springs, I had reached the outer limit of my endurance. I turned on my GPS to follow the arrow on the screen across the dark river to the boat ramp.

The approach to the motel looked completely unfamiliar. Thankfully, my GPS told me exactly where to go. I didn't know until I'd actually pulled the boat ashore that I'd arrived at the right place. My watch read 9:30 P.M.

When I walked into the motel office, I must have looked like hell and smelled like death. "I called earlier and made a reservation." I gave the lady at the front desk my name.

"The kayaker," she said, holding her index finger into the air. This was the same motel clerk I'd talked to earlier on the phone. I recognized her voice.

"The kayaker," I confessed. Then I explained it. "I'm in a race around the state of Florida and I think I'm in first place. At least so far. There's a guy on the river right behind me."

"Around Florida, you say?"

"We started in Tampa on the fourth. I don't even know what today is but I think that was about two and a half weeks ago. I'm sorry about my condition. I've been in the boat all day."

"How long will you be staying in the room?"

"Tonight for sure," I said. "But I may also stay tomorrow night if the weather turns really bad."

The woman typed something into her computer. She said rooms were available if I wanted to stay an extra night. I might have to change rooms, though. That shouldn't be a problem, I told her. I considered the luxury of sleeping most of the day and then wandering across the street to the restaurant for a nice meal, then sleeping some more before wandering back over to the restaurant for another meal. It sounded pretty tempting compared to slogging through what promised to be a vicious headwind all the way to the mouth of the Suwannee and then facing extraordinarily ugly and dangerous sea conditions in the open Gulf of Mexico whipped up by several days of high wind. "If the weather looks really bad I might just wait here for an extra day," I told her.

I suppose working as a night clerk in a motel you develop an instinct for fearlessness. She had been typing something into her computer, but she suddenly stopped and stared at me. I'd been among alligators and snakes for many days and nights, but the look froze me. "I thought you were in a race," she said, implying that it would be unacceptably slothful to lounge around a motel for an entire day with other racers out on the water sure to catch and pass me.

I tried to explain the weather situation. The wind would be blowing at least twenty and maybe harder from the southwest. It meant paddling all day in a nasty headwind just to get to the Gulf of Mexico and then having to navigate across very shallow and treacherous open water in what surely would be frenzied sea conditions all the way down to Cedar Key. I suggested maybe it would be better to wait out the storm in the luxury of the motel rather than ending up stuck for a day in some mosquito-infested swamp down near the mouth of the Suwannee.

She wouldn't leave it alone. "It's a race, isn't it?"

"Absolutely."

"Well?"

"Put me down for tonight. I'll have to see how the weather is. It is possible that I might leave very early this morning."

"Just leave your key locked in the room."

With that, I went to the room and immediately enjoyed the luxury of a sit-down flush toilet. Feeling quite civilized having now washed my hands with actual hot running water and a fresh bar of soap, I crossed the street to the convenience store. The restaurant, I had been informed, closed at 9:00 P.M. "No problem. I have food in the kayak and eating it will help make my boat lighter," I told the feisty night clerk at the front desk.

I wasn't sure what I'd purchase at the convenience store having pretty much fulfilled my convenience store shopping spree fantasies earlier that day at Branford. What I wanted was some kind of reward for accomplishing my goal of reaching the motel before ten o'clock.

Normally I don't like to shop, but this was special. It was an opportunity to satisfy all those little cravings that come up at odd times of the day. I literally walked up and down every aisle in the store— three times. First, to take general inventory. Second, to double-check that what I wanted and needed was there. Third, to select my purchases. I didn't buy much. I went for quality over quantity: A pint of orange juice, two giant Snickers bars, and a Hostess cherry pie. Then I returned to the motel room.

I can't recall actually eating a Hostess cherry pie since I was in junior high school. I mean once you pass a certain age you are expected to give up bubble gum and sugar-encrusted pastries sold on the same shelf as windshield wiper fluid and Drano. I tore open the wrapper. A Hostess cherry pie actually looks like a big piece of lard-soaked pastry injected with cherry filling and artfully disguised under a layer of sugar frosting. It is the kind of food product best consumed in the dark. It is essential that one not think too deeply about the ingredients or how substantially this small pastry might reduce one's life expectancy.

I took a bite and nearly passed out it was so unbelievably delicious. This little pie—dare I call it a tart—was perhaps the most tasty and satisfying pastry I've eaten in well over a decade. "Oh my God," I said aloud. "Oh, wow." I might have shoveled it down in a few quick bites, but no, oh no. I savored this cherry pie. I enjoyed the aroma, the bouquet. I took small bites, allowing the cherriness to swirl in my mouth, to fill my senses with the wonder of machine-made pastry. Thank you, Hostess. Thank you.

Enough indulgence. I needed information, good information, about the life-threatening mess I was about to insert myself into the next day. I channel-surfed on the motel television, looking for the local weather. I felt concern about the approaching storm and wanted to know the latest forecast. I needed to decide whether to press on the next morning or to simply sleep late and have a nice relaxing breakfast at the restaurant across the street.

I called Linda on my cell phone. I asked if she had any information about Manitou or Wizard. Nothing specific. I figured I could stay in front of Wizard at least until he got to the gulf, but I wasn't sure about Manitou. He might paddle all night and pass me as I slept in the motel. There wasn't much I could do about that if he did. I was tired. I needed sleep. Linda told me she'd been talking to my friend

Marty "Salty Frog" Sullivan, and he suggested that if I wanted to call him I could. Salty Frog had competed a few years earlier in the Cross-Florida Challenge. He knew where I wanted to go and what I might face when I got there. I called him around 11:00 P.M.

I asked him how the weather looked and how that might affect my trip the next day to Cedar Key. I said the reports I'd heard on my radio talked of pretty bad conditions in the Gulf of Mexico—small-craft advisory, etc.—and that I didn't want to get to the gulf and have no dry land for refuge if it became too rough to continue. He suggested that I leave at 2:00 A.M. and ride the outgoing tide to the mouth of the Suwannee. By the time I reached Cedar Key the tide would be rising and high enough to permit paddling through a backwater route to a motel called Mermaid's Landing, the last checkpoint in the race.

"I can't do that," I said. "It's already eleven o'clock and I need some sleep. I've got to get some sleep."

Marty told me the approximate times it would take to reach key points in the fifty-mile journey to Cedar Key. He said if I stayed on schedule I should be fine

Right then I made a decision. I'd leave at 4:00 A.M. I told Marty that was my plan and that if I wasn't in Cedar Key by tomorrow evening it just meant that the weather was rough and I would be holed up on the lee side of Deer Island south of the mouth of East Pass.

I hung up the telephone and turned on the television to watch Jay Leno. It felt good to have a plan, but I was worried about how severe the weather might get the next day. I sat up in bed watching TV, waiting for my exhaustion to catch up to me. I was too tired to sleep. Way too tired. I sat there staring at the TV and checking my watch every five minutes. I turned off the TV, lay down, and closed my eyes. I got up and looked out the window at my boat pulled up on the grass behind the motel. I closed my eyes. Nothing. I turned the TV back on. More Leno.

Finally, at some point after midnight, sleep.

The First

Remember the National Gallery of Art? It was sort of like a date, but really only lunch. We ate in the atrium. Caesar salad, or something. Iced tea. We both had to get back to the office. Deadlines. Calls to make. I didn't want to go anywhere.

We walked through the halls, slowly, looking at the paintings, but not really seeing anything. I wondered who you were, a savior or an assassin. I wondered if this thing started between us, how it would end. With slammed doors? Another massive hemorrhage from my meager bank account? Why did there have to be an ending?

Each step echoed in the giant halls. And my heart too. In my head, a debate raged. Finally, I surrendered. I don't even know what the painting was. I stopped there for purely selfish reasons. This spot was just out of the line of sight of the docent, as secluded as you could get in a museum filled with priceless works of art. I had to do it. If I didn't, I knew I'd regret it, perhaps for the rest of my life.

Do you remember? That little kiss, that first kiss, lasted maybe a few seconds. But, thinking about it, I don't know that it ever really ended.

Tuesday

I woke at 3:50 A.M. and felt pretty good. I got up and decided to go. It took about a half hour to repack the boat and drag it back down to the water. By 4:20 A.M. I pushed off from the concrete boat ramp at the Suwannee Gables and paddled out into the dark river. I didn't know it at the time, but Manitou was about fifteen minutes behind me up the river.

I assumed he had passed me during the night. I figured I had to keep up a pretty good pace to catch him. I used it as motivation. The bigger motivation, however, was to get downriver fast enough to catch and ride the outgoing tide to the gulf. The weather wasn't too bad, but if the weather forecast was accurate my day would be filled with wind and rain. The approaching storm was expected to get worse. Much worse.

As I sliced through the darkness, I watched for Manitou's boat up ahead. We'd been circling Florida for almost three weeks, but suddenly it was starting to look an awful lot like a race. That's when I realized what day it was. This was Tuesday—the third Tuesday of the Florida Challenge. I mentally reviewed the experiences of my prior Tuesdays. The first Tuesday of the race I spent a grueling, chilly night in the mud in Florida Bay. The second Tuesday I spent a grueling, chilly night on a mound of shells near Jacksonville. Now here it was Tuesday again. What are my prospects today? According to the weather forecasters, I can look forward to twenty-mile-an-hour headwinds all day with higher gusts, rain squalls, and probably dangerously high surf and powerful currents in the Gulf of Mexico. It had all the ingredients of a disaster in the making, perhaps the most terrible Tuesday of all.

Maybe I should have stayed at the motel and slept all day. I thought about it. The bed. The hot shower. Soap. The restaurant across the street. Another Hostess cherry pie.

The strange thing is, if I was making a mistake being out on the river it didn't feel like it. Not at all. First, I don't really believe Tuesday is a cursed day. Second, part of what makes the Florida Challenge interesting is heading into the unknown, just to see what's going to happen.

I told myself to paddle as hard as I could right off the boat ramp at the Suwannee Gables. There was only one place for me that predawn Tuesday morning, to be in the kayak and paddling fast downriver. I did not know what obstacles the river, or the gulf, or the weather might present later in the day. I had no idea what terrible ordeal I'd face, but I knew it was time to paddle.

As forecast, the storm intensified with gusty wind and band after band of rain squalls. Although the squalls complicated my trip, they did not delay me much. I'd drop my head and paddle a little harder to knife through the worst of it. At other times I hugged the shore to take advantage of the relative calm behind the tall trees on the south bank.

At 12:30 P.M. I emerged from East Pass and got my first look at the open Gulf of Mexico. The wind whipped the sea into a roiling torrent of waves and whitecaps. The turbulence churned up the muddy bottom, painting the water a kind of chocolate-milkshake brown. The steady blast of wind from the southwest launched white beads of spray off my bow. They stung my face with enough force that it felt like they might draw blood.

The passage between East Pass and Cedar Key can be particularly treacherous, with deceptively shallow reefs and hull-shredding oyster bars. I ducked partly out of the wind behind a spit of marshy grassland to assess the situation. I approached the issue in the same way I had navigated through other difficult sections of the race-course. I asked two questions: Is the door open? May I proceed?

I did not try to weigh the strength in my arms and my expertise in a kayak against the fury of the storm. This was not a mathematical calculation. I recognized this as a critical moment in my journey around Florida and perhaps a turning point in the Florida Challenge. It was not a question of my will or the depth of my desire to reach Cedar Key that day. It would be wrong and dangerous to force my way into the storm. Instead of defiance, what I most needed was submission. Instead of personal willpower, what I needed was permission.

Is the door open? May I proceed?

It's not about strength, or fancy paddle work, or even courage. It is about remaining faithful and obedient to the answer when it comes, whatever it might be. If the answer is no, if the door is closed, I could double-back ten miles or so to the little town of Suwannee. I could rest, have a nice meal, and wait out the storm. That would be easy enough and completely safe. If the answer is yes, what then? If I am faithful and obedient, I should have nothing to fear. In contrast, if I am willful and defiant and try to force my way through the storm, I would be on my own. That could be extraordinarily dangerous under these conditions.

Is the door open? May I proceed?

I have paddled through rough water many times, but I knew this would be particularly challenging. The shallow water in this section of the Florida coast meant I'd need to go at least a mile or two—maybe even three miles—offshore just to get into water deep enough to avoid breaking waves. I pulled out my chart and tried to decide on a route. The chart looked nothing like the coast. I actually checked to make sure I had the right chart. It was the correct chart. It just didn't look accurate. I tucked the chart away and decided to navigate by sight.

I was grateful to have reached this spot at midday, in daylight. I knew I had to somehow get from the mouth of the pass out into deeper water without being crushed by breaking waves. Then I had to stay far enough offshore to avoid even more breaking waves. My emergency fallback position would be to try to reach a series of small islands I could see extending down the coast to the south. If I capsized and couldn't get the boat bailed out, I'd drift in and camp on one of the islands. First there was Deer Island, then the Long Cabbage Islands, Spanish Bayonet Island, and eventually Rattlesnake Key. Spending time in a place called Rattlesnake Key wasn't particularly appealing, but I suppose one takes refuge at any port in a storm.

That was my safety plan. It was a risky plan, because between the deep water and the islands were a series of shallow reefs and oyster bars concealed under the white foam of breaking waves. To reach the safety of the islands, I'd have to survive being thrown by the surf into a washing machine with razor-sharp oyster bars. In addition, the tide was falling, extending the surf zone significantly farther out in the gulf. Mistakes were not an option.

There came a time when all I could do is pick up my paddle and go. There was no drum roll. No chorus of inspirational singing from above. No blinding bolt of lightning transferring superhuman power into my shoulders. Any of those things would have been nice. It was pretty much just a miserable day, but I knew deep down that I could do it and went to work.

The force of the wind surprised me. I tightened my grip on the paddle. I used a length of parachute cord as a paddle leash, but I was afraid if the wind somehow ripped the paddle from my hands the gust would snap the cord and fling the paddle a half mile away.

Paddling in rough seas isn't all physical toil. A key part of it—perhaps the most important part of it—is outlook, perspective. I thought of myself as a duck rather than as someone sitting in a hollow boat with a brittle hull that might crack and sink. Watch a duck on the water in rough weather. It floats over the chaos. The duck knows it cannot be touched by the tempest. It knows this. I tried to hold the same thought, the same calm understanding. The chop and waves may break around me, sometimes they might even break over me, but I will find a path through this and float safely over the turmoil. I will not become part of the storm. I will not allow the storm to shake my confidence.

As I hold to these ideas, something begins to happen. I start to see a way through the waves. I don't worry about the crashing wave ten feet to my right, or the building swell to my left. My eyes are locked on the water ahead and the emerging path revealing itself with each paddle stroke. I find myself moving between the most violent sections of water, floating over the big waves, and somehow skirting the deepest, most dangerous wave troughs. Several times I look down into the trough behind the swell and see less than a foot of water covering the seafloor. Sand. Oysters. Rocks.

When you see something like that, it provides a strong incentive to paddle hard toward deeper water. It happened several times. There were a few instances when waves crashed over my boat. My spray skirt held tight and the boat stayed upright. I just kept moving with firm, constant strokes. I basically ferried the kayak down the coast. Ferrying is a paddling technique used to cross a fast-flowing river. It is designed to compensate for the drag of the rushing water under the hull. The technique is to aim upriver from the spot where you intend to land and then paddle hard against the current, letting the force of the water pull you toward your desired landing spot on the far shore. In the gulf, it meant that even though I was headed to Cedar Key to the southeast, my boat was constantly aimed to the southwest, directly into the teeth of the storm. This was necessary, in part, to help me punch through approaching waves and avoid being hit broadside in a way that might startle me and flip the boat.

My goal, as always, was simple—just keep moving forward. My paddling cadence was relatively fast, and I discovered about halfway out to the deeper water that I was singing. This was no ordinary song, it was a testament to an epic maritime struggle, the very embodiment of man's quest to survive the brutal forces of wind and sea.

"Just sit right back and you'll hear a tale, a tale of a fateful trip . . ."

My singing grew louder and louder the farther out I got, until I belted out the words at triumphant top volume, loud enough even to compete with the roar of the crashing waves and the shriek of the wind.

Eventually I lost track of my bailout islands. They disappeared somewhere behind me. Instead, at some point I glanced over my left shoulder and saw houses. Houses? Houses! Am I there? Could that be Cedar Key?

I paddled to the lee side of a small shoal jammed with seabirds. The shoal offered shelter from the waves and wind. Perhaps it wasn't entirely dry land, perhaps it was even a little slippery and smelly, but it offered a safe place to rest in a corner of calm water. I held my nose, checked my chart, and confirmed that I was due west of Cedar Key. I had made it. I still faced several miles of paddling, but now the wind was off my right shoulder rather than in my face. The waves and chop no longer seemed so menacing.

Getting from the Gulf of Mexico to the checkpoint at the Mermaid's Landing Motel, however, wasn't as easy as it looked on the

chart. There were a series of long, shallow oyster bars protecting Cedar Key from the open Gulf of Mexico. I found every one of them.
I'd paddle a quarter mile to the east and then have to paddle a half
mile to the north or south around an exposed oyster bar. Then, I'd
paddle another quarter mile to the east and again run into shallow
water at the edge of even more oysters. Eventually, I poked my way
around and through them. Just don't ask me to do it again or retrace
my steps. As difficult as this was in daylight, it would be next to impossible at low tide in the dark.

When I pulled up at Mermaid's Landing in the early evening,
Chief stood by the water behind the motel. He filmed my arrival.
The first thing I asked, even before my bow touched land: "Where's
Manitou?"

Mermaid's Landing

It took about two hours to shower, drop off my dirty clothes at a
nearby laundromat, and shop for food for the last stage of the race. I
needed more bagels and some Snickers bars. That's about it. The final
leg was 120 miles—an easy two-day paddle.

Chief wasn't alone at the Cedar Key checkpoint. My friend Salty
Frog had rented a room at Mermaid's Landing and then stocked it
with a big box of fresh fruit, including large bunches of bananas.
Had he shown up and done this at the Suwannee Gables Motel it
would have broken the Florida Challenge rules and I would have
been disqualified for receiving unauthorized assistance from a friend.
Checkpoints are different. The WaterTribe was supposed to have rented

a room and kept it available for any challengers to use while at the checkpoint, but the race moved faster than Chief had anticipated. He did his best to keep up, but he had challengers still on the approach to Fort Clinch—all the way back on the Atlantic side of the state— and he had to be there for their arrival too. A week earlier that had been me struggling to reach Fort Clinch. I remembered it well. Now others strained to get there. Chief spent long hours crisscrossing north Florida trying to keep up, trying to be there for everyone.

At every checkpoint I completed a list of essential chores. First, all my dirty clothes had to be washed. Second, new supplies had to be obtained. Third, if at all possible one or two showers would go a long way in maintaining a positive outlook. It would also help counteract my increasing resemblance to a homeless person. Fourth, any opportunity to eat real food had to be exploited. I managed to do all four, including enjoying a nice meal with Salty Frog at a small restaurant down the street from the motel.

When we returned to the motel Chief asked about my plans. I said I'd launch at 8:00 A.M.

Chief was unimpressed. "You have a lead, man" he told me. "You should leave at four or five o'clock."

He had his reasons. Chief wanted a race. He wanted to see boats moving down the coast to the finish, neck and neck. I knew in my gut that it would be important to get a good night's sleep. Eight sounded about right to me. The last weather report I'd heard said the wind was about to shift from southwest to north and that it would blow hard from the north for several days. If it did, both Manitou and Wizard would easily pass me during the final leg. In addition, the last thing I wanted to do was leave too early and end up wasting my effort against a strong southwest wind amid an obstacle course of

Cedar Key oyster bars. I wanted to make sure the wind had shifted and start fresh in daylight.

Later that night I turned on my weather radio. The forecast had changed. It called for variable winds. When I heard it, it made me stop. I stood still in the center of the motel room. Variable winds? Did I just hear that right?

Salty Frog heard it too. He smiled. "You know you could win this race," he said.

"I don't think so," I replied. But I heard him say it. It was an idea—that's all—just an idea. Certainly nothing worth talking about.

At that point I was 120 miles from the finish line at Tampa. Even if I didn't come in first, I would still win the right to step out of my kayak and stay out of it for a long, long time. That's a powerful reason to paddle hard. It was that idea, and the impossible dream of dry pants, that stuck in my mind as I drifted off to sleep that night in a real bed, with real sheets, and a real pillow in a place called Mermaid's Landing.

I woke once in the night, disoriented. "Where am I?" I looked around the dark motel room at the floor. I fought the urge to stand up. I didn't want to get my feet wet. Water covered the floor everywhere.

PART VI

Chasing Something Real:
Cedar Key to Tampa Bay,
120 Miles

A Glorious Departure
from Cedar Key

By 6:40 A.M., I had completed final preparations to launch my sea kayak from the checkpoint on the back lawn of the Mermaid's Landing Motel at Cedar Key.

A magnificent sunrise of yellows and oranges painted the sky. A perfect day. Then I gazed out at the launch site and my heart sank. Instead of nice, deep water, I discover a creek chock full of slimy, black muck, with a consistency somewhere between hot fudge and used motor oil. All the water had drained away. This place was called Mermaid's Landing, wasn't it? Any mermaids attempting to swim ashore here would need wings.

After almost three weeks of near round-the-clock racing, I was primed to begin the final 120-mile "sprint" to the finish line. All I had to do to win the race was get in my sea kayak and paddle to the finish at Fort De Soto Park, near the entrance to Tampa Bay. That's all. Of course, there were two other challengers nearby—both in boats with large sails—and both closing fast from the north. The sailboats would have an advantage if there was wind from the north, east, or west. The forecast: variable winds, primarily from the north.

To me it was a surprise that a sea kayak was in the lead, beating sailboats in a race around Florida. I wasn't sure I could sustain the kind of paddling pace necessary to stay out front, but I was ready to try. Now, instead of open water and clear paddling ahead, I found myself staring at a maritime mosh pit, a potential neck-deep quagmire of oozing, stinking, useless mud. The finish line seemed so close I could almost smell it, if it wasn't for the stench of all that muck.

I hate mud.

As I stood at the edge of the muddy creek pondering my dilemma, I was sure that at that very moment Wizard was piloting his twelve-foot sailboat through several shortcuts to Cedar Key's back entrance. It is a route that can trim miles off the trip, provided you know the way. And Wizard knew the way.

Manitou had to be even closer, slicing through the gulf in his expedition canoe under a full sail stretched tight by a steady eight-mile-an-hour tailwind. He was close enough to read the words CEDAR KEY SHARKS on the water tower over the island. And he wasn't just sitting there sailing, he was also paddling—hard.

My first-place position in the Florida Challenge was due in large part to the decision to plow ahead into the turbulent Gulf of Mexico the day before when I emerged from the Suwannee River. I later learned that Manitou arrived at that same spot about four hours behind me. Instead of throwing himself into the storm, he decided to turn back and stay the night at the nearby town of Suwannee. He knew the wind would shift the next morning. His plan was to leave around two or three in the morning and use the tailwind to pass me.

Now his plan appeared to be working perfectly. In contrast, I went nowhere fast. Maybe Chief was right. Maybe I should have left at 4:00 A.M. The early departure would have had one great benefit, water. Few would dispute the necessity of water in a boat race.

I wasn't about to be defeated quite so easily.

I dragged my fully loaded boat to the edge of the creek and reluctantly nudged it into the ooze. The shiny white hull disappeared and seemed to be sucked down into the goo. I positioned a piece of driftwood beside the boat as a walkway. It sank so deep that I had to dive back toward shore just to save myself.

I wasn't asking for an ocean. All I needed was six inches of water. To be honest, given the circumstances, I think I could have made my kayak glide at seven miles an hour over a damp sponge. But this was no ordinary mud, this was mud with an appetite.

I yanked the boat out of the creek before it was wholly digested. A half inch of black sludge coated the white hull. I couldn't bear the sight of my beautiful boat covered in slop. I found a Mermaid's Landing garden hose and washed it clean. I considered assembling my portage cart and wheeling the boat about a quarter mile away to a launch ramp used by local fishermen. That would require unpacking and then repacking the boat. It would take too much time. I was sure at any moment I'd hear Manitou's familiar voice: "Hey, Warren, is that you?"

A motel patron came out of his room and offered to help. Just like that. "Really? Are you sure?" I asked. He must have been watching through his room window and seen my failed attempt at a glorious launch.

"No problem," he said.

We carried the loaded boat across the causeway, down the street a few blocks, and slid it into the water behind a commercial fishing business. I don't even know the guy's name, but thank you, whoever you are. This maneuver was legal under the race rules because the help came from a stranger. If my friend Salty Frog had helped carry the boat, that would have been a violation. Also, if we'd used a truck to transport the boat, that would have been a violation.

The mud cost me about a half hour. The motel patron's help saved me a half hour. I pushed off at about 7:30 A.M.

As I paddled south into the open gulf, I glanced over my shoulder for a sign of Manitou's orange sail or Wizard's white sail. The horizon was clear, but I knew they were back there somewhere, and coming fast.

Baseball

We sat in a coffee shop on Connecticut Avenue, too excited to return to work. It would have been useless even to try. You had the elementary school auction to organize and news stories to write. I don't remember anything about my work, my stories, my deadlines. All I saw were your eyes and that smile. It was cloudy and cold outside. Somehow we got from the National Gallery across town to the coffee shop.

We both ordered tea. Green tea, I think. Or hot chocolate. Something hot. The shop was jammed. Too many people for a Friday afternoon. We found a table. You wrapped your hands around your mug. I wrapped my hands around my mug.

Please don't let this end.

My mind was racing. For years I'd been plunging through a dark sky, bracing for that moment of impact, sometimes hoping for that mo-

ment. Now, I was in free fall, but in a different way. It had been so long I couldn't recognize it.

It can't happen this fast.

We traded pieces of our past lives in the same way people share a blueberry muffin. A little for you, a little for me, a little for you, a little for me. You grew up in Winchester, Massachusetts, outside Boston, the oldest of five children. I grew up in Red Bank, New Jersey, south of New York City, the younger of two children.

Your family dog was a dachshund. You called it a wiener dog. Fritzie. My family dog was a poodle. Tina.

The mention of New York hits a nerve. I can see it.

Baseball? There was tension in your voice.

"Yankees. My Cub Scout pack went to Yankee Stadium a million years ago in the 1960s. We sat in the left-field bleachers and yelled out to Mickey Mantle. 'Hey, Mickey. Hey, Mickey.' He looked up into the stands, directly at me—at me—and waved."

"I'm a Red Sox fan," you announce.

This is what I love about you—there isn't a fake bone in your body. You aren't going to pretend to be something you are not. The Yankees and the Red Sox are mortal enemies. You know that. You might have just smiled and said something innocuous like: "Baseball is nice." That's not you.

Your ex-husband lives across town with a younger woman but still keeps a car in the driveway behind your house. I don't understand this desire for young, inexperienced women. It is the spirit and soul that make a woman irresistible. I'm not talking about attractive, pretty, fetching. The word is "irresistible," and the power is immense. To me, wisdom is sexy. Intelligence is sexy. And your legs. Oh man. Those legs.

Where are you? What are you doing right now? Are you thinking of me?

The Crossing

Finally back in the boat, I began to ponder how I should approach this last leg of the race. I had always assumed that by the time I reached checkpoint 4 at Cedar Key navigation wouldn't be important and I'd just follow the coast south. The night before, while studying the chart, I could see that if I followed the coast east from Cedar Key it would take me on a twenty-mile detour into extremely shallow water.

What I really wanted was to travel almost due south directly to Tampa Bay. I assumed that would be the favored route of both Manitou and Wizard—a beeline for Tampa. That wasn't the right plan for me, however. I needed to stay a little closer to land in case the weather turned ugly. I had to figure out a way to cut the corner a bit. At a minimum it would be a thirty-mile paddle across open water.

As I rounded the last point at Cedar Key, I discovered the answer on the horizon. The wide vista from east to south was an open seascape of flat, featureless water—with one exception. To the southeast I could clearly see the cooling towers of the Crystal River nuclear power plant. Plumes of steam floated like white balloons over the towers. It was the only target on the horizon, but it was all I needed, something to aim toward.

I raised my downwind sail and started paddling. The breeze blew over my left shoulder and I moved at about five or six miles an hour.

Eventually, Cedar Key fell off the horizon behind me. I looked all around—water. Other than the nuclear plant's cooling towers, there was no land in sight in any direction. No worries. I reminded myself how comfortable I'd become paddling this boat and that even if the boat should flip, I knew how to get back in, bail it out, and keep going.

My sights were set straight ahead on the towers. Even though I couldn't see the shore itself, I could trust that those towers marked the location of Florida's west coast.

It wasn't so much that I needed the towers. They were more a convenience than a navigational necessity. I had a compass and charts. I could navigate using the rising sun. I could even get out my GPS at any moment. My intent was to move as fast as possible over a long distance, and it helps to pick a point on the horizon and then get there. That's what I did.

About an hour into the crossing the wind picked up, rising to about ten. It shifted slightly, blowing from the north, which meant it was almost abeam of my boat. Technically, I'm not supposed to be able to use my downwind sail effectively on such a sharp angle to the wind, but I adjusted the sail and somehow it continued to work. The wind blew steady and even. I hitched my body out the upwind side of the cockpit to counterbalance the force on the sail. The conditions were ideal. The kayak skimmed over the water with surprising speed. The sound of the water at my bow increased from the familiar gurgle of a five-mile-an-hour pace, to the steady splash of an actual sailboat moving at seven or eight miles an hour.

"This is good," I told myself. "This is very good."

The wind shifted from northwest to northeast and with each degree of movement to the east it built and began to gust. The gusts bent my sail backward toward the water zipping past on the downwind side of the kayak. I leaned as far as I could out the cockpit and into the wind, my balance becoming increasingly tenuous. I flew up and across the face of a rising swell. The kayak sailed along the knife edge of the white spray at the crest of the wave as it was about to roll over upon itself. Just as fast I was down in the trough and back up the face of another swell. It was an exhilarating ride, but also precarious. In a very short period of time the wind had transformed my trip from a gentle rolling cruise into a screaming, white-knuckle sleigh ride at the edge of a series of watery cliffs. I could see the disaster that was about to unfold. I had to get the sail down before I flipped.

My downwind sail had given me many hours of good service in a variety of windy conditions, but the sail has a dangerous design flaw. In high, gusty wind, it becomes increasingly difficult to take down. Of the four times I almost capsized during the Florida Challenge, three of those incidents occurred during attempts to take down the sail in high winds that were continuing to build.

The basic design of the downwind sail is ingenious. It is two fiberglass stays that suspend an inverted V of lightweight sail material above the forward deck. The hollow stays slide down over support posts that can rotate within a base assembly bolted to the top of the deck. The idea is that the sail catches the wind and helps push the boat forward. The problem arises in strong, shifting winds. That's when the support stays press too tightly against the base, making it difficult to lift the stays off the base to take the sail down. To reduce the wind pressure on the sail, I can either rotate the sail to move it into a luff position or turn the boat toward the wind to decrease the pressure the full sail exerts on the stays. While this is relatively easy in winds of five to ten miles an hour, it is unbelievably treacherous in choppy, stormy seas amid gusty winds of fifteen to twenty.

This was not the time to enjoy a refreshing dip in the gulf.

"This is not good. Not good at all." I said it out loud riding up the face of a wave. "Oh no," I said, swooping down the backside of the swell.

The force of the wind in the sail was so strong that it caused the sail mount itself to flex my fiberglass deck. I worried that the wind might break the sail mount completely off the deck.

I planted my feet hard against the foot pegs inside the hull and pressed the tops of my thighs against the underside of the deck in preparation for a violent, high-speed disaster.

Up another wave face, watching the feather of white water at the crest, blasting through it, and then bracing for the bottom to fall out. At that moment there was enough pressure between my upper and lower molars to slice a power cable. Again, I rocketed across the face of a wave, swooped down the back side, came back up again, balancing over the crest, and then went almost in free fall down the back side. Spray shot out from both sides of my bow where it sliced through the chop.

This would have been terrific fun on a Saturday afternoon on some bay, but it was way too reckless for me in a fully loaded boat some twenty miles offshore on the last leg of the Florida Challenge. Several times I tried to take the sail down. The swirling wind immediately refilled the sail, locking the sail stays in place and sending me, once again, on a wet and wild sleigh ride across the swells. Finally, I timed my effort to a lull between gusts. I yanked the entire support structure out of the base and pulled the sail down. When it was done, my hands were shaking and my mouth had gone completely dry. I took several long slow gulps of air and then tucked the folded sail away in my cockpit. I paddled for an hour until the wind inexplicably dropped back down to about five from the northeast. As fast as the wind arrived, it disappeared. The sea flattened. The day was, once again, peaceful and calm.

The Boot

There was that time I was staying in the apartment in Virginia, the one that looked across Route 50 at the Iwo Jima Memorial. You came over one morning. Instead of calling first, you surprised me. You just appeared at my door, like the Publishers Clearing House lady, except a million times better. I opened the door and there you were, smiling.

I hadn't seen you for three weeks. In the joy and excitement of the moment I forgot to ask, "Where's your car parked?" You had pulled up at the front of the building and decided to surprise me. It would only be a moment. There are signs everywhere. They all deliver the same message. No parking.

We were only about three or four minutes. Mostly kissing, but I also had to get my stuff and lock the door. We ran to the lobby and out into the morning, the entire day a present wrapped in a shiny bow for both of us. The apartment complex security officer had already discovered your car. She'd just finished affixing the boot to the front axle. To urban drivers the boot is worse than death.

"No. No," you said, immediately. "I was only a minute. I just ran up."

The security officer, a woman in a crisp blue uniform, had heard it all before. A thousand times before. "You can't park here, even for a minute," she said, her voice flat and professional. "Ma'am, this is a fire zone."

"No. No," you pleaded. I was surprised by how quickly you moved across the sidewalk to confront the officer. How forcefully you reacted.

The security guard started shaking her head, no. She'd heard it all before.

Then your tone changed. It became desperate, raw. Your hands pressed palm to palm. "Please. Please," you said. "You can't do this. You can't."

The officer shook her head.

Then you told her something I will always remember. "I'm a single mom."

The guard's head stopped moving.

"I have two children," you said. "Please."

Never in my life will I ever see this again. The expression on the guard's face changed, the professional indifference melted away.

"I have two kids," you repeated. "I'm a single mom."

The security guard in her crisp blue uniform had heard it all a thousand times before. But something you said—or the way you said it—touched her. There was a bond, an understanding.

I've thought about that moment, the level of desperation in your voice and how it came so quickly to the surface, like a little piece of that frightening gut sound that comes during childbirth. You can't fake that. It was genuine, a flash of perfect clarity into a strange and awful place deep, deep down inside you. The officer seemed to recognize it.

She produced a large, sturdy key. She bent down, and quickly pulled the boot away from the front tire.

I knew better than to say a word. I wanted to crawl into the bushes and hide. I felt I was an intruder, a witness to a moment I was completely unqualified to see.

We got into the car and drove for about fifteen minutes without anyone saying a word. No radio. Just the sound of the wind and the traffic.

I know what it is like to be alone and in pain, but until I heard your voice that morning, I had no real idea about life as a single mom. It was important for me, that moment outside the apartment building. It helped me see you more clearly. More important, for the first time in a long time I started to see my ex-wife in a different light, to consider how it must have been for her, the fear and pain, and the magnitude of her accomplishment.

We have our issues, but there is no doubt she's a good mom, a great mom. She loves Jason and would never let anything bad happen to him.

For the first time in a long time I started to feel something. It's like I could feel part of myself coming back from someplace far away. I could feel it.

Gratitude.

Compassion.

It is a strange thing to be dead and then suddenly alive.

It's you. You did that.

Getting to Tampa

There was almost no breeze but I put my downwind sail up anyway. I put it up just for the psychological boost it might offer. For most of the late morning and through the midafternoon there wasn't much wind at all. By two or three o'clock that changed with a slight breeze. It gave me a little push. I paddled at a pace faster than five, and because I'd had great sleep the night before and plenty of good food, I felt strong. The boat moved well. I didn't know how Manitou and Wizard were doing, but I was happy with my progress.

About four in the afternoon I passed a fishing guide with two clients anchored near an offshore island. "How far is it to New Port Richey," I asked.

"About forty miles as the crow flies," the guide replied.

"Thank you."

Near sunset, I called Linda. I knew my position report would provide important information about my location and progress to

Manitou and Wizard, but I figured they were probably well offshore and past me by then anyway. I checked my chart and guessed that I might be approaching Hernando Beach. Then I got out my GPS and read Linda the coordinates: N + 28°33'37.20", W - 82°40'11.94".

She filled me in. Manitou had arrived at Cedar Key at 8:30 A.M. and Wizard at about 11:30 A.M. She said they were only a few hours behind me when they left Cedar Key. Then she asked what to report for my plans that night. Was I planning to stop and camp or paddle all night?

"I'm not sure yet," I told her. "I'm going to play it by ear, but I'm leaning toward trying to go all the way through to the finish."

"Okay."

"Don't report that, though. Just leave it open. I'm really not sure, and I don't want to make Manitou and Wizard work any harder than they would otherwise."

I knew that if I stated as a fact that I planned to paddle all night, they would pull out the stops. I'd rather keep them guessing about how hard they'd have to work to catch and pass me, if they hadn't passed me already.

Linda had no information about the current position of either Manitou or Wizard. I wasn't going to call her back just to find out that I'd been passed. That would make the final miles even more difficult.

My Life

Did I ever thank you? I can't recall if I ever really thanked you. Not since we started this thing we have. What you have done for me is beyond any words I could use to describe it.

Where are you? What are you doing right now? Are you thinking of me?

Wouldn't it be great if you were there? If I came paddling in to that beach at Fort De Soto and you were standing there, waiting. Oh, that would be great.

What would I say? What would I do? I'd give you a hug and then a kiss. I'd get down on a knee. Just one, or both? No, just one. Two knees are for prayer. One knee is for proposing.

What would I say? "Linda, will you marry me?" That's not much, but I suppose it covers the essentials. No. There should be more. You might need some convincing—a little salesmanship might be in order.

What would I say? Thank you. That's what I'd say. I can't tell you how much I appreciate everything about you. No. That sounds too much like a retirement speech. We're colleagues at work, but come on. I have to just speak from my heart. I have to tell the truth, the complete truth without any fear of ridicule or rejection.

Part of growing up is learning how to put this mask on to deal with the world without betraying anything. In the most important relationships, however, that mask is worse than useless—it can be destructive. It is important to tell those we love how we feel. How else will they know. But if I really told you exactly how important you are, you might see me as some pathetic, weak man. Desperate. Clinging.

I'm not those things. That's not me.

What would I tell you?

We both know from experience that a full life includes hardship and heartache. It also must include triumph and love. Love nourished and cherished can survive. I believe that.

To love one another selflessly, unconditionally, is the noblest thing we can do as men and women. After being a good parent there is no higher calling.

You came into my life when I thought I had nothing. You saved my life. You did it not by giving me part of your life. You did it by showing me mine.

Oh No

I felt pretty good. I told myself to keep up a good pace, no need to kill myself. Even strokes. The steady sound of moving water pulsed at the bow with each pull on the paddle. Next thing I know my ears were filled with a sound of fingernails on a blackboard. *Screeeeeeeeeeech!*

The bow of the kayak slid fast over something substantial and sharp. The sensation took me immediately back to my precarious teeter-totter experience on the log in the St. Marys River. This sounded much worse. I'd run my kayak up on a pile of dark, barnacle-encrusted rocks just south of a boating channel. I backed off the rocks, gave them a wide berth, and immediately discovered I was in water two feet deep.

I had expected that by now I would be able to see Anclote Key. But since I hadn't seen it I assumed I wasn't anywhere near it yet. Instead of heading out into deeper water, I continued through the shallows toward a well-lit building to my south. Just keep going, I told myself. Just keep moving forward.

I didn't know what that well-lit building was up ahead. There was darkness all around and I was starting to feel tired. The water alternated between shallow and supershallow. In some places the sand wasn't even moist. I considered getting out and walking.

There was no moon, but there were so many lights to my east it made it difficult to develop any night vision. I checked my chart, comparing it to lights on the horizon. I was unable to spot anything that might match potential navigation points on the chart. I kept moving, aiming for the large, well-lit building to my south.

Before the race, I had studied the charts, looking for possible campsites. I'd even talked to people who had paddled in the Clearwater–St. Petersburg area for advice about the best routes to the finish line near the entrance to Tampa Bay. I never imagined, however, that after 1,080 miles the race would be close enough that even a minor navigational error might mean the difference between finishing first, second, or third.

The good news was that unless something went really wrong, I couldn't do any worse than third. Midway into that last run down the coast I began to appreciate the magnitude of my mistake. What I should have done was program a series of waypoints into my GPS to help keep me away from shallow water. I should have placed one waypoint about a half mile west of Anclote Key and then another west of Honeymoon Island. Anclote Key is a state park three miles offshore from the mouth of the Anclote River, near Tarpon Springs. The island is accessible only by boat and is uninhabited, with no prominent lighted features. Had I reached this point in daylight there would be no problem. I'd have recognized the island immediately on the horizon to the southwest, noted its position on my chart, and moved out into the Gulf of Mexico to avoid the shallow water and other obstacles in St. Joseph Sound. But by the time I arrived there was no daylight, and on a dark, moonless night Anclote Key is about as noticeable as an oil stain on a black tar driveway. If the island was out there somewhere, I couldn't see it.

Instead, my eyes locked onto on a giant rectangle of white lights. When I reached it I identified the building as a power plant. I drifted about thirty yards away, bathed in an eerie halo surrounding the plant. It emitted a steady hum. I examined my chart, pressing a wet finger along the line of barrier islands between Tarpon Springs and Clearwater. Why would they put a power plant out on a barrier island, I wondered. That makes no sense.

I assumed, mistakenly, my location was just west of Anclote Key. If this was Anclote Key, why didn't my chart note the presence of a power plant?

Just to be safe I checked the mainland from New Port Richey to Clearwater—again drawing my finger across the chart searching for a power plant. I found nothing indicating a power plant.

In reality, I was just north of the mouth of the Anclote River. There is a power plant at that location, but it is not marked as a power plant on the chart. The chart notes only the presence of a smokestack.

The problem is I could not see a smokestack in the white glow of the plant. Nor did I know I should look for it. I wrongly assumed I was three miles west of my actual position. I wrongly assumed I was already in the Gulf of Mexico and that all I had to do was paddle south.

This is what the Florida Challenge does. Physical and mental exhaustion undercut the ability to think. Anyone can paddle eighty miles down the Florida coast in daylight and good weather. Anyone can paddle at night from the Anclote River to Fort De Soto Park.

Combine those two things in the context of a race and add to it the accumulated toll of having already paddled more than a thousand miles in less than three weeks, and the undertaking becomes a bit more difficult.

At 11:00 P.M. I began to paddle again. I headed south, along what I thought was the coast of Anclote Key. As I paddled I felt a sudden surge of wind from the east. It was building. I could feel it on the side of my face, on my arm. I knew immediately this was bad news for me and good news for Manitou and Wizard. Both would be able to use the steady east wind to sail to the finish line. I was certain this east wind would mark the decisive turning point in the race.

But I had other, more pressing, problems. I was just south of a power plant that didn't seem to exist on my chart. Now I found myself crossing a dredged channel with lit navigation markers running east-west.

Had I not been so tired, had I not been so hungry, had I not been in such a hurry, I might have discovered the impossibility of my assumption that I was west of Anclote Key. I might have even recognized my actual location near the mouth of the Anclote River, or, better still, I might have taken the channel to the west into the open gulf and then headed south, but that would have been too easy.

What happened next helped convert confusion into fiasco. I turned on my GPS and saw I was only forty miles from the finish at Fort De Soto Park. A GPS is a wonderful tool. My friend Salty Frog frequently jokes about how I rely too much on charts and don't fully trust my GPS. In fairness, there are times when I have to ignore the GPS, especially when it is about to convince me to go in the wrong direction.

My task on this night was to get from my current location (wherever that might be) to the finish line at Fort De Soto Park. My GPS pointed the way—but in a straight line. Unless I decided to start flapping my arms and fly to the finish line, I'd have to confine my efforts to a watery route. Instead of proceeding southeast—as the crow flies—I had to paddle southwest to get around the protrusion of Clearwater and St. Petersburg Beach before turning south and then east to Fort De Soto Park. This is a lesson I had already learned many times during the Florida Challenge, but now, when I needed it most, I was too tired to remember.

"Go south," I said. But after seeing the GPS pointing to the southeast, I kept turning southeast, aiming toward the lights on shore. The water kept getting shallow—in some places just a foot deep. A causeway appeared, a solid causeway, like a dam of rocks across the water. *How is that possible? I'm in the Gulf of Mexico.*

Again, I consulted the chart, running my index finger along the barrier islands from Anclote Key to Clearwater, searching for a causeway extending out into the Gulf of Mexico.

"Where am I?"

In reality, I was just north of the causeway leading to Howard Park Beach near Tarpon Springs. This wasn't the Gulf of Mexico, it was St. Joseph Sound. But I didn't know that. All I knew was that my way south was blocked by a wall of rocks.

"Which way do I go?"

The tide was falling. I flashed back to that awful night spent on the mud bank in Florida Bay. I didn't want to get stuck in the muddy shallows on a falling tide.

"You've got to get to deeper water."

I paddled through a bridge under the causeway. On the other side I saw a well-lit park about a mile away and, more important, a fisherman. I paddled toward the fisherman, intending to ask directions.

"Excuse me. Excuse me. Do you know the way to Fort De Soto Park?"

I rehearsed the question as I paddled hard toward the park. As I drew closer, the "fisherman" disappeared, or I should say he transformed into a few fronds of a palm tree. I paddled to the park anyway, hoping there might be someone to ask directions. I just needed a little reassurance. I just needed someone to say, "Go that way. It's right over there." I just needed someone to say, "Yeah, you're still in Florida."

I paddled along a beach, and found no one. I checked my chart and was unable to see anything that looked like my current location.

In every WaterTribe challenge I've entered there is at least one moment of truth. It is a moment when I pause and take stock of the extraordinary situation I've gotten myself into and wonder how I am going to get out of it. I thought: "I can't believe that I've paddled one thousand, one hundred, and sixty miles around Florida, I am in first place in the Florida Challenge, and now, with only about forty miles to go to the finish line, I've gotten myself lost."

I was buffaloed. Baffled. Confused. I was tired. Sore. Dazed. Palm trees looked like fishermen. But I was also thinking how odd that I wasn't frightened. Frustrated, certainly. But there was nothing fear-inducing about it. Everything I needed I had right there with me. I could just pull my kayak up on shore at any moment to set up camp, sleep, and eat, and I'd be fine.

That little moment of calm helped break through the confusion. It happened as my boat floated in a dredged pocket near the park. As I consulted my chart, the kayak began to spin slowly around like the needle of a compass. When I looked up from the chart I noticed a small green light blinking way out on the dark horizon. The thought came to me: "Go that way." So I did.

The closer I got to the green light, the deeper the water. "This is good. This is good." After a while I saw a second green light, and turned slightly to the left toward that one. Then another. And another. I seemed to be moving in the right direction. The water was deeper. My pace was steady. I was racing again.

Then at some point I stopped paying attention to the green lights. I aimed instead for a cluster of white lights and buildings. Soon I noticed an island west of my position and signs prohibiting motorized boats from entering. "What? What?"

Buffaloed. Baffled. Confused. Tired. Sore. Dazed.

Again, I got out my chart. Again, I was unable to locate anything that looked familiar. I saw the lights of a bridge off to the east and thought, "Maybe I should go there." So I did.

After passing under the bridge, I saw a car parked on the causeway about a half mile away. Like the "fisherman" earlier, I was convinced that if I could only ask someone for directions I would be okay. I paddled toward the car. "Excuse me, how do I get to Fort De Soto?" I practiced the question again. Then I began to consider what might happen. My mind raced through the possibilities. I imagined a disastrous scenario.

"Hello? Hello?"

I can hear the squish-squish of my wet diving booties as I walk toward the car. I feel relief as I discover it is just a teenager sitting alone in his car. No problem. No problem at all. As I approach I can see his head is rocking slowly. He must be listening to the radio. I notice a bit of condensation on the inside of the car windows. His eyes are closed. He's asleep. No. Not asleep. He has this strange look on his face. His mouth opens. I can't hear what he is saying, but his lips form a perfect O. That must be a great song playing on the radio. He seems to be enjoying it. His face is moist. Is that . . . sweat?

I lean in toward the driver's side window. Now I can hear him through the foggy glass. "Oh-Oh-Oh, yeah," he says. I move closer. My breath is fogging the glass from the outside. I raise my hand to knock on the window. My fist, sheathed in a salt-stained, fingerless, paddling glove, hovers about three inches from the glass.

His eyes open. For a moment he seems to be studying the roof of the car. Then he turns slightly, sees me, and unleashes a hideous, high-pitched scream. Dogs as far away as north Georgia are rendered temporarily deaf. Fine crystal goblets shatter across most of west-central Florida. The roof of the car seems to balloon outward. It isn't just a shout. Or a yell. What emerges from his lungs is a terror-filled banshee shriek. That's not the worst of it. A head springs up from somewhere down in the shadows near the lower part of the steering wheel. A human head actually pops up out of the darkness, and the look on that girl's face is sheer terror. She screams even louder than the driver, which I wouldn't have thought possible. The sound of it and the sight of her face contorted into a mask of unimaginable horror, makes me scream. And that makes him scream even louder. I back quickly away from the car, tripping on a coconut and then a curb. I scramble in a kind of crabwalk sideways cartwheel, kicking up sand— feet and hands and elbows flying—all the way back to the boat. *Get me out of here. Get me out of here.*

By the time I'd thought through this scenario I was still about fifty yards from the parked car on the causeway. I couldn't see if there really was anyone sitting in the car, but I already knew it was not a good idea. Maybe it wouldn't happen exactly like that, maybe it would be different, but it was way too late at night to tap on the window of a parked car to ask directions. No good thing could come of it.

I tried to clear my head, to get my mind back into the race. *Think, think.*

This was the idea that emerged. "If I want to get to Fort De Soto the easiest way is to go out about a mile or two into the Gulf of Mexico, follow the shore south until I see the bridge across Tampa Bay. When I see the bridge, hang a left."

That actually made sense. It had the benefit of being relatively simple and easy to remember, and it just felt right. I pulled out my chart and studied it. This time I began to recognize the outline of the shore, the nearby island, the causeway. I identified my position just south of the Honeymoon Island causeway near Hurricane Pass. The chart showed the way to the open gulf through the pass. I decided to go for it.

Easier said than done. Hurricane Pass was choked with sandbars and I could hear rolling surf somewhere in the darkness ahead. There was no defined channel, at least not one clearly visible at night. I managed to avoid at least two sections of breaking waves, and then, just as I thought I might be in deep enough water to start heading south, I heard the rip of falling water just ahead of my bow as a wave broke over my front deck. "Do not turn. Do not stop." I paddled hard and fast through several more waves until I was about a mile offshore. Then I turned south and repeated my plan. I actually said it out loud, as if someone else was in the boat with me.

The most difficult ninety minutes of the Florida Challenge began around 4:30 A.M. I was beyond exhausted. Sleep deprivation hurts. I know now why the U.S. government tried to use it to coerce confessions from terror suspects. Human rights experts say it is a form of torture. "Okay, okay. I'm al Qaeda," I shouted. "Enough. Enough."

The pain was the least of my concerns. Mine was not the most stable boat in the world. Unlike Wizard in his self-righting sailboat or Manitou with his stabilizing pontoons, I was in a kayak. If I fell asleep and leaned too far to one side, I'd get wet. Worse, I might drown.

I told myself that to nod off a mile offshore alone in the darkness in my confused mental state would almost certainly be fatal. The scare tactic wasn't nearly as effective as splashing water on my face. Soon, I was so tired even the shock of the water couldn't rouse me.

At one point I felt the cold breath of something mean and unforgiving on the back of my neck. It made the little hairs stand up straight.

Flashing

They say at the moment just before death your life flashes before your eyes.

My mind was working slowly, like a computer about to crash. But it still worked. What flashed within the dusty cobwebs was not the totality of my life. It was not a comprehensive assessment of my being. These were selected images, memories I summoned to try to fortify myself against the intensifying ordeal.

Mohammed Saleh smiling back at me as we walk deeper into the Arabian desert.

Jason on a high mountain trail.

Linda walking beside me in Washington, D.C.

And a long night, day, and night in a Bahrain hospital.

Birthday

In 1988, I worked as a foreign correspondent based in Bahrain, a small island in the Persian Gulf. My wife was eight and a half months pregnant and I was researching a series of stories about unrest among the Shia Muslim population in Bahrain. I'd already been warned that the Sunni-dominated government was sensitive about the subject. If I produced another story, I'd be arrested and deported.

It would have been easy to stop, to just keep quiet. That would have been the safe thing to do, the smart thing. A reporter's job, however, is to find the truth and tell it.

I kept digging. I filed another story—the most important yet—on October 31, 1988. I remember it clearly because that night my wife went into labor.

I had mapped out four different routes through Manama between our house and the hospital. I had timed each one, during heavy afternoon traffic and with no traffic at all. We made the trip in fourteen minutes.

The rest of it took about eighteen hours. Our doctor was from South Africa. When I entered the delivery room I noticed his white rubber boots. They were the same boots commercial fishermen wear. I thought: "This must get really messy."

It didn't. At least not at first. Jason arrived at 5:26 P.M. He was small and skinny. Two weeks early. I didn't count toes or fingers. I just listened to him. That was more than enough. They took him away and then the doctor took me outside in the hallway. It was dark and the hall seemed to extend forever into a shadow at the far end.

The hospital appeared empty, closed for the night. The doctor told me there was some internal bleeding and that they might need more blood. I felt like someone was standing on my chest. *More blood?* I couldn't get any air in my lungs. I just nodded. He wondered if I had questions. I asked if I could be with her while she was being stitched up. "It would be best if you just stayed here," he said.

I nodded. I couldn't breathe. I sat down in the dark hallway, alone. I asked for help. It wasn't much of a prayer. "Please help me."

A voice came, but it wasn't really a voice. It was more a suggestion, a feeling. I didn't believe it at first. I was confused and tired.

Go.

I sat there, lost for a moment. The voice, the feeling, was persistent.

Go!

I started walking tentatively down the hall toward the nursery. The message came again as I turned onto a second hallway. This time it was unmistakably urgent.

Go!!!

I ran down the hall. When I arrived at the nursery, I could see him wrapped in a blanket in a little plastic tub. I expected it to be exactly like in the movies. It wasn't. Not at all. He was blue. Is he supposed to be blue? The nurses were busy in the back, preoccupied with something. I knocked on the glass. I pounded on the door. A nurse took him away. The pediatrician rushed in, and another, and another nurse.

I could see them doing something to him in the back.

My hands pressed against the window, but I couldn't feel the glass. I couldn't feel my own feet. My thoughts turned to my wife. Then back to the infant.

"Please help them."

I went completely numb, and started to feel cold. "This can't be happening." I tried to breathe. I tried to think.

If it had been possible to make a trade at that moment, I'd have agreed. No question. No hesitation. "Take me. Take me instead."

———

There are experiences in life that are inexplicable. They run counter to logic. They challenge any understanding of reality. In times of need we return to them, to the memory of them, as if they contain some nugget of truth, as if quiet reflection might encourage a reprise, a miracle, like plunging headlong into healing waters in a fountain believed capable of granting eternal life. If only it were that easy. I hope it wasn't all an accident, a coincidence, just luck. I hope it was something more. Something real and wonderful.

It isn't that they both lived, or that I was so completely prepared to give my life to let them live. The reason those eighteen hours in Bahrain are alive in my heart today is the voice. I can't explain the voice. It wasn't even a voice, more a suggestion, a feeling, an intuition. Who knows where it comes from. Perhaps sleep deprivation. Confusion. Wishful thinking. All I can do is fall back on my training as a newspaper reporter. All I can do is tell you what happened.

I stayed with them, to protect them, to guard them, or to at least try. When the nurses found me curled up on the floor beside my wife's hospital bed, they brought a foam mat and a blanket. Just down the hallway, Jason lay in an incubator with tiny oxygen tubes inserted in his nose.

People sent flowers and congratulatory notes. I wore a pathway between her room and that window at the nursery.

Slowly, slowly, the shadow lifted. But the experience stayed with me.

———

I carry a life jacket at all times in my boat, but I've never put it on. Not once. I've never felt the need. More precisely, I've never been told to do so.

A famous British explorer once said that no journey is ever truly an adventure unless you face a distinct possibility of death. Everything else is just tourism.

For a time I misunderstood that quote. I so admired the man who said it that I took it to mean more than it does. It isn't almost dying that defines the journey. It is what sustains the explorer in the midst of peril that defines the journey. It isn't tempting death that is important. It is overcoming the fear of death.

I don't have a death wish. I am not suicidal. It is the exact opposite. I want to live. I want to travel to the heart, to the precipice, to the depths, and live it on its terms, understand it on its terms, and then come back. When I push my way to the edge of that strange and distant place, I may be called many things, but tourist is not one of them.

Going Home

The sun rose at Clearwater Pass. To my left were high-rise condos and a beautiful white-sand beach. My lightweight carbon fiber paddle felt as heavy as concrete. At one point I thought I saw Wizard's sail up ahead, but it was just a buoy.

At times it seemed I was just clawing the water, like paddling with a pitchfork. That's when I started to look over my shoulder for sails. They had to have passed me.

I wish I could say it was easy, that surviving the night made the rest of it effortless. At one point I actually debated whether I should just slow down, stop pushing so hard. Manitou and Wizard are probably already at the finish line anyway. They are probably lounging in the shade eating Hostess cherry pies and sipping ice water.

I rejected the idea that I should slow down. That's not the way to honor the other challengers in a race. You honor them by bringing your best stuff, by doing the absolute best you can, by not leaving anything out on the water. If those guys beat me, at least I'll know I gave it my all.

Chief had asked that we telephone him about two hours from the finish so the media could be notified. After the night I'd just endured I had no idea how long it might take me to reach the finish line. I also wasn't sure I wanted a bunch of reporters and cameras on the beach when I came in. I wasn't sure I'd be able to stand up. I might have to crawl out of the boat and up the beach. I wasn't keen on the idea of those folks from the news media being there to record it. I just kept paddling. No phone calls.

I thought about Jason in his classes at school. I knew he was following the race on the computer in his school library. He'd point to the screen and my location on the map to show his friends how far I'd traveled. He told me later exactly what he said. "That's my dad."

———

I stayed about a half mile off the beach. I knew St. Petersburg was a long beach, but it just seemed to go on forever. As I paddled, I scanned the shoreline for a familiar building. Everything looked strange, foreign. Maybe this was the wrong St. Petersburg. Maybe I was in Russia. I even looked for my favorite prerace dinner spot, Gigi's Italian Restaurant. I never saw it. Finally, I just concentrated on finding the Don Cesar Hotel at Pass-a-Grille Beach. You can't miss the large pink castlelike building.

Around noon the wind shifted somewhat from east to southeast, which made it a headwind. Maybe eight to ten. Just something else to slow me down. I was tired, but I could still keep the boat moving. Perhaps the southeast wind was a gift to me. It would mean that both Wizard and Manitou would be unable to sail without tacking. Wizard might have to scull and Manitou might have to paddle. It probably didn't matter. By then I didn't have enough energy to take a drink of Gatorade. This wasn't a race anymore. It was an attempted self-rescue.

I turned inward. *Think. Come on. Think.*

Walking

Walking with you in Washington, you take hold of my arm while we are walking on the sidewalk. It isn't out of fear. It is just a pure act of companionship. We are together. You're with me. I'm with you.

Maybe it's a little bit of possession. That's okay. I'm yours.

Maybe it touches my heart because it would be so easy to simply walk apart side by side to get where we are going. Or maybe because you feel exactly as I do. Just being together—just being—is enough. It is everything.

Do you remember our first real date? Dinner and a movie. That Mexican place and then the big screen at the Uptown. The Green Mile, about a man on death row. Not exactly the best date movie. Who cares. We held hands in the dark the entire time, like a couple of teenagers. Every moment with you I'm home. That's when I'm at peace. The journey is getting back to you. Home is walking with you on a busy street in Washington and having you reach over and take my arm. Or holding hands in a dark theater. I love that.

The Pier

I worked my way down Pass-a-Grille Beach paddling close to shore to stay sheltered from the wind. Then I cut across the North Channel past fishing boats, plotting my final assault on the finish line. I was worried about what I'd do if there were large waves breaking on the beach.

The finish line was at a concrete fishing pier at Fort De Soto Park about a mile west of the beach where the Florida Challenge had begun on March 4. The day before the start of the race, I drove to the pier to familiarize myself with the surroundings. I knew if I did manage to get all the way around Florida, by the time I arrived here I would be the paddler equivalent of stone-cold roadkill. I got out my chart and walked around, trying to imagine what it would be like to stand at this spot after paddling twelve hundred miles. I thought, "Good, there are showers and a men's room."

The prerace scouting trip was important. There are two concrete piers at Fort De Soto, one on the Gulf of Mexico side of the park, and one about a mile away on the Tampa Bay side of the park. The finish line was at the second pier on the Tampa Bay side. I marked my chart by circling the second pier with a red marker. Then I double-checked the coordinates entered into my GPS.

Visiting the finish line was the last thing I did before heading across town to Gigi's on St. Pete Beach to consume massive piles of pasta and garlic bread in the traditional prerace carbohydrate load.

Now here I was, almost three weeks later clawing through the water trying to remember what that damn pier looked like. It is a bad sign when you start to look over your shoulder in a race. It is loss of concentration, loss of confidence. I was sure I had been passed by Manitou and Wizard. When I couldn't see their sails, it just confirmed it.

My goal was clear—get to the finish line and put an end to my suffering. There would be a shower, food, sleep. Of course, the worst possible thing to do in the final, difficult stage of an endurance race is to imagine the luxuries I would enjoy after the race. Every imaginable pain from the trip immediately came flooding back for an encore. I started to itch all over. My butt felt like it had been pummeled mercilessly by a heavyweight boxer. I had no feeling in the three center toes on my right foot. Mentally, I possessed the IQ of a doorknob.

I entered a kind of survival mode in which I picked a point and went to it, and then picked another point and went to that. At times I had to stop, lower my head, and close my eyes. I was so tired I couldn't even tell myself what I usually tell myself: "Just keep moving forward."

As the pier came into view, I strained to see the beach and any sign of another boat. My GPS pointed in the general direction of the pier, but something was wrong. One hundred yards off the beach the GPS said I still had 1.4 miles to go.

There were swells rolling in from the Gulf of Mexico and I wondered how rough the landing might be. I timed my move just right and scooted in between two waves. I hadn't been out of the boat since a quick drag over a sand spit near the Crystal River nuclear power plant roughly twenty-five hours earlier. I was surprised by how fast I was able to pop open my spray skirt, get out of the cockpit, and drag the boat up the beach out of the line of breaking waves before one crashed on top of me. Once on the beach, I doubled over with my hands on my knees and just tried to take a few deep breaths. I was dizzy and in pain, but grateful to be standing on dry land. It didn't really matter to me that there wasn't anyone there to cheer and celebrate my arrival. I hadn't called in a position report since 6:00 P.M. the night before.

Slowly, slowly the idea began to sink in. I'd made it. I closed my eyes and tried to stand up straight. That, too, was painful.

A chubby guy in a T-shirt and bathing suit walked over to me. I thought he might offer to call an ambulance. I guess I didn't look as bad as I felt. "Are these kayaks hard to paddle?" he asked.

I love kayaking and under normal circumstances I will gladly discuss the sport for hours with anyone. But there was this tiny voice somewhere way back in my head.

Hey.

Hey!

Hey!!!

Call Chief.

I told the man in the T-shirt I had to make a quick phone call but that I'd be happy to talk to him in a second. I dialed race organizer Steve Isaac.

"Chief, I'm here. I'm at the finish line at Fort De Soto."

"Where? Where are you?"

"I'm at the pier. I'm on the beach at the pier."

Chief, who was standing at that moment beside the pier at the finish line, said immediately: "Wrong pier."

"Huh?"

"You are at the gulf pier, the finish line is at the bayside pier. You have to come around the point."

As soon as he said it I thought of my GPS and knew my mistake. Then I asked: "Who else is in?"

The answer hit me like a two-by-four in the face. "No one. If you get here soon enough, you win."

At exactly that moment, a wedge of black clouds swept across the sky. The wind picked up. It started to rain—hard. I put the cell phone away. The man in the T-shirt waved as he ran for shelter. I dragged my boat back into the water and managed a clean launch between breaking waves. The combination of the short rest, the cool, driving rain, and Chief's information revived me enough to get back in the boat—a huge accomplishment. Rounding the point, my eyes turned for about the six millionth time to scan the horizon for sails behind me. Then I saw a beautiful sight up ahead—the correct pier and a small group gathered at the center of the beach.

As I drew near, I surprised myself. While paddling the final hundred yards, I scanned the beach searching for Linda. I knew she wasn't there, but I examined each of the faces anyway. Each one. My eyes followed the line of trees, the showers, the parking lot, in case she might be standing back there.

I knew she was in Washington, D.C., where I'd called her the evening before with my last position report. I knew it. I also knew she would have been there in a second had I asked her. I never told her what I'd been thinking, what I'd planned for this moment. Now having carried and nurtured the idea of proposing marriage on this sandy beach for twelve hundred miles, I would be lying if I didn't admit to feeling empty and disappointed when I realized she wasn't there and that it wouldn't happen.

I could see my parents, Chief, and a few others standing on the beach. It was great to see them and that finish line. They applauded and cheered as my kayak touched the sand at 1:48 P.M.

Fifty minutes later, Manitou Cruiser arrived at the finish. Wizard came in five hours after him.

Aside from winning, the biggest surprise for me was that all three of us—each in completely different boats with different strengths and strategies—finished so close to each other. I beat the thirty-day deadline, completing the challenge in 19 days, 6 hours, and 48 minutes. To do it, I averaged 60 miles a day and covered the last 124 miles of the journey nonstop in 30 hours and 18 minutes. Manitou made his final "sprint" in just over 29 hours.

A week later, on March 30, Pelican and Doooobrd crossed the finish line, followed three days later by Dr. Kayak and Sandy Bottom.

People sometimes ask why anyone would want to endure the hardship necessary to race around Florida in a small boat. It's a good question.

For me, it's not about the glory of winning. It's something more. I'm not a paddling superstar. I don't have the sleekest boat or the biggest sail, and in my sleep-deprived stupor I'm anything but the sharpest navigator. But something amazing happened during the challenge that I can't fully explain. I traveled each day and night to the point of physical collapse, never knowing if I would be able to continue the next day. I wore holes in two pairs of leather paddling gloves, but never developed a single blister on my hands. Most important, way out in the darkest place alone on the water, I realized I was completely unafraid. The fear had vanished, and with it all sense of pain. In that place I was more alive than I'd ever been.

Humility, not strength. Submission, not force of will. Listening for those voices. Those are secrets it took me fifty years and twelve hundred miles to discover. That's what I'm chasing out there on the water—the possibility that if I push harder and faster and longer I might glimpse something real, something eternal.

What is it those crazy sea kayakers say on that bumper sticker? PADDLE OR DIE. If I'm not moving forward I am dead. Lose the fear, pick up that paddle, and head for the horizon, just to see what's going to happen. That's my victory. That's my treasure.

Epilogue: Fort De Soto Park,
Near the Entrance to Tampa Bay

It took time to recover from the Florida Challenge. My shoulders and butt were sore for weeks. The kayak sat unused in the garage for almost nine months. I continued to see Linda on every trip to Washington. We took vacations and spent holidays together, but we lived in distant cities and the kids, hers and mine, were tied to separate places. Weeks became months. If only the planets would align. If only the earth would slow down just a bit. But it didn't. It couldn't.

Months became years.

Then, on a flawless sunny day in Florida, I decided to make good on a pledge long overdue. Linda was visiting from Washington. I picked her up at the Fort Lauderdale airport.

"Let's go do something," I said.

We drove together in the Toyota across the Everglades and up I-75.

"Where are we going," she shouted.

We crossed the Sunshine Skyway Bridge over Tampa Bay and headed out to a beach beside a concrete pier. I hadn't been to this place since the last day of the challenge. I'd circled Florida in just over nineteen days with a secret plan, but it took me three years to find my way back to the finish line, this time with Linda standing there on the sand.

It had been a long journey for Linda, as well. She'd left Washington before dawn that morning to catch a flight. By the time we drove across the state and arrived at the beach, she'd traveled nearly twelve hundred miles.

I waded out into the water to just above my knees. Then I came ashore and took her hand in mine. When she realized why I brought her to this beach she began to tremble. She pressed a hand over her mouth and started to cry. I tried to keep talking, but couldn't. Somewhere nearby, people, strangers, were clapping.

I won't reveal all the details. Sometimes the warmth between two hearts is meant to be felt, not spoken, or even written. But I will tell you three things. One knee. Sapphire and diamonds. She said yes.

Appendix: What I Carried

PADDLING GEAR

Current Designs Solstice GT sea kayak, fifty-six pounds empty

Two Werner paddles, one primary, one spare

Spray skirt

Inflatable life vest

Hand pump

Sponge

Inflatable paddle float

Inflatable seat cushion

Downwind sail rig (Spiritsails.com)

Handheld GPS navigation unit

Handheld VHF marine radio

EPIRB (emergency beacon transmitter)

Three emergency flares

Compass, watch, and whistle

Duct tape

Cell phone and recharger

Hypothermia survival kit, including space blanket and fast fire starters

First aid kit

Safety knife

CamelBak hydration system

One headlamp, two flashlights, and a rear-deck running light

Reflective jogging vest

Small, lightweight wheels to pull kayak over rocks or tidal flats

Nautical charts

Extra batteries

FM radio with earphones

Three bandanas

Three disposable cameras

Notebook and two pens

Reading glasses

PADDLING CLOTHES

Straw hat and baseball hat
Sunglasses
Sunscreen
Two O'Neil rash-guard
   long-sleeve surfing
   shirts

Nylon front-button short-sleeve
   shirt (for night paddling)
Fast-drying shorts
Diving booties
Paddle gloves, two pair
Waterproof paddle jacket

CAMPING GEAR

Jungle hammock
Inflatable air mattress
Sleeping bag
Four tent stakes
Assorted lengths of parachute cord

Eight-by-ten tarp
Bug repellant
Biodegradable soap
Toilet paper

CAMP CLOTHES

Fleece sweatshirt
T-shirt
Long-sleeve front-button shirt
Nylon running shorts

Nylon wind pants
Smart Wool socks
Mosquito head net
Fleece hat

COOKING GEAR

Food for five to seven days
   (resupply at checkpoints)
Backpacker's propane stove
Titanium pot
Three cigarette lighters

Matches
Plastic containers to carry up to
   four gallons of water
Plastic knife and spoon
Pocketknife with can opener

FOR THE FORTY-MILE PORTAGE

Portage cart (Paddlecart.com)
Running shoes
Silk sock liners (for use with the
   Smart Wool socks)

Small backpack with rope to tow
   the kayak

Acknowledgments

Books don't just happen. This one might never have been published but for the efforts of two people—Janet Reid and Matt Martz.

Janet Reid is a literary agent in New York City who plucked my query letter out of her slush pile and decided to take a chance on an unpublished writer named Sharkchow. Thank you, Janet, for your courage, your wise advice, and those hilarious emails.

A good editor is like a GPS: They both always show the way forward. Matt Martz is a great editor. He understood that for me these weren't just words on a page. Thank you, Matt, and the entire team at St. Martin's Press, for the privilege of working with you.

Behind every race and every story is a supporting cast. Mine begins with Steve Isaac, chief of the WaterTribe. It is his vision and his hard work that made it possible for me and so many others to discover something new about ourselves out on the water. My appreciation extends to the entire tribe, the greatest assortment of ragged humanity ever assembled on a Florida beach. To Chief, Ridgerunner, Greybeard, Kneading Water, Kiwibird, Dave on Cudjoe, Sand Dollar, Nitenavigator, Nitesong, Crazy Russian, SnoreBringGator, JungleJim, Tyro, Paddle Carver, Roo, Tinker, Lumpy, Bumpy, Porky, Dances with Sandy Bottom, Etchemin, Lugnut, Root, River John, DaveD, PeteD, Black Sun, SOS, River Slayer, Slackjack, Vanman, Water Rose, Weed Warrior, Danimal, Jarhead, Shallow Minded, Savannah Dan, Paddle Maker, Sharkstu, Sirbobsalot, Beer Slayer, dabiscuit, Boo, and many others, thank you all.

My own journey into the world of sea kayaking was enhanced by the competition and friendship of two speedy paddlers—Marty "Salty Frog" Sullivan and Matt "Sore Shoulders" Coiro. Marty and Matt, it is an honor just to have been on the water with you guys.

When you share hardship and triumph, you forge a strong bond. That's how I feel about those who competed in the Florida Challenge. To Mark "Manitou Cruiser" Przedwojewski, Matt "Wizard" Layden, Nick "Pelican" Hall, Donald "Doooobrd" Polakovics, Dawn "Sandy Bottom" Stewart, Leon "Dr. Kayak" Mathis, Dexter "ThereAndBack-Again" Colvin, Gregg "Alaskan Seahorse" Berman, and Marek "Wayfarer" Uliasz, you are all heroes to me. I salute you.

To Team Sharkchow—my sister, Carolyn; brother-in-law, Walt; stepson Evan; stepdaughter Rebecca; and last but not least, my wonderful parents, Marge and Roy Richey, thanks for your help, your cheers, and all the other support. You are in my heart always.

To Jason and Linda, this book is for you.

24.99   7/22/10

LONGWOOD PUBLIC LIBRARY
800 Middle Country Road
Middle Island, NY 11953
(631) 924-6400
mylpl.net

LIBRARY HOURS

Monday-Friday	9:30 a.m. - 9:00 p.m.
Saturday	9:30 a.m. - 5:00 p.m.
Sunday (Sept-June)	1:00 p.m. - 5:00 p.m.